BRIGID PROCTOR

Counselling Shop

An introduction to the theories
and techniques of ten approaches
to counselling

BURNETT BOOKS
in association with ANDRE DEUTSCH

First published 1978 by
Burnett Books Limited in association with
André Deutsch Limited
105 Great Russell Street
London WC1

Printed in Great Britain by
Lowe and Brydone Printers Ltd.
Thetford, Norfolk

ISBN 0 233 97042 8

Contents

Part 1

Introduction

THIS book is intended as a resource for those who are involved in counselling. It contains interviews in which I ask, of a variety of practitioners, the questions that I wanted to know the answers to, and which I wanted my students to be asking. These questions are arranged in a structured questionnaire for purposes of comparison. They are intended to make clear the theoretical assumptions on which ten current approaches to counselling and therapy are based, so that counselling practice can be seen to be intelligent rather than mystical. They are also designed to give my contributors an opportunity to share with readers the methods and processes of their counselling practice. My principal objective is practical rather than academic. It is to encourage counsellors to practice more effectively and inventively.

In drawing up the questionnaire, conducting the interviews, presenting them and commenting on them, I was not an impartial or disinterested scientific observer. My intentions are scientific in the sense that I wish to encourage anyone practicing counselling to understand better the assumptions from which they operate, to communicate them clearly, to inform their practice with fresh theory, and to monitor their resulting practice. However, since I act from the centre of my personal, sub-cultural, and cultural world, I am no more impartial than any of my contributors. To offset this partiality, I have tried, throughout, to make clear my own assumptions and my methodology. It is for readers to decide what among the ideas, viewpoints and, practice presented could be usefully incorporated within their own counselling philosophy and personal style. In the final section of the book, I offer some ideas which I hope may make this task easier.

Primarily, the interviews are intended for students of counselling, social work and clinical psychology who want to acquaint themselves with the various methods of counselling being practised in Britain today. I first thought of such a project when I became involved in self-directed learning communities as a method of teaching counselling. Although my students were directing themselves, I wanted to retain the residual power of the educator: to ensure that students would ask the questions I thought they should ask, and receive thoughtful and comprehensive answers. I do not feel that need any longer, but there remains a general need for readily available resource material, and I hope this book will add its to provision.

It should, too, be useful for those practitioners of counselling who are interested in, or puzzled by, all the new ideas there are abroad, but who have insufficient time for reading or attending the proliferation of courses and workshops. It will serve as an introduction to the current best-known approaches and should allow for better informed investment of time and energy. I conceived it at a time of personal transition from psychoanalytical assumptions to humanist/existential assumptions. The interviews reflect that passage and serve to make clearer to me, and I hope to others, the points of difference and the points of agreement between what are, on the face of it, divergent viewpoints and practice. The sixties saw a proliferation of 'new therapies' imported from America. There are books on all these readily available, but I was interested to see how British counsellors used and adapted these to their own culture. It has been a powerful incursion, and there must be many people who, like me, need an opportunity to meet, consider and absorb what is useful in these new ideas, alongside a consideration of more familiar models.

Since it was clear at the outset that there were no agreed definitions of 'counselling' and 'therapy', the two words are used interchangeably in the interviews. I asked contributors to explore what, if any, is the distinction for them, and have drawn some conclusions about their replies in the final section.

I did not ask contributors to talk about specific settings, although I did ask about the influence of their 'client population' on their practice. Instead, I wanted to know about underlying generic principles and practice. One or two of the contributors work largely with groups, and one almost entirely with families. The differing approaches may well be thought to have particular value in certain settings, or with certain clients. However, they are likely to be of interest to people who perform a counselling task, in whatever social setting they operate, or in whatever professional or voluntary role. Thus I hope this will be a useful resource book for social workers, clinical psychologists, psychiatrists, doctors, health workers of all sorts, personnel managers, youth and community workers, those involved with pastoral care in religious and educational settings, as well as for school and college counsellors, marriage guidance counsellors, and others who carry an official 'counsellor' label.

The task of counselling is the subject of considerable debate in Britain and other countries at the present time. In the United States, counselling, like social work before it, has become an established and proliferating profession. In Britain, and other countries where counselling is at the same developmental stage, social work has already become a profession and begun to show some of the undesirable spin-offs of 'professionalism'. Should counselling, too, become a profession? Or is it, in fact, a set of skills which should be made available to anyone who occupies a professional role in relation to individuals or groups of people, and to voluntary and non-professional workers who are called upon to counsel?

Against the backgroun d of this and other dilemmas of definition and boundaries, the British Association for Counselling has been formed. Within the next few years, counsellors of all sorts – voluntary and paid, full-time and part-time, in voluntary and statutory agencies, carrying a wide variety of professional roles in medical, educational, youth work, community and pastoral settings have to discover what, if anything, they have to gain from and give to each other. Within their ranks there are people who hold differing ideas about the nature of man and social institutions. They carry out their counselling from the basis of these assumptions, and with these ideas in mind. The words we have developed as an in-group – relationship, caring, autonomy, accepting, task-centred, non-directive, hidden agenda, etc – can be useful shorthand in sharing our ideas and practice. Sometimes, however, they hide quite divergent ideologies, and at other times they are used to signal certain ideologies, without necessarily communicating clearly what those signals imply.

In my interviews with the contributors of this book, I have tried to separate out the various 'strands' that make up a 'model' – its view of the human species, its view of society, its view of groups and families, its view of the individual in relation to all these, its view of the purpose of the counselling interaction, its view of the process of learning and change, its view of the limits of counselling. By doing this in a way that allows comparison, I hope people will be helped to recognize more clearly what they have in common with those with whom they might suppose themselves in disagreement, and what they do not share with those who seem to be fellow spirits. I think that true cooperation is only built on a clear recognition of differences and an acknowledgement of similarities. To quote Fritz Perls, 'There is no integration without separation'.

Last year, a British Association for Counselling working party on training suggested that one of the best ways of creating and maintaining standards of counselling training was to create informed consumers. Students should be helped to know what kind of training is available, and also to know the kind of questions to ask of any training course they are contemplating joining. I hope this book will help in that process of consumer education.

I also believe that the most healthy and open way to create and maintain high standards of counselling practice is to educate consumers of counselling. This goal is, at present, a very distant one, but I would be delighted if this book were used by prospective 'clients', to help them clarify what they are hoping for when they approach a counsellor or therapist.

The Counselling Context

Counselling is an activity and like any activity takes place in a context. When I set out to talk with practicing counsellors and counselling trainers about what they did, and how they did it, I first of all wanted to know the context in which they perceived themselves doing it. It seemed important to understand the social implications of such a private activity. I asked them to put on the 'conceptual spectacles' of their preferred counselling approach to look at the world and at their counselling practice in terms of that framework. Objectively, they all live and work in England to-day. Subjectively, they live in different perceptual worlds in some respects – not necessarily in conflicting worlds, but within co-existing perceptions which frequently inter-relate, but which remain separate and intact. I had to find a common frame of reference within which I could talk to each of them, sharing enough language to communicate effectively. Since I wanted readers to be able to compare and contrast the ideas and practice of each, this framework needed to be wide enough to encompass any perceptions of the world contributors might have, and exact enough to allow details of practice to be spoken about.

At the end of the book I have inserted the questionnaire that I devised based on that framework. Along with the questionnaire goes a declaration of my assumptions when I started this enterprise, an outline of the issues I wanted to explore, and a description of the difficulties I had in drawing up such a questionnaire. I suggest that readers look over the questionnaire, and even try to answer some of the questions, before reading the interviews on the different counselling approaches.

Models of Counselling

The idea of 'models of man' is fairly recent. When I trained as a case-worker, the psychoanalytic view of the world was not, as I remember, offered me as '*a*' view, but as '*the*' view. The new insights it offered me were so powerful at the time that I was quite prepared to believe that it was the only true view. A Probation Officer with whom I worked had developed a common-sense programme that helped juveniles from poor, disorganized homes become interested in turning up for appointments on time, looking fairly tidy. He saw that as their first step on the road to getting a job, which would allow them to earn some money and make a life for themselves. That seemed to me very naive, though I knew I would be happy to have him as my Probation Officer. Today, he could call himself a behaviourist, and a new Probation Officer might be suggesting that he was foisting society's goals on youths, rather than help them define their own. At that time I thought he should be addressing himself to the psychodynamics of the situation. I know he was an excellent case-worker and I think I was quite 'good' as a Probation Officer too. Most of the people I worked with ended up a bit less frustrated with themselves than they started. Working from a rather different set of ideas I think I am a rather more effective counsellor, but I suspect I would have become more effective with time anyhow.

One conclusion I draw from my experience is that it does not matter much what counsellors believe about the nature of human beings and society. It is the way that the counsellor *is* with a person that matters. I do not think that it matters much whether it is 'because' of modelling, or conditioning, or resolving the transference, or 'experiencing Another', or all of those things Nevertheless, to want to understand why things happen as they do and to be able to predict most accurately what is likely to happen is both a human trait and a responsibility for anyone who has undertaken to help someone else. It was an enormous relief to me, and I know to my students, to come in contact – in the first instance through books – with new ideas that made better sense of the world. I became aware that the ideas about the world that I held were not only illuminating, but also restricting, to myself and others. That is, they held in a bright light certain patterns, but the very brightness made it difficult to see what lay outside and beyond. Some of what was beyond were certain aspects of myself, and other people, our culture and so on, and when I got some new illumination, those bits, in conjunction with those already on show, had quite a different meaning.

This process of altered illumination obviously happens continuously. I suspect, however, that the social and biological sciences after a slow and patchy start are reaching a stage of coming together with a quite formidable body of insight about the human condition. All of us who are concerned in more than a passing way with helping individuals, groups and social systems be more satisfying may have to get used to quite sudden bursts of illumination, which throw our world pictures out of kilter. To pursue the metaphor perhaps unduly, like night driving, it is perfectly possible to get more used to dazzle, and I think it is a skill we need to develop. (In driving, it is done by keeping your eye on the kerb.)

In choosing which approaches to include in this book, I had in mind a two-dimensional spectrum. One of those dimensions is the psychological/sociological dimension. The approaches represented here focus their practice on different points along that spectrum. At the psychological end, certain models focus on processes happening within a person. Around the middle, other models focus on processes happening between people – the inter-personal processes which are the province of social psychologists. At the sociological end, yet other approaches focus on processes 'out there', through and by which people take their place as social entities – processes like learning new behaviour, goal setting, and role choice and performance.

Along another dimension I tried to present a range of political consciousness – from pairs of spectacles which did not focus at all on social or political issues, through those with high awareness of family and small group power issues, to those whose spectacles picked out the underlying power issues in every social situation. As I said in my questionnaire, I started with the hypothesis that any public action which endorses one world view against another, or values some activities and issues more than others, adds weight to the total social energy which supports that view and set of values. I do not believe that counsellors can ultimately work in a 'pure' way with individuals, without being affected by, and affecting, social systems. Some social workers hoped to dodge such issues, but found it not possible, and I think counsellors will find the same. In a social system based on often covert conflict of values, it does not seem to me to be possible to operate a totally co-operative counselling model. My choice of contributors, and the question I asked, were intended to illuminate any underlying conflicts among counsellors, and between counselling assumptions and those of wider social systems.

Over and above such categorisation, I was concerned to present any model of counselling or therapy which I had encountered which seemed to be useful to me or to my students. One or two interviews I conducted were, sadly, eliminated under pressure of space. These were interviews which did not sufficiently represent a particular 'school', but whose main interest lay in their dealing with counselling in a specific setting. I would like to have included a more whole-hearted look at bioenergetics, but it seemed to me that although Reichian theory is useful, and informs the practice of counsellors, bioenergetic methods have not yet been devised which are suitable for use by those counselling in most traditional settings. Albert Ellis's Rational Emotive Therapy, and Kelly's Construct Theory both interest me as theories, but I could find no one who used a developed counselling methodology based on those ideas.

When I invited people to contribute to this book, I only did so if I knew that I would be glad to make use of their counselling skills myself. That is, that I would consider their counselling model one which might be helpful to me at certain times, as well as considering them, as people, to be 'wise counsellors'. So I knew before I started that I did not regard the different models as either/or's. My experience in making this book has reinforced this view. At the outset, the image I had was of a series of differing maps of the same territory, the total territory being human social experience. The maps differed in scale, and thus in the detail or range 'mapped'. They also differed in the purpose and focus of the mapping – physical, political, geological, climatic, etc. According to this analogy, these interviews constitute pages in an atlas. Of course, as someone once said to me, maps give you a feel of safety before visiting a territory, but when you actually arrive in that territory the experience is something totally different.

Methodology

These interviews are edited versions of original, face to face interviews, which were taped and transcribed.

Each contributor received a copy of the questionnaire in advance so that they could think over and prepare the ground. Few brought written notes with them to the interview. Those who did bring a few, as an aide memoire, did not speak from them, but used them as a quick checklist at the end of a section. Since the questionnaire spelled out the issues I wanted to raise, my assumptions and my difficulties, there did not have to be much discussion to establish common ground before starting the interview. Occasionally my assumptions or motives were questioned before starting.

My object in the interviews was to supply space and guidelines for each of the contributors to display their ideas and explore their practice. I saw my role as being to focus and guide that process, and to reflect, clarify and summarize when it felt appropriate. I did not set out to confront. It seemed to me that the interviews themselves when published together would be their own confrontation to each other. Nevertheless, if I encountered inconsistency, or found myself dissatisfied with something said, I did confront. In retrospect, I was aware that I used the interviews as an opportunity to grind some of my own axes. Where this seemed particularly obscure or irrelevant, I cut the passages out.

The Questionnaire consists of five sections. The first I called 'The Game Strategy'. The questions in it were designed to elicit the overall view of human social functioning which emerges as the contributor looks at the world wearing his or her pair of conceptual spectacles – Rogerian, behavioural, psychoanalytic etc. One question dealt with the widest context, two with the current social context, one with 'purpose', one with historical context and the final one with the interaction of individuals within those wider contexts, and the place of counselling.

The second section was called 'The Game Rules'. This was designed to look at the resources which are valued by the different schools of counselling and at the responsibilities people perceived as belonging with counsellor and client. It explored the issue of making overt or implicit contracts. It looked at the similarities and differences between the counsellor role and other, in some respect similar, roles which the contributor played. In exploring these issues, the related issues of professionalism, and the politics of counselling were raised and looked at.

The third section offered a chance to look at the activity of counselling. There were questions about focus, climate, and types of response and intervention. There were also questions which asked about the place of some of the processes that are said to go on between counsellor and client at work – transference, modelling and conditioning – and a chance for the contributor to talk about processes of growth and change within people, or any other processes between people, that are recognized and used within the various models.

Although the words counselling and therapy were both used by most of the contributors, sometimes interchangeably and sometimes distinctively, that did not seem enough attention to give to that much vexed question. Section 4 therefore asked about the 'Game Limits' – what if any demarcation there is between the two, and if there are dangers in the uninitiated going 'beyond' counselling to therapy.

In the final section I asked three personal questions, which went beyond the 'conceptual spectacles.' It seemed very important to know to what extent the use and maintenance of any particular model was affected by the client population with which the contributor worked. I was purely curious and guessed that readers might be, to know if the contributor had dilemmas in counselling. And I wanted to give an opportunity for them to think and say whether the answering of the questionnaire and their discipline of 'wearing spectacles' had slanted and distorted their presentation of their ideas and practice.

Any editing has been primarily to make interviews more easily readable, so a lot that was repetitive and tentative was cut out. They were then edited by author and contributor. The contributor had a chance to alter or cut out anything he or she wanted and to add anything which he or she thought a significant omission. One or two contributors were invited to add something because I felt they had not dealt fully with a particular area. Nevertheless, the bulk of the interviews are original. They therefore represent, much more than a written account, not only the continuing viewpoint of the contributors, but also the interaction between interviewer and interviewed, and the interests and concerns that each contributor brought with them on the particular occasion of the interview. As you will see from the questionnaire, they were not invited to give a full and comprehensive account of the model of counselling which they represented, but to indicate what is in their awareness when they practice counselling.

The editing has done away with a good deal of the struggling for ideas and words that took place. Most of the finished interviews sound more clear cut than the original tapes. Some of the interviews were more of a struggle to mutually adjust language and concepts than were others.

Part 11

The Interviews

Ellen Noonan

I   Psychoanalytic/Object Relations

Ellen Noonan, who was born and educated in America,
trained as a clinical psychologist and psychotherapist at
the Tavistock Clinic, and worked on the staff there for
five years. She is presently Tutor Organiser of the London
University Extra-Mural Certificate Course in Student
Counselling, and is also Student Counsellor at City
University.

The Psychoanalytic/Object Relations school of
psychotherapy, of course, developed from the work of
Sigmund Freud (1856–1939), the Viennese
originator of Psychoanalysis. The British school of
Psychoanalysis is most notably represented by the work
of Melanie Klein, D. W. Winnicott, and Henry Guntrip.
Whereas Freud concentrated on the problems of managing
the unconscious sexual conflicts of the Oedipal child and
his parents through the verbalized free-associations with
adults, Klein furthered the understanding of the primary
mother-child relationship, the infant's phantasy life, and
the significant role of aggression through non-verbal play.
Winnicott and Guntrip concerned themselves with how
each individual gathers all his chaotic feelings and
impulses into an organised, recognisable separate being
in the first place.

SUGGESTED READING:
Brown, J. A. C., *Freud and the Post-Freudians*,
    Harmondsworth: Pelican, 1963.
Guntrip, H., *Your Mind and Your Health*, London:
    Unwin Books, 1970.
Salzberger-Wittenberg, I. *Psycho-Analytic Insights and
    Relationships: A Kleinian Approach*, London:
    Routledge and Kegan Paul, 1970.

PROCTOR : What pair of spectacles are you going to wear for the purpose of this interview?

NOONAN : My training and background is in the Psychoanalytic orientation. I think perhaps it's important to say at the outset that most of my work has been as a therapist. The task in the counselling component of my work now is the adaptation of the classical analytical techniques and theoretical points of view to counselling work. In terms of the actual analytic field, if I had to identify myself with any school within that, Freudian, Kleinian, or the object relations/Winnicottian school, I'm probably in the last one. The Psychoanalyst is really clinical at base, so the emphasis is equally on what is right developmentally about people and what is wrong developmentally about people. In my work, I tend to see first what's gone amiss and secondly what's gone right – that is, what resources and capabilities the individual has for coping with what's gone wrong. So the things I'm going to say are what I see as being amiss with people. In contemporary society perhaps one of the most striking things is that people's approach to life is basically an anxiety approach. Their view of what's available to them in the environment is determined by their particular anxieties and is a very narrow view, a blinkered view. It means that they don't often see all the possibilities that are open to them. I would contrast that with curiosity, and exploration – risk-taking – 'anything's possible.' People are limited in the sense of what they can see and what they can do, consequently it often appears that people are dedicated to a life of dissatisfaction. That they make short *term* decisions, or short *view* decisions about their lives – remedies for immediate dissatisfaction, immediate tensions, immediate pains – which soon are seen as inadequate in the long term. I think the 'Access' advert – 'Take the waiting out of wanting' – is very typical of what I'm talking about; people want something now, don't want to think of the long term.

PROCTOR : Putting it in wider terms, looking at the world in that way – what could man be? What would be his optimal way of working?

NOONAN : Obviously the ideal person is one who is free of the kinds of anxieties that get in the way of actually making full use of what's around. I take the view that people function on their defences all the time. Some defences are necessary. It's like with the human ear – we can only hear a certain amount. We can't hear everything because that would be too painful, break our eardrums or whatever. So it's necessary to be able to shut out or not to partake in certain kinds of experiences. But people on the whole function with defences that are limiting rather than protective, and it's getting rid of the limiting aspect of people's defences that I'm interested in.

PROCTOR: To take it away from individuals, what are the kind of relationships within groups and wider systems that you see as being innate to the human species?

NOONAN: Well, Freud said – I can't remember the exact quotation – that 'man's true place is in the gutter.' I really don't subscribe to that. The implication of that view, certainly, is that man is basically agressive and destructive. I'm not sure about that either; I think that the kinds of social organisations and institutions that we now have to live in means that we are constantly working on a survival level and our survival methods make us sometimes very base. Certainly in contemporary British society, the economic situation, the political situation, the social situation, and just getting through day by day, mean that people don't have a lot of freedom to be doing the kind of curious exploring that I see as being optimal. I don't know whether there ever was a time when that was so. We think of primitive society as being gloriously free, but they were on about survival too, perhaps on different terms, but probably with the same kind of anxieties.

PROCTOR: So as you see it, if you have to fight too hard to survive, you automatically aren't using your potential?

NOONAN: One doesn't always have the opportunity to do other things.

PROCTOR: So you see most of the social system as being against individuals rather than for them. Is there anything in it which is good and which you want to encourage?

NOONAN: Again, I'm thinking very much in terms of British culture. One of its great assets is the celebration of eccentricity. There's a tremendous amount of freedom for people to pursue individual ideas, to do what they want to do, and not have to risk a lot of interference from other people, even if it seems to be crazy or mad. And I do think that's quite important. Compared to America, which is my native country, there's more respect in Britain for the individual and less guilt-inducing pressure to conform. But I think I'd like to approach your question from a different angle. One of the traditional criticisms of Psychoanalysis is that it ignores cultural and social issues and focuses on the individual, and to some extent, that's true. But the question that I think Psychoanalytic people would ask, and which certainly I ask, is how can the cultural things that exist, the cultural state, be maximized? I don't see it as a thing to be contended with. In my work I'm interested in helping people to be their own agent, to get them to take responsibility for what they do. The individual is in a dynamic relationship with his groups and his culture, and he *allows* society to help or hinder him above and beyond whatever benefits or constraints society itself provides in reality.

PROCTOR: Presumably the question of your hidden agenda with the client is very different, if, like Freud, you believe that man belongs in the gutter, and is bound to be at war with any culture – or if you believe what you personally believe, that the culture creates the climate that reinforces man's aggressive and destructive potential rather than the reverse of those. So I guess that how you approach your client, the kind of expectations you have of your client are quite different?

NOONAN: They are very different from Freud's! Another one of the criticisms of Psychoanalytic work is that it attempts to mould people into bourgeois, bureaucratic, everyday, ordinary men. Indeed whatever values I have are necessarily going to influence my work and what I expect. But I don't really accept the criticism of the radicals that this is what we're all about. Thinking about the feminist movement, for instance, I've seen several clients who are in some ways very committed to that movement. I'm not a feminist. But what distresses me about those people is they're committed to it, but they can't get on with it. And it seems to me that my task is to remove the clutter; if they genuinely want to be feminists then the task is to explore within them what their reasons are, what their motives are, and get rid of all the things that are stopping them from actually getting on with it. So that at some level, one does suspend one's values and one's own expectations in order to enable this person to do what she wants to do. So I guess that I do have certain ideas about what people can achieve, and even about what perhaps they ought to achieve.

But it seems possible to suspend that and help people to achieve something which might upset my whole system. Within limits, of course!

PROCTOR: I notice when you talk about your framework, quite a lot of what is usually thought of as an analytic framework we haven't actually talked about. Could you very briefly say something about that?

NOONAN: There would be two ways of going about trying to set the framework. One is in more personal terms. The analytic view is that certain early experience with significant people, or a style of being responded to by those people, very much determines how one relates to people and the environment and how one goes about running one's life later on.

It determines the kind of relationships which you try to set up, determines the kinds of experiences that provide satisfaction and don't generate anxiety and the kinds that do. It determines the kind of needs you seek to have satisfied by people – appropriately and inappropriately. It determines the kind of relationships you want to avoid.

People find themselves in relationships or in situations, even in relation to themselves, which are unproductive but somehow compulsive, leaving them in pain, tense, confused. They simply can't understand it. And their failure in understanding has to do with the fact that the motivation behind it is often unknown; they are unconscious feelings, experiences, and intentions which were relegated to the unconscious because they were painful at the time. They remain there, shut off from modification or reality testing by later experience. Although the unconscious is conceived of as a kind of repository of all that's unwanted, it's an extremely active entity. Always. It drives people to do certain things, to see things certain ways. It demands attention, it never wants to be ignored. That's what analysis is about: you see how the unconscious operates in your life and you try to bring what's there under conscious control. The useful way it was explained to me is that the process of analysis frees the client to live in the present. So long as there are unconscious forces from the past, the individual is living as if the past were the present. By making the unconscious conscious, those early experiences are turned into memories which can then be put into their rightful place in history, where they still have meaning now, but no longer rule current life.

PROCTOR: In what historical context was this Psychoanalytic set of insights developed?

NOONAN: Freud has the place of the founder and the first developer of the Psychoanalytic school. The theory was very much determined by his particular personal circumstances. He lived in late nineteenth century Vienna which was a society that repressed any kind of feeling. He was a neurologist, which influenced how he looked at human functioning. At the time the physicists were working on theories of dynamic flow and energy and pressures. All those things came together to give Psychoanalysis the particular sort of theory that it had – hydraulic theory. Perhaps the concept of defences themselves and certainly the concept of repressions are based on that. Many of Freud's ideas are now regarded as outdated and that's because they were so directly influenced by the social and scientific environment. Klein developed the Freudian ideas – I think that her development reflects the fact that she was a woman and had different sorts of personal preoccupations than Freud had. Her time was also different. And then Winnicott developed Klein's ideas.

PROCTOR: You haven't actually mentioned Melanie Klein et al in the interview. Could you say how they developed Freudian ideas?

NOONAN: The first thing is that Klein moved everything back in chronological terms; Freud had his phases of development: the oral, the anal and the genital. These are age-linked so that the genital phase was supposed to have occurred roughly by five. Klein pushed it all back so that those processes, which she also called by different names, occur within the first year of life, occur within the mother-child relationship rather than with the mother and then with mother and father together as parents. She focuses much more on maternal relationships. Also, Freud's ideas are very much about the person in relation to himself so that, for instance, the oral, anal and genital stages all reflect the fact that the individual is in relation to his body and are determined by what goes on inside his body. There is very little in fact in Freud about the relationship between the individual and the others of his environment or his environment in general. Klein took the view, that we are in relationship right from the start, and that the people around us react dynamically with what's going on inside us. Consequently her theory is called 'Object Relations'. She was much more interested in developing the dynamic processes that go on between people, without in any way ignoring what happens inside us. She put a lot of emphasis on what happens inside us, unconsciously, in terms of phantasy.

PROCTOR: When you say she used different names, and terms . . . ?

NOONAN: She transformed stages into processes. Rather than talk about the 'oral incorporative stage' for instance (which is about taking things in either to consider them or to attack them), she talks about 'introjection', which is a process rather than a static phase. Similarly the expulsion aspect of the anal stage she links to projection – of putting things out. Not just putting them out but putting them out with a purpose in relationship with other people, to keep the unconscious level of the relationship active and to keep people in touch.

PROCTOR: She actually talks about people maintaining a process to maintain the relationships?

NOONAN: Yes. Another way of putting it perhaps is like this. Both Freud and Klein try to say that the physical, physiological development of the individual very much influences the way that individual sees the world and relates to it. Freud put it in terms of 'bodily pre-occupation,' that the infant is occupied with mouth-things and then genital-things and that those pre-occupations really do colour people's view of the world. Klein does the same thing, but she talks, I think, more in terms of developmental progressions from the point of view of how the individual manages his internal world. That is, not only his physical and physiological processes but also his phantasies and his feelings about himself internally, affect how he sees the world externally. He views the world as he views himself. And she comes up with the paranoid-schizoid position and the depressive position. The paranoid-schizoid position being a very simple way of organizing the world into good and bad. It's a defensive way of dealing with bad aspects of yourself and bad aspects of the world. And the depressive position is about integrating the good and the bad and holding it all together in some fashion, and this reflects the infant's view of himself. It takes him a while to develop a concept of himself as a person, that is sometimes good, sometimes bad. Sometimes happy, sometimes sad.

PROCTOR: And Winnicott . . . ?

NOONAN: Winnicott devoted his work to discovering how we come to get ourselves together as a self at all. Klein makes the assumption that we somehow manage to become ourself. Winnicott doesn't make that assumption, but is interested in how it happens, and he also focuses primarily on the maternal relationship as a whole caring relationship. He is much more likely than Klein to look at the relationship between the real and the phantasy – Klein gets very involved in the phantasy life, excluding the real one sometimes. Winnicott seems to understand that they're intimately connected and takes the view that some people experience real traumas and that often the task in life is managing to survive that trauma as a whole person.

PROCTOR: So, presumably the way you, as a 'Winnicottian', see the counselling task would be slightly different from the way more traditional psychoanalytical counsellors might or indeed a 'Kleinian' might?

NOONAN: Yes, I think the styles of the three are really very different. They obviously have a lot in common and in order to look at the differences, you almost have to caricature them, and that makes it slightly inaccurate and unfair. But the Freudian approach focuses very much on anxieties and the defences against those anxieties. The Freudian interpretation would be, for instance, something like, 'You're doing this, because you're trying to avoid that, in case some sort of catastrophe happens' – it's very much an internal thing that Freudians are focusing on. Kleinians go straight for the unconscious phantasy about what actions and feelings mean, and straight for the symbolic relationship of adult activities to infant activities. Whatever an adult does is in some sense related back to the very primary interactions between the mother and the baby. It's basically again an interpretive approach to the problem. The Winnicottians seem to me to be much more concerned with creating a therapeutic environment which offers space for the individual to find out who he is. So the therapeutic action isn't so much an intervention as a relationship protecting the client from impingements, so that he can have a sense that he exists and continues to exist. Maybe the best way to describe the Winnicottian approach is to use his words:

'The mother *is* something more for the infant, and that is greater than that she *does* for him'.

The therapeutic task is to be something for the client rather than to do something. If you know who you are, then what you do is related syntonically to who you are, whereas if you don't know who you are, then you do a lot of things to try and find a way of defining yourself or to fill up a horrible sense of emptiness. It's a much quieter sort of therapy.

PROCTOR: Syntonically – I don't know that word.

NOONAN: In line with – in agreement with. That you do things that arise naturally and spontaneously out of who you are, rather than doing things in order to find out who you are. All that is rather abstract – it's a very theoretical statement. I think theory always has to be slightly transformed to be useful in a practical setting. Perhaps what we need to do now is to draw out some of the implications of the theory for the counsellor in interaction.

PROCTOR: What then would you say is the therapeutic process?

NOONAN: I think that the therapy partly depends on the nature of the person that you're treating. On the whole in a counselling relationship, the process is enabling the individual to understand the patterns of his life, the defensive actions of his life, and that this insight leads to some sort of mastery and control, which they didn't have before. With longer term work, with more disturbed people, the actual insight, as it were, doesn't matter so much. What matters is the experience of having been in that sort of relationship where they can explore what their feelings are, and this leads onto the whole question of play – the opportunity to try things out that they've never had the chance to do before safely. Freudians would say that the therapeutic process was the transferences, the elucidation of the transference and the reality testing that goes on, as a consequence of developing transference relationships.

PROCTOR: And what resources do you see yourself bringing to the counselling task?

NOONAN: I think there are two major sorts of resources that I bring – that anyone brings. One of them is simply who I am, the person in the relationship. The people in the relationship are the basic tools and I am here for better or for worse. My experience comes into that, my intellectual style comes into it, my personal style comes into it. Within that, quite specifically, the important thing I bring is the capacity to listen, not only to what's overtly said, but to what is not being said, to the unconscious message – that is, what's being hinted at, which the client does not actually know about but which he's talking about, has a lot of feelings about. The other major therapeutic resource is the capacity to contain the communications, to hold them for the client, until it's timely to send them back in a way that's then useful to the client. Clients communicate ideas and feelings which aren't useful because they are threatening, frightening and alien. I have to hear the message and the overtones and transform them into ideas and feelings which can be accepted and used by the client. And it's almost a judgemental timing thing, hearing these and sending them back in a meaningful way.

My training, obviously, is something that I bring. I have absorbed the experience of my teachers, my supervisor. I feel they're part of me, not in a plagiaristic way, but as a sort of positive identification with these people. So I bring a lot of knowledge to the client, as well as the more intuitive aspects that I've been talking about. My own self-awareness I guess.

PROCTOR: Through your own analysis?

NOONAN: Partly through my own analysis – yes. Self-awareness is a very immediate process. It's a listening in a third quarter if you like – listening to the client, listening to the unconscious message and then listening to what's going on inside me, so that I can sort out 'that's me, that's him'. And perhaps within self-awareness, in counselling, one of the major dimensions is having a grip on caring and hating. We're in a caring profession but there are ways of caring which involve hating. This seems to me to be something I'm always working on.

PROCTOR: Could you enlarge that bit?

NOONAN: I think that in the layman's eyes, certainly, and even in the eyes of some clients and counsellors, we are in a caring profession, so we should be nice to people; we should be supportive, helpful. Indeed, we should, but I personally take the view that counselling and psychotherapy are quite aggressive occupations. You're confronting people with aspects of their experiences which they just don't want to know about. You have to be in touch with the hating part which enables you to make that kind of aggressive approach to people without bullying, without being moralistic about it, without putting the client down, or making him feel ashamed of it. And I think that's a very important part of the caring.

PROCTOR: When you get into a counselling interaction, what do you see as being the responsibility of the client and the responsibility of the counsellor?

NOONAN: Immediately, the first responsibility is to do some work; it sounds simple, but it's not. It *is* work. It requires a lot of energy and discipline, so I think that in many respects the responsibility of the two are possibly the same. My first task is to make sure that I do respect the client, that I take him seriously, that I don't mess around with him in any way, that I don't use him. Secondly, my responsibility is not to collude with the client in any avoidance, but to approach it and work on it. And, finally, I guess, to be there for the client, while he's there. It's his time. And I have to be there as fully as possible.

PROCTOR: And the client – apart from 'to work' – does he have any responsibility?

NOONAN: What I said about the counsellor describes the work of the client as well in some respects. I do anticipate that the client will be curious. I have to require that of him, I think; otherwise, it's a non-starter. Curious and willing to explore and a certain amount of courage to confront those bits of experience, I think, is his responsibility. I think again, it's part of the conception of the counselling role, that someone can come and see a counsellor in the hope that the counsellor will sort things out. It's not that at all. The clients ultimately do the sorting out themselves.

PROCTOR: Do you have ways of trying to ensure that your client and you see those responsibilities similarly and have similar assumptions about the nature of the counselling task?

NOONAN: Oh, indeed. Certainly in the initial stages, and usually in the first interview with somebody, I do try and discuss what it's about and in some ways to establish a contract with the client, not only over time, but over task. Usually this doesn't have to be done in an explanation sort of way, although sometimes it does. Often in the first interview, the material is about what their expectations are and what they think the counselling is all about and they present me with information and a demonstration of how they try to establish relationships. Through using what they actually do in the relationship and in the interview, some of that explanation can go on; it can be related directly to the relationship they are in, saying 'This seems to be what you are trying to set up', and contrasting that with a more work-oriented counselling encounter. So certainly part of what I do is to elicit expectations and explore them and then compare it with what's actually going to go on, as far as it can be predicted. As far as the theoretical viewpoint goes, at some point, either in the course of using the material or in a more didactic way, it seems to me to be sensible to offer some sort of explanation about how I see people, how I'm going to approach that, and what my style of thinking is, and see what they think. We don't always share assumptions and expectations. Sometimes there's a workable way, sometimes there's not. There are clients for whom my sort of work is of no use, and they would be better to go somewhere else, and see someone else.

PROCTOR: Is the counselling encounter different from encounters you have in other roles?

NOONAN: The other major role that I have is teaching, training, supervising. There's a lot of overlap. The kind of awareness that over the years I have developed, the principles that I operate by, these are very much inside me, I can never get away from those. They operate all the time. I'm always hearing the second message in anything I do. What I choose to do with that differs. I could choose to ignore it or store it, in case it's necessary later. I use it for myself, to see where _I_ stand, where _I_ am in relation to this other person or this other group, just as a kind of orienting process, but I may not actually make it public. Sometimes I do make it public, if for some reason the relationship, either with an individual or a group, comes to a halt, or is unproductive. Then I use it – the information that I have and that I've stored – and try to intervene in a way that will get things going again.

PROCTOR: It sounds as though you take the counselling skill over into another role.

NOONAN: Yes. The issue around that seems to me to be about adapting that skill and being very clear in my own mind about when I'm dealing with clients or patients, and when I'm dealing with colleagues. The important thing is to be clear about the level of relationship in which I am operating. It's difficult to keep the distinction clear sometimes. It's ready to be used, but it needn't be used.

PROCTOR: So it's the difference in how you see *the task* in different roles, rather than *skills* and *insights* which might be interchangeable?

NOONAN: Again, I think it feeds back in on itself in the sense that when you're moving from one task to another, even with the same group of people – from coffee to teaching – an alertness about that boundary helps to keep things straight and I like keeping things straight – very much! In friendship I think one tends to not use the skills. The counselling task is very much keeping one's distance – and in friendship you can't keep your distance in that sense.

PROCTOR: The counsellor tends to focus on certain aspects of a client's interaction with the environment. Do you focus on any particular processes or engage some faculties rather than others?

NOONAN: In the questionnaire you mention feeling and emotion and phantasy, imagination, behaviour, awareness. Certainly all those are aspects which I would focus on and make use of – the others, communication skills, goal-setting, decision-making: probably not so much. Quite a lot depends on the task of the counsellor. I think the tasks differ. For instance, vocational guidance is a different thing from personal counselling. Techniques are the same, but the goals are slightly different. I might focus on decision-making and other factors then, but usually I don't make much use of those. To get away from the categories you provided me with, a major operation in counselling is sorting out phantasy from reality; finding out what really is there as opposed to what people think is there, what they feel is there. Another important kind of work is linking up feelings with experiences. People often come along and say this and that happened, and I did this, this and this, without bringing in any feelings about what they did or reactions to what they did or what other people did to them. And similarly linking intention together with behaviour. He can say 'I did this and that' but in order to make that behaviour meaningful, it's important to understand the intention behind the behaviour which will often explain why things have gone wrong and why things didn't turn out the way he thought they would turn out. Particularly in counselling work, I put a lot of emphasis on demonstrating how their own personal experience and early relationships have left them with certain expectations and certain assumptions. They tend to impose these on the world, and then try to make the world like they want it to be, or again, be upset if it isn't what they want it to be. And also, demonstrating how their assumptions affect their perceptions, which comes back to what I said right at the beginning about the anxiety-ridden approach to life. A lot of the work is saying, 'well, you're seeing certain things because you're so pre-occupied with this and you're not seeing other things in this distorted perspective'. That is another way of sorting out phantasy from reality. I find it very difficult to generalise, but I suppose those are the kinds of tenets that I have in mind when I actually see somebody.

PROCTOR: What kind of climate do you seek to develop and how do you see it being important for your joint task?

NOONAN: I suppose primarily what I try to generate is a serious atmosphere, a reflective atmosphere and then perhaps paradoxically, a play atmosphere. By reflective, I mean clients usually come in a state of anxiety or excitement – excitement being both good and bad – and I try not to get caught up in that, not to get panicked, not to respond to the implicit question '*Do* something, can't you help me?'. I try to sit back and contain it, and help the client to become more reflective too about the situation. It *is* a serious business. Not necessarily solemn but certainly serious.

PROCTOR: Like in a kindergarten? Serious but not necessarily solemn?

NOONAN: Ha! Yes And that comes into play I think. At some level play is a non-serious occupation. It doesn't have any purpose except to be what it is and that is exciting and fun and exhilarating and totally immersing. By play I also mean generating, if you will, a magic circle, a space in which people can take symbolic risks, to discover something about what might happen. To generate that kind of space where they can try things out, play with ideas and with the relationship they find themselves in. Tolerance is also something I think is quite important. People are coming because there is a part of themselves they have avoided or are afraid of, or humiliated by, so a kind of friendliness is important, perhaps more than tolerance. I often use the phrase with clients that they seem to be unable to make friends with, say, their anger. I say, 'I seem to like that part of you more than you like it': that kind of friendly atmosphere.

PROCTOR: It sounds more like very positive valuing of bits of them. Definite permission to be that way.

NOONAN: It is a kind of sanctioning, although I find myself bristling at that. I don't like terms like 'positive valuing' because again, I think that fails to look at the other half. By being friendly in that sense, you positively value but I am also challenging and saying indirectly, 'Look, what's wrong with you, that you don't like it or can't stand it?'. That's where the aggressive aspect comes in, of constantly confronting them with what they don't want to be confronted with, albeit in a friendly way. One of the important things about the atmosphere, too, is that there has to be a certain amount of anxiety, otherwise nobody does any work. You do have to mobilise a lot of energy. It's not a secure, comfortable relationship at all.

PROCTOR: And does that happen automatically? If it isn't happening, are you trying to raise the level?

NOONAN: It's a situation where you try to keep the anxiety at a productive level, neither too high nor too low. If there's too little anxiety, no one does any work and if there's too much, no one does any either.

PROCTOR: What other ways have you practiced responding to people's requests for help?

NOONAN: Well, the obvious sort of way is through interpretation in a straight, analytic sense. Listening to clients and putting back to them some sort of hypothesis about what I see. 'This is the anxiety that you are experiencing, this is the way that you are trying to avoid that anxiety'. A lot of the interventions are clarifying, trying to enable the client to say something a bit straighter, more directly, a bit less muddled and confused than he's actually saying it. Linking is another sort of intervention. Where I begin to see a pattern in the various kinds of relationships, various kinds of experiences that a client has, I try and put them together for the client so that he can see and understand the pattern and, hopefully, by understanding it, will be able to examine it, what's behind it, and what it's for. That's all part of an exploratory process. Asking the right questions and making comments that perhaps enable the client to see something differently from how he has seen it so far. I talk about confronting; it's not the kind of confronting that people might ordinarily understand. Certainly in my mind, confronting is wrapped up with bullying but in 'confronting', the tone is not necessarily aggressive. It's a kind of doggedness, a persistence, a refusal to let them avoid an issue. Clients are in a dilemma, they seek counselling because part of them no longer wants to avoid an issue that another part is still wanting to avoid. It's sticking with it and facing them with their conflicts that I see as being the confronting aspect.

PROCTOR: Are there any responses that you deliberately soft-pedal?

NOONAN: I don't give advice. I don't make decisions. I don't see that I have any right to do that. It's their life and they have to be making those kind of statements for themselves, or those kinds of decisions. I'm there to enable them to do that. Ethically or philosophically that is quite important and links up with the things I was saying right at the beginning. One of the tasks of counselling is to help people to be their own agent, and to be prescribing for them in any way is a direct contradiction of that. Obviously, it never works out quite so purely as that!

PROCTOR: How do you see transference?

NOONAN: Oh, in all sorts of ways. The classical, the literal definition of transference, of course, is that the client is unconsciously projecting or imposing on the counsellor attributes which belong to somebody in their early experience – he's turning the counsellor into somebody else, proceeding as if she were somebody else, and reacting to her as if she were somebody else. And, in counselling, you sometimes use that very directly, making the link, 'You're seeing me as your mother'. Other times that seems to be inappropriate in a very brief counselling encounter. I don't see people for very many sessions, so that the transference I tend to use is a broader definition which would be more correctly called the 'here and now'. That is, I make use of the relationship to demonstrate how they're trying to set up relationships, what they're perceiving and not perceiving, the kinds of assumptions and expectations they are making. It's tremendously valuable; you can sit and listen to someone talk about what goes on out there forever. Without doubting the veracity of the client in any way, you don't actually *know*. But, if it's going on between you, you can both see it, you can both look at it and talk about it.

PROCTOR: How do you check out what is their transference and what is actually here and now? What is happening between you and them in reality, as opposed to phantasy?

NOONAN: Well, at some level, of course, there's not a lot of difference between the here and now and transference. But, I think the major way of checking it out is to check myself out, to find out what I'm putting into it, to find out where I am at, psychologically and relationship-wise. If I'm being attributed with something which I know, as far as I can, doesn't belong to me, then I start checking out in transference terms. In both, I'm using what this client is making me feel, the counter-transference, and using my awareness of my feelings to elucidate the relationship. I don't think it's necessary to *say* 'you're making me feel. . . .' Sometimes it is, but I can use that to focus back on the client or on the relationship.

PROCTOR: Do you see yourself as being a model for the client? And if so, what are you modelling?

NOONAN: I think one inevitably is a model. I don't set myself out to be a model in a conscious way. I am what I am. Or, I am what I am in that setting, and different clients will choose to pick up and identify with different aspects of myself. In that sense, yes.

PROCTOR: What does it model?

NOONAN: I think one is often set up as a kind of corrector or counter to another model they have somewhere else. Particularly as a woman, I often get set up as the 'not my mother' especially if the mother is seen as being not the right sort of mother. Yes, inevitably that happens, and it has to be talked about rather than left unmentioned. Another way I function as a model, and this is perhaps more conscious, is that I offer the clients my way of looking at themselves – through the interventions that I make, through the way that I relate to them and understand them. I offer them a framework for thinking about themselves, and this I think goes quite well. Often clients do take this away. They come back saying, 'I wondered what she would've said about that?,' and they try to say to themselves what I might have said about it.

PROCTOR: Are you aware of positively conditioning some responses and behaviour within the counselling relationship and negatively conditioning other communications?

NOONAN: Well, again I think it's inevitable. Just because of the classical theory of operant conditioning. It is, it's there. I don't set out to do that, and I feel very uneasy about talking about training clients, but one does train them into one's way of thinking, if the relationship is going to operate. It works the other way, too; I mean, I get conditioned by my clients. That's important to say. Through the language that they use, through their particular viewpoint too, I get conditioned. In more specific terms I think there is another kind of conditioning that goes on. As I said, I do very brief counselling and in the first interview, I tend to begin in my own mind to decide on a focus. I ask the question of myself, and usually of the client, 'What can we usefully do in the time that we have?'. And, by defining that area of work and responding only to material that is in that area, it's a kind of conditioning; they bring that kind of material. But again, they have to cooperate; they have to be willing to accept that. So I'm not sure that you can call it conditioning. I remember one patient I had, where I did a ten-session intervention and a follow-up. There had never been any discussion with her in the therapeutic contact about the focus per se, but she came back with an extraordinarily vivid statement of the focus. We talked about how she *had* felt focused and conditioned in a very positive way. It was a nice piece of feedback that this is in fact what goes on. She put the focus better than I could!

PROCTOR: She had inside information! Do you see a demarcation between counselling and therapy?

NOONAN: I think I'll have to say that this really is personal, because there are a lot of people who disagree with me. I think that the techniques used in counselling and psychotherapy and psychoanalysis are basically the same, using the same resources as it were. The difference comes in the depth of the intervention. Psychoanalysis is much more oriented toward an unearthing of the unconscious. It's aimed at total personality change, modification. It's almost like a structural change, like taking down a building and re-building it. Consequently, the relationship is a much more unequal one, in the sense that the therapist or the analyst has, as it were, far more access to the unconscious or to the unknown than the patient does. And this has all the implications of the dependency generated there – the patient is in reality quite reliant on the analyst's insight.

In the counselling relationship, the objectives *are* different, the goals are much more limited. One isn't seeking to effect a large-scale modification. One is taking on a more limited task either in choosing to work on a particular area of difficulty or working only to a certain level. One taps only that which is most available of the unconscious rather than that which is really submerged.

And again, I think, one of the implications of this is that the relationship is more equal in counselling. Certainly for myself, with both my client and my patient, I tend to set up an alliance, a working alliance, a therapeutic alliance: with my therapeutic patients, that alliance is more about trusting me at a primitive level. In counselling, the alliance is much more with the working ego of the client, so that I try to say in a much more direct way, 'Look, let's you and I work together as peers on this problem'. I'm primarily mobilising the ego resources. That doesn't mean to say that doesn't happen in analysis as well.

PROCTOR: I get a picture of your patient actually taking his hand off his own ego strings in analysis.

NOONAN: Maybe one way of describing it is to say that in counselling, I'm operating far more on a conscious level. I'm always in touch with the client's positive wish to do something about the situation and using that part of the client as a companion in working out the problem. In therapeutic work, I think the level of operation changes, so that sometimes I'm working in much the same way as counselling. I'm working in an 'adult partnership' with the patient looking at his child part. But other times I'm dealing with an infant directly. This is the real transference. The adult part of the patient somehow disappears and is taken over by primitive attitudes. We go back and forth in time. Sometimes I'm with the adult, sometimes with the child, sometimes with the adult observing the child. One of the reasons I'm having difficulty in trying to describe it is that in my own work, I find it very difficult to differentiate the processes because they evolve naturally as the work goes on. I don't know, as it were, when I'm counselling and when I'm doing therapy. I think the other thing is the language I use. In my own counselling work I tend to use more adult words, and in therapy, more child words.

PROCTOR: If there is a difference, there must be dangers that counsellors will somehow try to be therapists? What would the danger be?

NOONAN: Well, I think that the deeper you get – and this isn't necessarily to do with any line of demarcation between counselling and therapy – but the deeper you get, and the further you move into the unconscious, the further you move into transference and the more you're in the area of subjectivity. You're moving away from what you and the client actually see and hear into what's not seen, what you have heard with the third ear. And once you get into that area of literally interpreting the material, that's the point at which awareness of one's own unconscious is very important. To make sure that you're sorting out what's in you and what's your patient or client. I think this is the danger area. I'm actually not so convinced about the danger. I think the disaster is of failing to understand the client. When you get into that area, and you don't understand, that really is a terrible assault on the patient. I have unlimited faith in the defences of my patients. If one makes a wrong intervention or a premature intervention, or a not-quite-right intervention, their defences are there to protect them. At some level, that's a cop-out and I'm not saying that the patient has to defend himself, that I don't have to be careful, responsible, or respectful in my interventions but it's important to recognise that they do have self-protective mechanisms.

PROCTOR: It's a question of being more or less effective, rather than actually damaging them?

NOONAN: New counsellors, new therapists who have not been through a lot of training or who are only in the early stages of their own analysis or psychotherapy do astoundingly creative work and are sometimes much better therapists than the very experienced and trained psychotherapists.

PROCTOR: A very generous comment!

NOONAN: There are reasons for this. One is that because, if they're responsible people, they will know their limits and they will tend to be very discreet about the kind of people they take on, and they will be very discreet about how far they go. They're making safe judgements all the time. In fact they are probably only one or two steps ahead of the patient. That means they have to stay very close to them, they don't have a massive theoretical framework out of which they can make textbook intepretations. They have to listen: they really have to stay with the patient; the only thing they've got is what the client tells them. And that for the patient can be tremendous. And because they are new they put a tremendous amount into it. Sometimes it's that freshness that gets lost. It needn't. I certainly know that for myself. I can think of one patient who said to me 'Surely you must be able to tell me what's wrong, and what I must do to make it right. You see lots of patients'. My answer to that is 'Yes, I have, but I've never treated you before'. So that's a way of staying in touch with the freshness that's necessary.

PROCTOR: Does the client group with which you work influence the way you counsel?

NOONAN: Yes, in two ways. One is that on the whole my clients are intelligent, agreeable, usually articulate and in a sense, they have nice, middle-class problems! So that the talking therapy on the whole works with these people. They have the basic equipment it takes to manage this approach. The other thing is that in my patient, as opposed to my client, work, I see more disturbed people. I find myself very interested in working with the borderline personality and in the course of working with these people, I've found that the classical, Freudian theoretical orientation is inadequate which is why I've moved more and more to the Winnicottian approach. They've made changes in the way that I look at things. It's not that they've made it – I've chosen it. And I find this reflects back into my counselling work and I do it differently than I did three years ago. One of the most important things for me is that I'm always in a process of change myself – personal change leads to intellectual change, which affects the work I choose to do and that affects me personally, and so on!

PROCTOR: And do you have any personal dilemmas in your counselling work?

NOONAN: My inclination is to say, 'Oh, masses!', but as far as actually naming them, I find it fairly difficult to say what they are. I have a basic confidence in my theoretical approach and it seems to work. But there are times when it doesn't work. I feel that by being committed to one approach, perhaps I am missing something: that perhaps I'm not offering people what is right for them, what they really need, or what they can really make use of. I don't know how much that is a dilemma except when I am actually dealing with a particular person. I think, in a broader sense, what that is masking is a fundamental doubt about any kind of therapy which is such a symbolic process. There are times when I feel that symbolism simply isn't enough. Something else is required. This is where I see the value of the Encounter movement, for instance, or Gestalt therapy or any of the other more active, involving sort of therapies around at the present. I see those as extremely valuable.

I think that part of my wish would be that counselling could take away all the pain – wipe out the past. But it doesn't, and I sometimes wonder why. I think that's a despairing cry – there are so many people who are in so much pain, so much of the time.

PROCTOR: Talking of the new therapies how do people express the connections they make between their experience and their feelings?

NOONAN: It varies, certainly. In the counselling setting where there is less time, sometimes it seems that the encounter is kept very much at a thinking, intellectual level. The clients gain understanding, rather than the emotional experience of working through, although the intellectual understanding itself would not be very useful unless it is also emotionally linked. Certainly there is a good deal of emotional expression and in the 'in-depth' therapy encounter, it is critical.

PROCTOR: What exactly is 'working through?'

NOONAN: Working through, as I understand it anyway, in the therapeutic relationship, and in the transference, is literally working through. Re-experiencing the same relationships over and over and over again; setting them up, finding out how they work and how they don't work. It's repeated until the anxiety behind it is mastered or until they find a new resolution to the interpersonal pattern – a resolution that is no longer self-defeating. And that has to be an emotional thing. There's no way round it. It's something you have to feel every time not something you can do in your head.

PROCTOR: Having read the interview back, is there anything you want to add?

NOONAN: The interview contains some inaccuracies and inadequacies in explanation which serves to demonstrate two essential tenets of psychoanalytic theory. The first is that the current internal state of the perceiver or doer (that's me) dominates what he says or does. For instance, the emphasis on play and on the aggressive component reflects the areas which I was struggling with at the time. Today the emphasis might be quite different. Although the emphasis changes, the points are not invalidated. The second is that in order to communicate an idea or substantiate an argument, evidence is used selectively and is even distorted. For instance, my earlier attempt to define the differences between Freud, Klein and Winnicott has resulted in a gross misrepresentation of Freud and Klein.

Again, the facts are not, strictly speaking, wrong, but they are misleading because their use is motivated, not neutral. Rather than put it all right now (which might simply result in more of the same anyway!), perhaps it is best to let it stand as an object lesson.

Pat Milner

2 Rogerian Counselling

Pat Milner, who began her career as a teacher, took a
Counselling Diploma at Reading University. After
working as a school counsellor, she received a Fulbright
Scholarship to The State University of New York in
Buffalo, where she earned an Ed.M. in counselling. She
was founder/chairman of the Association for Student
Counselling. She was founder editor of the journal, *The
Counsellor*, and wrote *Counselling in Education* in 1974.
At present, she is Tutor to the South West
London College Counselling Courses.

Carl Rogers, the founder of 'client-centred' therapy,
believed that his approach was rooted in the educational,
social, and political philosophy of American culture. In
Counselling and Psychotherapy, originally published in
1942, he first presented the 'non-directive' approach and
became the focus of an extensive controversy in the
American psychological world. Almost ten years later, in
1951, his book *Client-Centred Therapy* extended and
elaborated on this approach and offered a theory of
personality to support it. *On Becoming a Person* was
first issued in 1961, after Rogers had worked for thirty-
three years as a psychotherapist.

SUGGESTED READING:
Rogers, Carl, *Counselling and Psychotherapy*, London:
   Constable, 1942.
Rogers, Carl, *Client-Centered Therapy*, London:
   Constable, 1965.
Rogers, Carl, *On Becoming a Person*, London: Constable,
   1967.
Rogers, Carl, *Freedom to Learn*, Columbus: Charles
   Merrill, 1969.
Rogers, Carl, *Carl Rogers on Personal Power*, London:
   Constable, 1977.

PROCTOR: What pair of spectacles are you wearing for the purposes of this interview?

MILNER: I am looking at counselling, at life, and at people, through the eyes of Carl Rogers, the man who developed client-centred counselling, or non-directive counselling as it's sometimes called.

PROCTOR: And looking through Roger's pair of spectacles, what comes into relief about the nature of man and the relationship between individuals and the groups and social systems of which they are a part?

MILNER: I think to begin with, this is essentially an optimistic view of human nature, it's full of hopefulness about the way people are and the way people live their lives, and this is one of the things that's most attractive to me about it. I don't think it's as naive as some people suggest; it recognises things like evil, but its essential basis is a positive one. It's, I suppose, humanistic in its outlook, it's phenomenological in its outlook. It suggests that man is basically good, he's not neutral and he's not evil; basically he's good. He's rational in the things he does and he has some measure of freedom over his own life. It's very American and belongs very much to American history and American culture, which I find has an enthusiasm, an optimism about life. So it's suggesting that people have a basic movement, a basic propensity towards friendly, co-operative, constructive behaviour.

When it looks at the problem of evil, as it does and as it must, when considering man, it accepts that people can be incredibly cruel, horribly destructive, anti-social, and can hurt one another, but it also suggests that all these things stem from defensiveness, fear and frustration, which lead to a distortion of people's more natural inclinations. It also believes that people's development for good or for evil can be and very often is influenced and controlled by cultural conditions. In this sense as children we learn to be what other people say we are. We learn to behave in ways that other people will approve of, we conform to group expectations, to social systems, to family values, because we hope that this way we will get love or acceptance or status or security or whatever we think it might bring. In doing this, in conforming to the human external values, Rogers thinks that we somehow distort our own natural nature. It's this distortion which leads people to have difficulties which cause them to come into counselling or lead unhappy lives.

PROCTOR: But those distortions aren't inevitable?

MILNER: No, he doesn't think they are inevitable, he somewhere has a fantasy that if you could bring up a child in the way that he is suggesting, when a child does have freedom to choose and is able to be his natural feelings, then a lot of the difficulties and maladaptive behaviour that adults seem to be faced with wouldn't happen. It is a phantasy; I don't think anyone has ever done it, or ever will. But I think it's rather nice, it has a lot going for it.

PROCTOR: What is the purpose of human energy?

MILNER: Man uses obviously quite a lot of energy for what you might call biological purposes, the very business of living and existence. But aside from that energy, which we take as given, I think people use their energy to learn things like self-awareness, and self-direction; in this way they transcend the biological animal pattern with language, with culture, with relationships with one another, and with control over their environment. They come up against the problem of choosing, sometimes choosing between good and bad, which in turn faces them with the problem of values: what is good, what is bad? And that in turn I think, brings up the problem of meaning. How do I know what is good and what is bad and what am I basing it on? I think a lot of human energy goes into this, without people really being aware of it.

PROCTOR: And for Rogers there isn't a set meaning? Life's about finding your own meanings?

MILNER: Yes. I think this is very important in his point of view because he suggests that a person's most basic striving, that is, where most of his energy probably goes, is to maintain that part of his phenomenological field, which is what Rogers calls the 'Self'. There is a tendency for human energy to be directed towards growth and towards making whole, in other words, getting to this real self and pushing aside the distortions that we've learned and developed. Rogers suggests very firmly that if a person can clarify his experience and get in touch with his real feelings, his basic self, he will choose personal growth, he will choose positively, he will choose to be friendly and co-operative. That doesn't mean to say he will never be un-cooperative or angry. When it's appropriate, he will be angry but he is much more in control of what's going on because he knows more about it and himself.

PROCTOR: And able to take into account other people's points of view?

MILNER: That's right.

PROCTOR: When did this approach originate and why did it happen? What gaps in thinking about men did it fill?

MILNER: Where this sort of approach seems to me to fit in relation to other ways of looking at man is somewhere between what you might call a Psychoanalytical view of man and a Behaviourist view of man. It's neither of these. It seems to have arisen partly because neither of those seem to offer a satisfactory explanation of the way man really is. One suggests that man is very much at the mercy of unconscious drives and instincts. The other one seems to suggest that man is very much conditioned by his own environment and almost at the mercy of that. And trying to grow a bit higher, I think, than these is this point of view which says 'No, this doesn't really seem to be it; from the experience we have of working with people, this doesn't really seem to be the way they are.' So this approach to counselling is fairly recent, very much mid-twentieth century.

PROCTOR: Perhaps that was the time man had choices; a great number of people had choices they never could have had before because of survival needs?

MILNER: Yes. You had to spend most of your energy on just existing, whereas now, these areas like 'who am I' and 'what does my life mean to me?' become really pressing; you can't afford the luxury of these questions when you are just fighting to exist.

PROCTOR: What processes or structures in British society today stand out as being helpful to the realisation of man developing the way that Roger's fantasy would have him develop?

MILNER: I find this difficult because all the structures that we have can be helpful. I can't think of any that are necessarily unhelpful, but having said that, I don't in fact think that they are as helpful as they could be. I think much of education is unhelpful; it need not necessarily be that way, but it is. In order to become this true self, if I can put it in those terms, it is necessary to be able to think and to feel, to discriminate and to choose, and I don't think education fulfils any of those functions.

If you see man as having a potential for choice, some degree of freedom, some ability to reason, a basic need to develop his own values consistent with his own reality, then any structure that you have that tries to rigidly control the behaviour of people is likely to produce distortions and maladaptive behaviour. So schools in which children feel too threatened to be themselves, to acknowledge their own experience, are likely to produce maladaptive consequences for the children although not necessarily for the schools. And I don't think you can work with students for any length of time without realising that some schools are very efficient at denying children's own reality experience, they do this remarkably well.

Then there are families, another group, another sort of structure that does this too. The motto of a lot of families, certainly I think mine, seems to be 'Every other person must think, feel and believe as we do.' This is something I find very difficult, and I think it is one of the reasons why I moved into this area of counselling or this way of looking at life. It feels as if all my life I have been fighting against this, and I have been fighting to be me.

PROCTOR: And Rogers gives you that permission?

MILNER: He does, yes. And his way of looking at life and people helps me a great deal. So it's very much a function of who I am and what I've experienced that I've chosen this way.

PROCTOR: Does he have anything to say about power in society, power in systems at all? Is it basically a way of looking at people that is going to be supportive of existing power structures, or does it undermine them?

MILNER: Rogers describes the revolutionary nature of his ideas in *Carl Rogers on Personal Power: Inner Strength and its Revolutionary Impact*. He suggests that his person-centred approach is the spearhead of a quiet revolution. This approach does not give power to the person; it never takes it away; it changes the nature of psychotherapy, marriage, education, politics. A quiet revolution is underway shaping a different future built around a new type of self-empowered person.

PROCTOR: Sharing power more evenly within existing systems?

MILNER: Yes. It doesn't strike me as being revolutionary, but it is challenging, and it does strive to help people, to understand their possibilities and their limitations.

PROCTOR: So, what do you see as the objective of the counselling task?

MILNER: I think most people come into counselling with a problem or a concern which they can describe in fairly practical terms, like difficulty at work, difficulty with study, some unhappiness in relationships, maybe some feelings of loneliness in themselves or inadequacy that they can perhaps talk about and present. But underneath all that there seems to be another question more often than not, what life means to them. Underneath all the worry about the practical living of life, there is this 'who am I really?' and 'how can I find out who I am?' 'how can I find out who my real self is?' Sidney Jourard suggested that this was a search to be that self which one truly is, which I think is a very good way of putting it. It's been described by lots of people in various ways. Rogers calls it – and I don't like this phrase much – 'being a fully functioning person.' Maslow talks about a self-actualizing person, other people talk about people who are autonomous. I think they are all talking about the same thing. I suppose the objective then is to provide a situation in which a person feels safe enough to lower the defences which he's made to protect himself against thoughts, feelings, events that threaten him, by creating an atmosphere in which he feels accepted, understood and valued. And this somehow seems to give freedom to look at real feelings and thoughts which are often fairly negative and have often had to be denied or distorted.

PROCTOR: And what resources do you see yourself bringing to the counselling task? What gives you your authority?

MILNER: Myself first of all. And wherever I am in my journey to become the real me. So it's my own self-awareness of my own strengths, plus my needs and tendencies, my hang-ups, my attitudes, my prejudices. I think some knowledge of human nature and some experience of what it's like to be out of touch with yourself helps. Basically, faith in people's capacity for growth, their resilience, a tendency to accept people where they are, trying to give them space, to listen is important. One of the things the students used to say was that I let them do all the talking. This was their description of what happened in counselling. And sometimes I seem to have the ability to get at the essence of what is happening in an encounter, which is quite a useful resource.

PROCTOR: Have these resources come from your natural abilities, your life experience or your training?

MILNER: They must have come from all of these.

PROCTOR: What would you say of your training as part of that resource? What is it that you've got out of training that's helped you?

MILNER: The important thing I think about the training was that it stopped me dead in my tracks and caused me to question all sorts of assumptions that I had about education and people and children. It really was quite a shock, and I wasn't at all sure that I could do it. So I tended to blame the approach and say, 'It'll never work, it'll never work in our schools,' but when I look back on it, it was me – it was really shaking me right to my foundations. But then from listening to the way it was, we went into schools to try and practice it and when it was put into practice, then it began to be a possibility and it wasn't just a theoretical thing about which I could say, 'This will never work,' because when I got into the situation, it did. It happened.

PROCTOR: So one of your resources is that you have learnt to question assumptions and that you have concepts that make sense of life for you, and that you are able to use this part of you in a way that they become you, rather than using Rogers?

MILNER: Yes. I think whatever theory you choose to work from, you have to make your own personal style, because I am me and not Carl Rogers. I can't work as Carl Rogers works. I can approximate perhaps, and I can take as guidelines what he says. This I think he would agree to, because it's inherent in his own beliefs that my experiences will dictate what I believe and do.

PROCTOR: What do you see as being the responsibilities of the client and the counsellor in a counselling interaction?

MILNER: In this way of working with people, much of the responsibility is deliberately put on the students or clients, or whatever you want to call them, because the assumption is that they have within them the capacity to resolve their own problems or difficulties. So that usually, the counselling will be self-initiated, and usually it will be self-terminating. In other words, the students will decide when they feel they've had as much help as they need or want at that particular time. What I as the counsellor take responsibility for, I think, is time keeping, providing the place and, as far as is humanly possible, my undivided attention, bearing in mind that I have needs of my own, and I may have certain things on my mind that day. But as far as I can giving my undivided attention to that person for that time, and in that sense putting aside quite a lot of my own needs for the moment, being able to work with them. I have the responsibility for trying not to deliberately use the situation to meet my needs. Having said that I am very well aware that I learn a great deal from being a counsellor but that, I think, is something rather different. I take the learning away and do it somewhere else, as it were, rather than thinking about it there and then in the counselling situation. That hour or whatever it is, is primarily for them. I think I have a responsibility to that person.

I feel, too, that many people who come into counselling have two different pictures of themselves. One is painted in very bright colours and contains all the things that are good about them, and the other is very, very dark and is usually not on show but kept in a locked room somewhere, and it's what somebody called the canvas of self-condemnation. I feel a responsiblity to try to help people bring these two pictures together, so that the bright one gets some shadows from the other one and thus some depth. And similarly when you're looking at yourself in the dark colours you can never see anything good about yourself, but by bringing these two pictures together, you help people along the way – both things are part of them, both pictures are part of them – it's putting them together that makes them a whole. This relates very much for me to the question of colour value in painting; the colour value of a painting has to do with the light and the shade and their relation to each other within the picture. When a picture is out of value it means that the light and the shade are not in balance with each other, and that's a very good way of looking at people for me.

PROCTOR: Do you have any responsibility for clients not going crazy, or that kind of thing?

MILNER: No. I'm not quite sure what you mean by 'going crazy', but there may be a need for that part of them to come out; although I would find it very difficult, I don't feel a responsibility to stop it. What I do feel responsibility for is the limits of the counselling situation. If somebody is going to 'go crazy', it would, I think, worry me a bit because they are there safe for an hour and then they have to go out into the world and I feel some responsibility for that.

PROCTOR: Would you do anything about that?

MILNER: I don't know quite what. I might do several things. One might be referral, one might be extending the limit of time because of what has happened. I haven't really thought that one through.

PROCTOR: You've talked about the way the counselling encounter is different from encounters you have in other roles. Do you want to say anything more about that? You've said, for instance, that in that encounter the time was for the client.

MILNER: I think that in the sense that the main purpose of the counselling encounter is to be with the other person and to be alongside them in an entirely neutral situation (neutral in terms of the outside world) with usually uninterrupted time, which is different from any other encounter that I have. In some ways it's artificial in the way it's set up, although not artificial in the way you relate to each other.

PROCTOR: Different from a teaching encounter?

MILNER: Yes, I think there are quite a lot of differences. The biggest difference is the whole feel of the experience – when I teach, or when I've finished teaching, I feel stimulated because the teaching situation and feed-back is mainly on an intellectual level, and is often a stimulating experience for me. When I've been counselling, I tend to be much more reflective and quiet, almost withdrawn I think. I am not in touch with that more extrovert part of myself that teaches. It's as if I have a teacher in me and I have a counsellor in me and they're almost different people. They obviously have a lot in common as well, but I don't bring the two together very easily at all. There are people I know who teach and counsel, who find these quite compatible. I don't.

PROCTOR: Do you have ways of trying to ensure that your client and you have similar assumptions and objectives about the nature of the task and the interaction?

MILNER: This is what I would call structuring and it is quite important because people come into counselling with absolutely no idea of what's going to happen, what's likely to happen, what it's all about, what they need to do. I think it's important to share, not all at once in a great big introductory mouthful, but as time goes on and things come up, like, 'Well, we have fifty minutes (or an hour), let's see what we can do and we have an hour next week or the week after'. As it seems appropriate, I share that I don't have answers specifically, I don't have solutions to problems but that I see myself as being there to listen and to relate and perhaps to make things a bit clearer as I listen – to help them to find solutions. If we don't share this assumption, we get at cross-purposes. But it's unhelpful to say right at the beginning, 'I don't have any answers, I don't have any solutions', because then they think, 'Well, what do you have? I've come for answers.'

I think the silence that often occurs in counselling sometimes bothers people and they may need a bit of help, particularly children, because teachers often use silence as a punishment. If you go to a teacher and you stand in silence it tends to be because you've done something wrong or you feel you have; whereas in counselling, of course, silence can be very positive as well as very negative. So particularly with children, it's not enough to let the silence go on without helping them to live with it, and to use it, and to try to understand what's happening.

PROCTOR: Do you focus on any particular processes or engage some faculties more than others?

MILNER: I think that at different stages in the counselling encounter I do focus on different things, different aspects. For example, I think initially most of the focus is on feelings. The idea is to try to help the person to release emotions and feelings which they are often not aware of, which have become buried, denied, but which nevertheless are very much influencing whatever it is they thought they came to talk about, even though that may have been presented in a fairly practical way. If you can, in the beginning, focus on feelings, what seems to happen is that it helps them on to yet another stage which has to do with exploring attitudes that they have, either to the problem that they've mentioned in the beginning, or to people, or to relationships or to you as the counsellor.

It does seem very important to get in touch with these feelings, otherwise you go along on this practical, sometimes superficial level, and never get at what's really important. When you come to look through the feelings at the attitudes that people have, what seems to happen is that they become more aware of the things that they have been denying. For example, if they can express the anger they have about a situation, this in itself gives them a picture of their attitude to that situation. If they didn't know before that they were angry, when they discover that they're angry about it, their attitude to it seems to be different, because they've discovered the feeling. Then they are more aware of this anger and other things previously denied and that seems to be another stage. When this awareness comes, it changes the way they look at themselves, it changes their perception of themselves. From being a person who didn't know they were angry, they become aware that they are sometimes an extremely angry person, which is a different personal view than they had at the beginning. And then it seems that the acknowledgement comes, that anger in this situation is all right. I can be an angry person, this is acceptable, but what am I going to do with my anger? So this slowly leads on to things you can do, which is a fairly practical thing, to an acceptance of yourself as having feelings that you haven't been able to acknowledge before: to seeing yourself in a different light because you've previously been unable to do this, and from that to develop, gradually, new attitudes to your problem, new ways of looking at your life, new ways of seeing yourself. And I suppose that these in turn finally lead to greater satisfaction with life and relationships, to being more real, to being more nearly yourself than you were in the beginning.

PROCTOR: What sort of climate do you seek to develop? How do you see this as being important for your joint task?

MILNER: I would just like to read Carl Rogers on this because he does explain it beautifully, and much better than I can. He says, 'If I can create a relationship that is characterized on my part by a genuineness and transparency in which I am my real feelings, characterized also by a warm acceptance of and a prizing of the other person as a separate individual and also characterized by a sensitivity to see his world and himself as he sees them', then Rogers suggests that the other individual in the relationship will experience and will understand aspects of himself which previously he repressed, which is what I was saying when I talked about focussing on different things. He will also find himself becoming better integrated and more able to function effectively. He will become more similar to the person he'd like to be, so he's that much further along this road that I mentioned before. He'll become more self-directive, more self-confident, he'll become more of a person who is unique or self-expressive. This seems also to lead a person to be more understanding and more acceptant of others, which has to do with the greater satisfaction in relationships that he gets. So that he'll be able to cope with the problems of his life more in his own way.

PROCTOR: Does the idea that people tend to recreate old patterns of relating in a counselling relationship, i.e. transference, have much significance for you? If so, what do you do about it?

MILNER: I think that transference occurs in all kinds of relationships, and it certainly occurs in counselling. It's not something which is just the prerogative of an analytical situation, it's a human experience. I think that people recreate old patterns of relating in counselling as in life. I think I deal with transference by being there as me in a relationship. In other words, I don't try to use it or deliberately encourage it by being enigmatic, withdrawing myself more as a person from what's going on. I try to use the feelings involved in transference in the same way as I use other feelings that come up in counselling. So it would be helping people to be aware of them just like any other feelings that arise, and then gradually leading on to explore the attitudes involved in those feelings.

PROCTOR: Do you regard yourself as a model for the client and, if so, what do you model?

MILNER: I think in this approach to counselling, the counsellor is a model and I think what the counsellor is modelling probably most of all, are the three things that Rogers stresses as being very important to a therapeutic relationship – the holy trinity of counselling – empathy, warmth and genuineness. To the extent that the counsellor contains these qualities, so the other person seems to respond in the same way. I'm not sure how much this is modelling and how much it's conditioning.

PROCTOR: Are you aware of conditioning? If so, what communications do you tend to positively condition, what communications do you tend to negatively condition?

MILNER: I'm very aware that, for example, I use nodding an awful lot. I find myself sitting there with my head going up and down, and I use nodding as a positive reinforcement for behaviour which is more genuine – I can nod when a person is being angry, they don't have to be being warm, but if I feel they're being real, I'll nod, and that's a definite form of reinforcement. I smile too, as a form of reinforcement, usually positive reinforcement. Occasionally I make jokes and I introduce some humour and this I think too, is a positive reinforcement. I seem to do it for that rather than to relieve tension. I don't usually make jokes if the situation is particularly tense.

I think I use silence as a reinforcement. Sometimes I've noticed that I use silence when I've noticed something that appears to be happening and I don't want to interpret it. I don't want to say what I've noticed because it's more helpful {the other person can come to it themselves and they're not ready yet. So I almost consciously bite my tongue on those occasions. I do find myself, though, having done that, rather gently leading the person in that direction. Instead of saying what I've seen, I will gently suggest that they look at that area. Sometimes they will see it, sometimes they won't until very much later.

PROCTOR: Are there any other patterns of interaction which you would identify as a process, which you habitually recognise or make use of?

MILNER: One of the most effective things in counselling is to hold back the responses that can make ordinary relationships comfortable, which is one of the reasons why people need counsellors. If I can use a personal example, my flat has recently been burgled and it has upset me very much, and I've talked to different people about this experience and I had very different responses. Some responses have been at a practical level, and say something like: 'Well you were silly, you know, to leave that key there, why on earth did you do it'? I left it there because I didn't take it away – there is no answer to that question, and when people are in the kind of discomfort that I am over this, it seems to throw them into a place that's not relevant. So that's an area to avoid in counselling. Another response I've had to this burglary is sympathy – a genuine response like: 'Oh gosh, that's happened to me and I know how I felt, you really must feel awful.' And this sympathy has been much more helpful than the practical response, but it's really not helped me to get in touch with what *I'm* feeling, it's helped me to understand how other people feel and it's hit on something of what I feel, but yet it's not really touched it. It has been supportive and I've valued it very much but it's somehow not got to me. And another sort of response I've had when I've said how I feel about what's happened is: 'What do you mean'? and that too, has taken me right away from where I am because I don't know what I mean. I only know at this stage, what I feel about what happened and the meaning of it is really not at all clear. To be asked what I mean just confuses me because I don't know.

PROCTOR: Have you answered the question about what responses you have worked on being able to use effectively?

MILNER: It seems perhaps to have to do very much with trying to be where the other person is. This seems to be most helpful. If you approach somebody from where you are, it just isn't touching what's really the core of what's gone wrong. It seems important to move around in their shoes whilst realising that there's a part of being in your own shoes that's universal because they belong to everybody else as well.

PROCTOR: And what ways do you have of letting them know that you can see things through their eyes?

MILNER: I think in this way of working, the way in which you reflect back their feelings, their perceptions to them for clarification, to give them a new look at what they have said and what they are, is very important. You may say: 'It feels to me as if what you're saying is that such and such happened', or 'You feel that's terrible', but the whole focus is on what they're feeling rather than what you're feeling. However when what you're feeling is intruding on what their feeling is, you've got to bring it out and talk about it.

PROCTOR: Are there any responses that you have deliberately soft-pedalled?

MILNER: The soft pedalling has to do with the ordinary every-day interactions of people; and interpretation which I very rarely use. Partly because it's from me; any interpretation I make is mine, it's my way of seeing rather than their way of seeing and this is why I use it sparingly. Although I am aware, as I said previously, that I do sometimes have the capacity to get at the essence and when I feel that, then I might make an interpretation.

I think the client's own world view makes sense in their own world. It may not make sense within my world but that's not what we're there for, to make sense of my world. It's to help them. And I think their world changes and their world view changes as they're helped to see it more clearly, rather than giving them another world view which is mine and saying: 'Well, this is the way I see it, this is the way you see it, which are you going to choose?'

PROCTOR: Do you see any demarcation between counselling and therapy?

MILNER: No. Rogers doesn't really differentiate between counselling and therapy. He uses the terms almost interchangeably in this approach.

PROCTOR: Are there no dangers in the uninitiated going 'too far'?

MILNER: I think that most of the dangers which come in counselling generally seem to be in the area of disturbing the *modus vivendi* that a person has created for himself. If you have a fairly seriously disturbed person who has created his own little world, it seems to me that the danger is that somebody will come along and shatter that world and give him nothing with which to replace it. Counselling is not a good place to do this because we're not able to give the constant care needed when this happens. But with Roger's approach, by trying to stay with the person in their world, there seems to be very much less danger that you will shatter it and make them feel very vulnerable, as you might with some of the approaches.

PROCTOR: Presumably there is a difference in the range of effectiveness. You won't help much if you are not very aware.

MILNER: Right. In one sense it's one of the easiest approaches to learn and yet it is one of the most difficult approaches to be and it's being it that's the effectiveness rather than learning it.

PROCTOR: Does the client group with which you work, or largely work, influence the way you do counselling?

MILNER: I think probably it must. But it is important to remember that Rogers first developed his approach with problem children. I've done a lot of work with students and they are, generally speaking, resilient. They're young, they're at a stage in life where they can be capable of really quick growth – very often from one week to the next – and this must encourage this sort of optimism. But I've also done quite a lot of work with children and here I think there is undoubtedly a difficulty in the area of helping a child to both transcend and accept his dependence on other people. Children are dependent on their parents and they depend on their teachers, too, in a way that students do not.

PROCTOR: In reality, you have power over them, control over them?

MILNER: Yes. That's it. And I am aware that this affects the sort of work I do with children, whereas it doesn't affect the work I do with students.

PROCTOR: Have you used it with less articulate clients?

MILNER: Oh yes, with children particularly. When a person is not very articulate I lend them my way of verbalizing feelings. What seems to happen is that we sit there and I try to pick up what they are feeling and speak it to them. Sometimes it's not successful, but very often it just seems to hit right on the mark and they say: 'But how do you know that that's what I'm feeling'? And I think with people who do have difficulty in speaking, this non-verbal communication which can develop between you if the relationship is good is terribly important. I've often found children more inarticulate than students and the children that I've worked with have been of a very wide ability range. For some children, I had paints and toys available, even though I was working in a secondary school, and we would use poetry, we would use anything that was for them, a way in which they could communicate. With the painting, they would just paint. They wouldn't necessarily have to talk about it but they'd paint it and leave it with me and talk about it when they were ready.

PROCTOR: And you wouldn't interpret their paintings?

MILNER: No. I might ask them to tell me, but I don't tell them.

PROCTOR: Have you any personal dilemmas in your counselling?

MILNER: One of the things I find most difficult about counselling is the amount of holding back that I do. People often say about counselling: 'Oh, you must give out an awful lot.' I think you do, but what is most difficult for me is what I hold back in counselling, rather than what I give out. It's what I can then do with what's held back, in terms of my own life which is one of my dilemmas in being a counsellor. I think another possible dilemma is that I see counselling as being available for everybody, but perhaps that's ambitious. If you look at analysis and psychotherapy which are available to a few people, and if you look at the benefits of social work, which tend to be given to people who are materially deprived in some way, I see counselling as being a source of help for people who are in neither of these groups, and that's what I mean by 'everybody'. And yet I am aware that there are few counsellors really, so should we be spending most of our time working with individuals or even with groups, or should we be spending more and more time helping people to help each other? And I think what I did as a counsellor in school, particularly, more so than with students, was to spend a fair amount of time helping staff to help children, not actually seeing the children themselves. And I felt that was very important. So in a way, I suppose that was my way of doing something about that dilemma.

Dougal Mackay

3   Behavioural Counselling

Dougal Mackay is now Principal Clinical Psychologist at St. Mary's Hospital, Paddington, London. His clinical interests are wide, but he has specialised particularly in the application of behavioural techniques to sexual and social adjustment problems. He is the author of *Clinical Psychology: Theory and Therapy*.

The term 'behavioural therapy' was first used by B. F. Skinner to refer to operant conditioning work with psychotic patients, but the emergence of a 'school' of Behaviour Therapy is normally associated with H. J. Eysenck. Two 'sub-schools' of Behaviour Therapy can be identified: one of behavioural 'technology', the proponents of which are interested in devising standardised techniques both for individuals and in systems (such as 'token economies' in schools and mental hospitals); the other might be called 'behavioural psychotherapy' which, while using the same techniques, is more interested in the behavioural analysis of individuals in order to discover which stimuli are the significant ones for that person in his situation. Dougal Mackay places himself in the second school.

SUGGESTED READING:

Jehu, Derek, *Learning Theory and Social Work*, London: Routledge and Kegan Paul, 1975.

Krumboltz, J. D., and Thorenson, C. E., *Behavioural Counselling: Cases and Techniques*, New York: Holt, Rinehardt & Winston, 1969.

Krumboltz, J. D., and Thorenson, C. E., *Counselling Methods*, New York: Holt, Rinehardt & Winston, 1976.

Mayer, Victor, and Chesser, Edward, *Behavioural Therapy in Clinical Psychiatry*, New York: Jason Aronson, 1971.

PROCTOR: What sort of spectacles are you going to wear for this interview?

MACKAY: I think I'll wear my Behavioural spectacles today since I feel most comfortable in them.

PROCTOR: Looking through those pair of spectacles, what comes into relief as to the nature of human beings, and the relationships between individuals and the groups, social systems, and ecological systems of which they are a part?

MACKAY: We'll deal with the nature of human beings first of all. Although I think few Behaviour therapists nowadays would deny the existence of thoughts and feelings, we tend to focus more on the *behaviour* of the individual. Each human being is seen as a collection of learned responses, a unique behavioural repertoire if you like, which has built up as a result of his particular past conditioning experiences.

PROCTOR: And to what extent is that repertoire built up purely by chance and how is it that people come to acquire certain conditionings and not others?

MACKAY: The behavioural repertoire develops in a relatively random fashion as parents, teachers and peer group members wittingly, or unwittingly, reinforce certain types of response. So they, in effect, shape the way in which the individual's behaviour, and subsequently his thoughts and feelings, develop.

PROCTOR: And is this entirely by chance and purposeless?

MACKAY: Right.

PROCTOR: And so the sum total of human experience that has accumulated is purely a series of haphazard conditioning events?

MACKAY: Yes. The Behavioural model is a very deterministic one. The individual may think that he is free to decide on a particular course of action, but in fact he is just behaving as he has been trained to. What he 'chooses' to do at any particular point in time is a direct result of past environmental experiences which have themselves occurred in a fairly haphazard sort of way. So the individual is just the product of his past experiences.

PROCTOR: How can you make a choice if you are just the sum total of your responses? What does 'choice' mean?

MACKAY: I don't see the individual as having total freedom to decide what he is going to do in a particular situation. What I am trying to say here is that so-called 'choice' is a direct result of past experience. In other words, if I knew everything about that person's past conditioning programme, I could predict what response he would 'choose' to make in any given situation. So choice is something which one can predict for the individual, if one is in full acquaintance with the facts of his past experience. Thus, he isn't really capable of being free in any meaningful sense of the term.

PROCTOR: If an individual is the sum total of his past experience then presumably social systems are sum totals of all those people's past experiences and it doesn't much matter what situation the person finds himself in. There isn't anything good or bad about a system.

MACKAY: On the contrary, I believe that there are both good and bad systems. In my model, a good system is one in which all individuals functioning within the system are getting a number of positive reinforcers, or rewards if you like, from participating in this system. A bad system is one in which the positive reinforcers are unfairly distributed. In other words, one or two members obtain more than their fair share of rewards while others are, consequently, deprived.

PROCTOR: In other words, what you are advocating is maximum pleasure for the maximum number? This is the purpose of human life?

MACKAY: That's it exactly.

PROCTOR: And what processes or structures within British society stand out as doing that effectively – that is, rewarding the maximum number of people?

MACKAY: Well, let's deal with the family first of all. Ideally the reinforcement administrators (i.e., the parents) should create a situation whereby each child knows what he has to do to obtain a reward, for instance, approval. He should also feel that he is just as likely to receive such gratification as his siblings. However, few families come anywhere near such an ideal. For instance, younger children may be unfairly judged by the same criteria which are used to evaluate the behaviour of the oldest. Furthermore, the 'halo' effect may apply, in that one particular child may regularly receive rewards for what he 'is' rather than for what he 'does'. Another way in which the family can fail its members is by the over-use of punishment (or threat of punishment) to produce acceptable behaviour. As a result, the individual will engage in activities, not because he 'wants' to, but just in order to 'keep the peace'. Thus, at its best, the family unit encourages the child to be actively engaged in the process of development, confident in the knowledge that he is functioning in a fair system. At its worst, it can produce anxiety, suspiciousness, hostility and a host of maladaptive behaviour patterns.

Many of these points also apply to the skills situation. Behaviourists prefer individual programmed learning techniques to the more traditional classroom teaching methods. In the individualistic operant system, all pupils have equal opportunities for accumulating rewards, instead of just those who are capable of surpassing the norms of the group. Furthermore, programmed learning, with its emphasis on positive incentives, dispenses with the humiliation tactics which are often employed in the traditional system.

PROCTOR: If people's behaviour is actually conditioned, and their idea of rewards is conditioned, how do they actually know what is rewarding and what isn't?

MACKAY: Well, Behaviourists tend to dodge this particular issue. A reward is operationally defined as something which the individual will work hard in order to obtain. We do not feel that it is useful to speculate why it is that such rewards as, say, approval and respect are apparently universal. So we would rather not attempt to account for what is going on in the individual than add to the long list of untestable theories.

PROCTOR: Do you feel any need to answer the accusation that such a view of life, and the technology attached to it, lends itself to being used by people with power and resources to minimise other people's awareness of the possibility of intrinsic or greater rewards, in order to have them serving *them* for quite nice rewards?

MACKAY: I think this is a good question. Of course, Behavioural techniques can be used to support a dictatorship. However, I don't see this as a flaw in the Behavioural model as such. Behaviourism provides a set of techniques which can be used for autocratic or democratic ends. Therefore, any misuse is a reflection of the administrator rather than the methodology he employs. From my point of view, the attraction of the Behavioural model is that it doesn't encompass a particular value system. It is a technology, not an ideology. In fact, I think that many of the so-called non-directive approaches are more guilty of 'blinkering' the individual than the Behavioural one. The illusion created by such therapists is that the individual is free to grow and develop in this unstructured situation. In fact they are conditioning their clients to behave and think in line with the value system associated with that model. In contrast, the Behavioural therapist directly manipulates the behaviour of his clients in order to help them attain goals which they have chosen. Thus, in my model, Behavioural techniques are employed to serve the needs of the individual rather than of society.

PROCTOR: Can you tell me briefly how, when and where your approach to counselling and therapy originated, and why?

MACKAY: I was attracted to the Behavioural approach because I dislike working with ambiguous material. Having been trained as a scientist, I like my goals clearly defined. I like to be able to measure what's going on. I personally find it rewarding to get something tangible at the end of doing a piece of work. Using the Behavioural model, I can go home at the end of the day knowing exactly what I have achieved. I would not derive the same degree of job-satisfaction from operating within another conceptual framework.

PROCTOR: When did that kind of way of looking at people actually begin?

MACKAY: Well, I think my approach to counselling is the original one. Since time began people, and even animals, have used rewards and punishments to bring about changes in the behaviour of others. However, the actual skill of Behaviourism, which gave this approach a jargon and a methodology, began in the 1930s in America and has rapidly developed ever since.

It arose because of dissatisfaction within academic ranks concerning the various schools of psychology of the day, which looked at subjective data exclusively. Since different researchers were producing contradictory findings, and there did not seem to be any possibility of arriving at basic truths through introspection, a certain group of psychologists decided to study behaviour in order to produce certain unequivocal laws and principles. The original idea was not to restrict psychology to the observation of gross behavioural responses. It conjectured that thoughts and feelings could be studied objectively as well at a later stage, once psychophysiological devices had become more sophisticated. However, as yet, this is something which hasn't materialised. This school developed when it did to meet a growing need for objectivity.

PROCTOR: What do you see as the objective of the counselling task?

MACKAY: In my view, the purpose of counselling is to give the individual as broad a repertoire of behavioural responses as possible. As specific anxieties are eliminated and as new skills are developed, he will presumably be better able to adapt to, and control, his environment.

PROCTOR: What resources do you see yourself bringing to the counselling task?

MACKAY: There are two main things I feel I have to offer. In the first place, I am capable (hopefully!) of being objective. By virtue of the fact that I am not emotionally involved with the client's problem situation, I am able to see things somewhat more clearly than he can. To be an effective Behavioural counsellor, one must be capable of convergent thinking when faced with complex, relatively intangible, material. A second important characteristic is enthusiasm. Because this is a very directive approach, you can only really make it work if you are able to push yourself forward and sell your ideas to the client. Once he has told you what his goals are, it is up to you to persuade him to go out and achieve them. Furthermore, this enthusiasm should be used as a positive reinforcer so that the client will feel motivated to make progress. You can't be impassive and diffident and do effective Behaviour therapy!

PROCTOR: Presumably, your actual training helps you to acquire these skills?

MACKAY: Well, I can see how one might think that a training course which emphasises learning theory would place a great deal of emphasis on the coaching of clinical skills. However, in practice this is not the case. The reason for this is quite simply that the training courses are run by 'first generation' Behaviourists who traditionally play down the importance of therapist variables as being unscientific. Going back to your question, I think that people who want to be actively involved, and dislike ambiguity, are attracted to the behavioural approach. In other words, it is their past conditioning, rather than their conditioning on the course, which determines whether they will make good behaviour therapists, or not.

PROCTOR: What do you see as being your responsibilities and the responsibilities of your client in a counselling interaction?

MACKAY: It is up to my client first of all to state his objectives. I am not going to tell him in what direction I think he should be going. Let's take a very concrete example. If (as has happened to me) a homosexual were to come along, complaining of impotence in that setting, and requesting help to become a potent homosexual, then I would see it as my responsibility to help him achieve this goal. In other words, contrary to popular opinion, Behavioural counsellors do not have any preconceived ideas of 'normality' which they are trying to sell to their clients. Now, I am not going to do a complete whitewash here. There are some situations where if somebody came along and wanted to change in a particular way which I personally felt – you will pick me up on this, I know – to be inappropriate, then I would not be able to offer him anything.

PROCTOR: Can I ask you what areas those might be? For instance, maybe thirty years ago it might have been making a homosexual potent. Would it have been one of the areas you would have found unacceptable?

MACKAY: If he did not want to become heterosexual, then, yes. Mind you, there are things that I find personally unacceptable at the moment yet I go along with. For instance, I regularly help high-drive business men, who develop psychosomatic complaints because they are too 'soft', to be even more ruthless and competitive than they were. I feel no more able to judge life-styles than sexual tastes. However, if a person was seeking to not only deprive certain sections of the community of some rewards, but wants to actually inflict punishment upon them, then I would draw the line. I suppose I am really talking about criminal offences. In other words, if I felt that by helping a person to maximise his rewards, then that would involve painful stimuli being applied to other members of society, then I would feel obliged to withhold my services. Apart from that, I think I am accurate in saying that I would go along with the goals which the individual sets for himself.

PROCTOR: What about the responsibilities to the person's own organism? The high-drive businessman may become more ruthless at the expense of his own total organism. He might die of a heart attack, or something. Is it your responsibility to do what is 'good for him'?

Well, the high-drive businessman example is a fairly
~~o~~ deal with. It is the ones who are attempting to be
~~ut~~ who are not very good at it, who are liable to get
~~heart attacks~~. By making them better at it, I hope I am reducing
the risk to the total organism. A more difficult example might
be of a patient with cirrhosis of the liver, who had lost confidence in social situations, who wanted assertion training to
enable him to return to his old drinking haunts. In such a case,
I would probably go ahead and help him. The overall state of
the organism is, in my view, the responsibility of the client,
assuming that he is in possession of all the relevant information.

It is essential that the client should play the major role in
determining the goals of therapy. By this I mean everyday
goals rather than ultimate objectives. It is also up to him to
decide which of the various techniques which have been described are most likely to work in his case. Finally, no worth-
while change will take place unless he is prepared to work hard
outside the sessions. In fact, I make an unwritten contract
with the client that he must take on responsibility for objectives,
decide which techniques should be used, and carry out 'homework tasks', otherwise it's no go. My task is to help him
clarify his goals, give him the information about techniques
which he requires, and make sure that he does not set himself
goals which he is unlikely to reach in the first instance. If he
attempts too much and fails, then therapy will become associated with noxious rather than pleasant experiences. So the
responsibility is very much shared between us.

PROCTOR: Is the counselling encounter or interaction different
from encounters you have in other professional or personal
roles?

MACKAY: We'll deal with assessment first of all because
obviously a lot of my professional time is spent using psychometric devices. I must emphasise that I don't use tests just so
that a label can be attached to the individual patient. Rather
I see the purpose of assessment as being to help the individual
realise what his assets and limitations are. The information
should be available to him as well as to the consultant in charge
of the case. If testing has a role it is to enable the individual to
see clearly what sort of goals are realistic for him to attain. So,
as you can see, there is no discrepancy between my two roles as
assessor and therapist. In both cases, I refuse to classify the

individual and tell him what he should do to get 'better'. I simply provide him with the necessary information and help him to make some use of it.

My other main professional function is teaching. Once again I try to make my material as clear and precise as I can, rather than to emphasise the areas of ambiguity. I also play my salesman-type role because teaching, like counselling, is all about promoting change. In order to achieve this you have got to somehow stimulate the consumer. The big difference is that since I am usually involved in lecturing to large groups on a one-off basis, I have to determine the objectives myself. Under these conditions, it is not appropriate to try to find out the goals of each individual student. Thus, I attempt to change their attitudes in a direction which I think to be important. I am far less directive as a therapist.

PROCTOR: Do you have ways of ensuring that your client and yourself share similar assumptions and objectives about the nature of the task and the interaction?

MACKAY: Certainly, many prospective clients feel they cannot share my assumptions about human behaviour and the purpose of existence. Where this is the case, I have nothing to offer that person. He must be able to accept the basic assumptions of my model before he is going to get anything out of my treatment approach. I would certainly not try to force, if you like, the Behavioural philosophy down anyone's throat. I present it to my clients as the model within which I work. If they feel they can utilise it, fair enough. If not, then this is a 'free operant' situation and they can 'choose' another brand of treatment. It's a very simple model as you have no doubt appreciated, and anyone, regardless of intellectual level, can comprehend what it is we are talking about. A major advantage of the Behavioural approach is that it is so tangible and so easily understood.

Now let's turn to objectives. This is, I think, another major strength of the behavioural approach. We take pains to ensure that the day-to-day, or week-to-week, objectives are clearly defined. A nebulous goal, such as 'be a little bit more effective in personal relations' would be unacceptable to us. A more tangible assertion task would be 'talk to individual "A" for thirty seconds about his recent holiday'. Neither he nor I will be able to decide whether a reward is appropriate or not unless we have a clear idea of the nature of the task.

PROCTOR: Are there any other particular processes or faculties which you engage?

MACKAY: Well, as I said at the beginning, I am not denying for a second that the individual experiences thoughts and feelings. The reason why I prefer to work at the Behavioural level is because these responses are tangible and can, therefore, be manipulated relatively easily. However, I do not want to give the impression that I ignore thoughts and feelings totally. What I find is that, as a person's behaviour changes, so he becomes aware of different thoughts and feelings. This is very important to stress because, I think, a lot of non-Behaviourists feel that we just do a little bit of cosmetic work to make the real problems less obvious. I do think that profound changes can take place at all levels through behavioural intervention. Furthermore, new techniques have emerged in recent years which do operate at a cognitive level, and I think that in a number of cases, this is a useful level to work at. Some of the things we say to ourselves act as stimuli for unacceptable forms of behaviour. For instance, the thought 'I'll never be able to do this' may elicit a weak response from the individual. We attempt to teach clients to say out loud different things to themselves and then to whisper them, and finally to emit them sub-vocally. In other words, thoughts can be looked at as if they were overt behavioural responses, rather than as semi-mythical concepts which aren't open to direct manipulation.

PROCTOR: And what about phantasies?

MACKAY: As you are well aware, the original Behavioural technique, systematic desensitisation, operates at a phantasy level. The person imagines progressively more anxiety-arousing situations while he is relaxed. As a result of this, behavioural changes, as well as phantasy changes, take place. So I don't think it's true to say that behaviourists ignore thoughts and feelings. We find them more difficult to work with than overt behaviour but, in many cases, we believe that they are the most important areas to concentrate on. However, we maintain that it is still possible to use the Behavioural model when attempting to produce such a change.

PROCTOR: Would you explain a bit more what you mean by behaviour?

MACKAY: Behaviour is basically anything the individual does. It includes such diverse occurrences as going one stop on the underground train, becoming sexually excited, negative thinking and increasing one's heart rate.

PROCTOR: And what kind of climate do you seek to develop as being important to your task?

MACKAY: The first thing I have got to do is to get rid of any idea that the client may have that I am a sort of expert. Working in a medical setting, they are usually referred by their GP or psychiatrist, and therefore expect me to play an authoritative role, and encourage dependence on their part. In order to dispel this notion, I insist on using first names, I never sit at a desk, nor do I take any notes during a session. We just relax and chat in a everyday fashion. One thing about the behavioural approach which makes it possibly unique is that we will actually go out together to the situation which the individual finds difficult. This means that any mystique which I still possess when in the consulting room vanishes rapidly. I mean you can't stand at a bus stop with a client in the pouring rain and still pretend to be detached and clinical. So we deliberately try to demystify ourselves and have a freindly – fraternal if you like – relationship with the client. This is very very important otherwise he is not really going to be able to say 'Well, I don't think much of that idea, can we do it this way?' and 'How about this for an objective?', and so on. It is essential that we have a very informal and relaxed atmosphere.

Something which irritates me is that because the Behavioural approach is very directive, people tend to think of it as also being authoritarian. However, the two don't necessarily go together. The non-directive approaches can, in fact, be more authoritarian than the Behavioural approach.

PROCTOR: So, the making of the contract and the relationship you establish clearly puts the client in the position of directing his own course, and you are only directive in the way that you know how he may pursue it?

MACKAY: That's exactly right. In fact, I won't even begin to introduce techniques to the client until I feel we have established that sort of relationship. It would be wrong of me to go ahead and try to tell him things, or deal with his first suggestions, until I feel he is totally relaxed with me and able to speak freely. And I achieve this often, quite deliberately, by going out for a walk with my client, if I find that the stimuli which impinge upon him in my room are preventing him from talking. I'll have a drink with him in a café, if necessary. Anything to get him to relate to me as a person rather than as a detached specialist.

PROCTOR: Does the idea that people tend to recreate old patterns of relating in a counselling relationship have significance for you?

MACKAY: Yes. Transference is very, very easily translated into learning theory terms, at least in my mind it is. But we would prefer to call it 'response generalisation'. Having learned to respond to a parent in a particular way, when one finds oneself faced with the person who looks similar, one tends to make the same sort of responses. Also, since, as I said earlier, thoughts and emotions will tend to be consistent with one's behaviour at a particular point in time, it follows that patients will experience irrational feelings towards their counsellors. In fact, not unlike the psychoanalytic therapists, I make use of this relationship. I feed back to him the effect of his behaviour on me. I let him know how he makes me feel, hoping he might learn from this and attempt to behave in different ways if the present way is not appropriate. Also, as I said earlier, I try to make myself positively reinforcing for that person, so that he will want to do things which meet with my approval. And, by trying to please me, he will be helping himself along the way. I unashamedly use myself as a carrot to encourage the person to change. Again, I must stress that the direction of change is determined by him.

PROCTOR: How do you give him permission to get rewards which aren't associated with pleasing you?

MACKAY: In the early stages of treatment, and I very much emphasise this point, I am the big, positive reinforcer. I begin each session by saying 'Well, what did you achieve during the week?'. The client will then come out with various things which are tied up with objectives which I have already defined fairly sharply for him. When appropriate I will say 'That's really good. It must have been difficult for you'.

In time, however, they start to reward themselves. This is a very crucial stage in treatment. They start saying, 'Well, I was quite pleased with that'. Where the client doesn't do this, where he is still looking to me as the extrinsic reinforcer, then I will actually coach him in self-reinforcement, so that he will learn to pat himself on the back. This is a very, very important part of the treatment in my view. A lot of the people who come with problems just haven't learned how to evaluate their performance, appreciate that they have done well and give themselves a cognitive pat on the back for so doing. So initially I do all the reinforcing, but later I 'fade' myself out and encourage them to take over the role of positive reinforcer.

PROCTOR: Do you regard yourself as a model for the client, and, if so, what are you modelling?

MACKAY: Although I often use modelling quite deliberately I don't really encourage my clients to attempt to be like me. It is important that they should retain their individuality. To counteract this, I bring in co-therapists at various stages of treatment. There are various reasons for doing this. I don't want to encourage dependence upon one person as some of the other therapists do. By bringing in other therapists, the patient doesn't invest too much emotionally in one individual.

If I could talk more specifically about one sort of treatment – social skills training – I think my views on the whole modelling issue will become clearer. I do very little modelling here. I may do some at the beginning to give the client some idea as to what role-playing is all about. But as far as possible I would rather put the client in the situation and say 'Do what you usually do' and then feed back to him how people felt about his performance, than say 'Watch me chat up this girl and then you try to do it like that'. In other words, I concentrate on rewarding appropriate responses which are already in the individual's repertoire.

But modelling can be useful in some of the less controversial areas of my work – for instance, something like handling a spider. If I can approach the spider, and pick it up without anxiety (which I just about can!), then the client generally finds it a little easier to do this as well. I am not quite sure if I have fully answered that question.

PROCTOR: If you are an important person in your clients' lives, doesn't that automatically mean they are likely to try on your behaviour for size?

MACKAY: I think this is a very fair question and I am sure that this does happen. For let's face it, they are aware, and I am aware, that I am more successful in my life than they are in theirs. They may, therefore, try to copy some of my behaviour.

However, if it doesn't work for them then they will drop it just like any other unrewarding behaviour. This is presumably most likely to happen when the simulated response isn't fully integrated with the rest of their behavioural repertoire – or personality, if you prefer.

I am aware, of course, that if modelling of this sort does take place then this leaves me open to the charge that I am inevitably propagating my own particular value system. My attitudes are inevitably revealed through my facial expressions, and such. This could clearly influence the sorts of objectives the client sets himself. However, this is not something that is unique to Behaviour therapy. So far as possible, I try to cut down these cues to a minimum.

PROCTOR: What kind of behaviour do you expect to sanction and encourage in a client? Are you aware of positively conditioning certain communications and negatively conditioning others?

MACKAY: I'll say! As I've already said, the client sets up the targets and I, therefore, expect him to carry out the responses which have been decided upon. I do everything I can to encourage him to do this and, of course, when he comes back I reinforce any appropriate behaviour which has occurred. So far as negative conditioning – punishment – is concerned, I play this down as much as possible. Principles of learning seem to indicate that punishment is a very ineffective way of changing behaviour. Also, of course, it can have an adverse effect on a relationship in that it may lead to an association between myself and anxiety. I would far rather put the emphasis on positively conditioning appropriate behaviour.

PROCTOR: Are there any other patterns of interaction which you would identify as a process which you habitually recognise and/or make use of?

MACKAY: Yes, I feel this is a question about what I actually do in a therapy situation. As I have already said, the emphasis here is very much on 'behaviour' so we are *doing* things in a therapy situation, rather than sitting about and *talking* about them, although the latter is an important part which I shall come to later.

I suppose the basic techniques are, first of all, *systematic desensitisation*, which is simply helping individuals to overcome anxiety in certain situations. This is all part of the behavioural expansion idea which is, so far as I am concerned, the main aim of therapy. We have to eliminate all those sources of anxiety which inhibit the individual from responding appropriately in particular settings. Then there is *flooding*. This involves putting the person in at the deep end, so to speak, and creating the worst imaginable situation for him. Basically, we put him through an experience he typically avoids until such times as the anxiety has been extinguished. Incidentally, before beginning such a programme I would, of course, talk over the approach with the client. He can choose whether he wants a slow and easy desensitisation approach or whether he would rather get it over quickly by going through a programme of flooding. This is another occasion on which the client has a big say as to what the treatment is going to be all about.

Where the individual wants to give up a particular habit, such as gambling, drinking or abnormal sexual behaviour, then anxiety-increasing techniques are employed. *Aversion therapy*, which involves pairing shocks with the unwanted stimulus, is a traditional method for achieving this. However, it is rarely employed these days because it is so crude, cruel, and not altogether effective – at least, by itself. Nowadays we tend to use *covert sensitisation*. Here the individual is told to imagine himself carrying out a particular activity which he is not happy with and is then instructed to imagine that he is feeling unwell. In this way we try to build up – cognitively – a negative association between anxiety and that particular activity.

Another much used treatment is *social skills training*. In the first place, we help the client to get over his anxieties by using a systematic desensitisation approach in a group setting. We then coach him in the basic skills of social interaction. Once again, the emphasis is very much on rewarding appropriate behaviour.

There are just some of the basic techniques which one might use during the course of Behavioural counselling.

PROCTOR: In systematic desensitisation you are actually focussing on physiological responses some of the time?

MACKAY: This is not necessarily so. We find with many of the phobics we treat that the problem is basically a cognitive one. In other words, a client may *think* he is frightened of something but there may be no evidence of this at either a physiological or behavioural level. In other cases, the client may deny anxiety, remain physiologically unresponsive in the presence of the object, but take steps to avoid it. Furthermore, in other cases, the individual presents with a psychosomatic symptom but is not aware that he is anxious, nor does he avoid the stress situation. It is essential to find out whether it is a cognitive, physiological or behavioural type of phobia, and to use the appropriate techniques.

PROCTOR: Given that there are a fairly limited number of ways that we can respond to a request for personal help, or seek to intervene in another's personal exploration, are there any responses that you have worked on being able to use effectively?

MACKAY: My big hobby-horse is *assertion training*. Not just for people who lack social skills, but for almost anyone, regardless of the diagnostic label that is attached to them. I think a certain amount of assertion training is appropriate in most cases. By this I mean helping the individual to exert more control over his environment than he has done in the past. It is not aggression-training, as a lot of people tend to think. The aim of assertion training is to help people to get what *they* want without eliciting hostility from others. If hostility does result then the strategy has been self-defeating. So, whether it is someone who presents with a simple spider-phobia or someone who is involved in a complex marital or family situation, I think specific training in assertion therapy (and this can involve shouting, punching pillows, learning to argue, learning to interrupt and to compete) can be an important component of the treatment approach.

PROCTOR: Perhaps if you find you have to train a lot of people in assertion therapy then maybe social systems in our present culture have systematically failed to train people in assertion, and actually punish them for unharmfully asserting themselves?

MACKAY: Right, I feel strongly about this. We have conflicting standards, in my opinion. On the one hand we say 'Be your brother's keeper' and 'look after your neighbour' and, on the other hand, the big rewards – money, status, even attractive mates! – go to those who are the best competitors. In other words, we place the individual in a double-bind situation: he is punished for standing up to parents and teachers, but is still somehow expected to learn to compete and push himself forward.

PROCTOR: It seems to me you would not be willing to work with homosexuals who wish to be potent to-day, if there had not been homosexuals in the past who had asserted their wish to be homosexual, over and above the point that it gave pain and displeasure, and apparently did create hostility in other people in society. Clearly, an ultimate reward, like satisfactory homosexual relationships, may depend on behaviour that is extremely unrewarding for some clients, like being ostracised and cut off from family, and so on. I think my first question is, are you bound to settle for the objectives your client first sets himself? The second question is: don't you carry quite a lot of power in deciding which norms in society a person has a right to ask you to make him assertive over, and which norms of society you decide he should stay within?

MACKAY: If I can leave your two questions for a moment and go back to your earlier statement concerning the need for militant homosexuals to assert themselves in a way which did not meet initially with positive reinforcements. It is quite understandable (although unusual) in Behavioural terms to conceptualise the individual as delaying gratification in order to receive a more pleasurable reward. Many of my clients prefer to struggle with immediate hardships (e.g. family rows, upsets at work) rather than settle for 'an easy life'. It is the belief that the ultimate rewards will far outweigh the intervening unpleasantness which leads them to assert themselves and perhaps even over-assert themselves. However, now to return to your questions. So far as the first one is concerned, I never automatically accept the objectives the individual proposes. I want to be sure that he really believes in the goals he is setting himself. I do not challenge his assumptions as a rule. I merely give him plenty of opportunity to be absolutely clear in his own mind why he is asking to go in a particular direction. And, of course, his targets can be changed at any stage in the treatment. A fair number of my clients who set off in a particular direction decide to change their ultimate objectives in mid-stream. For instance, a homosexual who was undergoing a treatment programme aimed at changing his sexual orientation said, after half-a-dozen sessions, 'I have changed my mind. Really what I want is a satisfactory homosexual relationship'. At which point, we just change the treatment and set off in a new direction. We do not fully commit ourselves to an ultimate target at the outset. We re-evaluate the objectives throughout the treatment programme. So far as your second question is concerned, I can only recollect one occasion on which I refused to help a client because of a value-system conflict. This was a case of a client who had been a child-molester. He was referred to me because he had lost confidence and could not interact with anybody any more. The problem, so far as I was concerned, was that if I made him more assertive there was a fair chance that he would be back in the streets, in the toilets, and in the cinemas, picking up small boys again. And that is the only case – that I am aware of, anyway – where my values became very apparent to me and I acted as an agent of society and refused to offer my services to help an individual to do something which *I* felt to be inappropriate. As I say, that is the only occasion where I have been aware of doing this *explicitly*. I would not deny for a moment that I am signalling covertly to my client and that he may be reacting to this. However, all therapists are undoubtedly guilty of this.

PROCTOR: If people ask you to take away pain and you very kindly, and with the best motives in the world, agree, then maybe that leaves unchanged the systems in which they live, in which power is really used not in their best interests. If enough pain was felt they would co-operate in making themselves heard. To that extent, by taking away the pain are you preventing this from happening, and therefore, acting to an extent as a major social conserver?

MACKAY: Yes, I would not disagree with that. But I do not see that it is my place to evaluate social systems and push one type forward at the expense of another. While sympathising with your social conservation argument, I am very concerned about those psychotherapists who have extended their role to that of social agitators. My brief, as I see it, is simply to help the individual to maximise his rewards in society as it exists at present. I feel strongly that I would be misusing my position were I to promote one type of social change at the expense of another.

PROCTOR: Do you see any demarcation between counselling and therapy within your framework?

MACKAY: I see a fairly clear dividing line. Counselling involves discussing with my clients strategies whereby they can function more effectively in their environment. When I engage in Behavioural counselling, I simply teach people how to set objectives and how to evaluate their performance relative to these objectives. I also teach them how to reward themselves. Thus, *counselling* is *talking* about responding and reinforcing. When I engage in Behaviour *therapy*, I actually *reinforce* certain categories of behaviour and therefore change responses directly. So, as I see it, counselling involves talking about strategies whereas therapy implies actually conditioning the individual.

PROCTOR: You do not see, as a psychoanalyst might, a distinction between the degree of illness of the client you are working with?

MACKAY: Obviously, counselling tends to be used more often with 'well' clients. However, in my model, counselling refers to the set of techniques rather than to the depth of intervention.

PROCTOR: So, there are not any dangers in the uninitiated going beyond counselling to therapy?

MACKAY: Oooh! I do not know whether I go along with that. Yes, I think there are dangers, in fact with both types of approach. The first obvious point to make is that the uninitiated person might be ineffective, thus making difficulties for the person who has to follow. A client will become disillusioned with the approach and will, therefore, derive relatively little benefit from that sort of treatment in the future. There are cases where the uninitiated therapist can do actual positive harm. For instance, let's take a very simple-sounding technique, such as systematic desensitisation. If you do not control the anxiety level carefully enough, then you may, in fact, strengthen the phobia. Many enthusiastic amateurs have not quite grasped the significance of the word 'systematic'. However, the greatest risks probably surround assertion training. Bringing angry and hostile feelings quickly to the surface by direct methods is a form of Behavioural intervention which should only be carried out by a skilled therapist who knows when and how to put the brakes on, if necessary. As you can see, I am very much against people tinkering with Behavioural techniques.

PROCTOR: Looking at *you* personally, and taking off your spectacles, does the client group with which you work, or have largely worked, influence your way of working and the model that you continue to use?

MACKAY: Quite frankly, I believe that the behavioural model is applicable all across the board. I have worked with children, sub-normals, teachers, businessmen, psychotics, neurotics and physically handicapped patients. Unlike many other brands of psychotherapy, the intelligence and verbal fluency of the client has no bearing on whether or not he is suitable for this approach. I have chosen to work with the Behavioural model simply because I find that the most economic and effective way of dealing with the large majority of problems which my clients bring to me. However, I would like to modify that by stating that there are certain clients – and I could go on to talk about this – for whom the Behavioural model is more appropriate than for others.

What one basically needs in order to practice Behavioural therapy or Behavioural counselling with a client is a clear objective. If a person says 'Well, my life's not going very well, I'm confused, I don't know where I am going' and is unable to come forward with a more precise objective, then there is no way I can get a programme off the ground. Occasionally such clients may come back to me at a later stage having formulated their goals through group therapy or some other kind of approach. The second point here is that there is no way in which I can make progress with someone who is not prepared to take responsibility for his own behaviour. So the totally passive patient is unlikely to be taken on for Behaviour therapy with the obvious exception of patients who are subjected to ward management regimes. So, the model works best where the problems are clearly defined and where the client is willing to become involved in goal setting and in carrying out the appropriate tasks.

However, I do not want to give the impression that the model is only appropriate for mono-symptomatic phobias, as many people believe. Many problems which might be described as – using the word very loosely – existential might seem, at first sight, totally inappropriate for Behaviour therapy. However, many of the people with these sorts of ill-defined problems find the structure of behaviour therapy particularly useful to them. It enables them to set up day-to-day objectives and actually achieve something in their lives. Many come to feel that it is more useful to engage in some sort of activity than just to discuss their problems vaguely in a non-directive setting.

PROCTOR: Do you have personal dilemmas in your work?

MACKAY: Not dilemmas, so much. I am very envious of the other models in the sense that I think people practising the various psychotherapies derive more intellectual stimulation from their work than I do. The a-theoretical nature of Behaviourism deprives its practitioners of theoretical 'meat'. However, I think it is regrettable that a number of people would appear to have moved towards particular models because they are getting something out of it personally rather than because it is particularly effective with the client population with which they are working. I must confess that in my own particular unit I get a lot out of going to staff groups, and so on. I find this a stimulating and (for me) helpful experience. However, I attempt to distinguish between what I like to do and what is useful for my client. I personally get very little job satisfaction out of desensitising clients to simple phobias. However, I would not allow myself to – well – indulge myself in playing quasi-philosophical games with them, if I really felt that the best thing I could do would be to get them to lie on the couch, relax and look at pictures of spiders. . . .

PROCTOR: I feel a bit rebuked! Do you feel that what you have said in answer to these questions represents your practice and experience fairly fully, or has it slanted it in such a way as to make it not easily recognisable?

MACKAY: It seems to be a fair reflection of what I do. The trouble is that when I talk about it in this sort of setting it comes over, I feel, as very cold and mechanistic. I talked to you briefly about the therapist/client relationship – which I feel to be a very warm and friendly one – yet the jargon makes it sound very impersonal. It is not like that at all. It is very difficult to get the feel of Behaviour therapy across to people. I think that those who have worked with me and have sat in on my sessions feel that the dignity of the client is very much maintained. He is not just some object being shaped, twisted around, according to the whims of the therapist, as so many non-Behaviourists maintain.

PROCTOR: It did not sound as if he was to me.

Francesca Inskipp

4   # Developmental Counselling

Francesca Inskipp was trained and worked as a teacher until she took a Counselling Diploma at Keele University in 1970–1. She subsequently worked as Training Officer for Essex Youth and Community Service. Since 1973, she has, as Course Tutor, been responsible for the Diploma in Counselling and Pastoral Care for experienced teachers at North East London Polytechnic. She is a member of the Standards and Ethics Committee of the British Association for Counselling.

Developmental Counselling has grown out of Carl Rogers' Client-Centred Counselling. It was developed in America by Leona Tyler and Donald Blocher. It combines developmental theory with Client-Centred and Behavioural methods. Within the broad category of Developmental Counselling, Roger Carkhuff and recently Gerard Egan have been influential.

SUGGESTED READING:
Blocher, Donald, *Developmental Counselling*, New York: Ronald Press, 1974.
Egan, Gerard, *The Skilled Helper: A Model for Systematic Helping and Interpersonal Relating*, Monterey: Brooks Cole, 1975.
Tyler, Leona, *Work of the Counsellor*, Englewood Cliffs: Prentice Hall, 1969.
Hamblin, Douglas, 1978.

PROCTOR: What do you see when you look through a pair of 'developmental spectacles'?

INSKIPP: It's a model of man, and a way of conceptualising what you're doing in counselling.

PROCTOR: Looking through that pair of spectacles, what comes into relief as to the nature of human beings, and the relationship between individuals and groups and social systems of which they're a part?

INSKIPP: It's looking at a human being as being in a constant process of growth; that growth, both physically and psychologically, is sequential. Man goes through a whole series of stages which are fairly well-patterned but which are unique to every individual. The patterns are set in a way that he moves from one stage to the next and in those stages he needs to acquire different ways of coping with his environment. It is the response of the growing individual to the environment which determines whether he is living effectively or not.

PROCTOR: Presumably that must be culturally conditioned. Does what is required of him at different stages vary?

INSKIPP: Yes, Developmental Counselling takes into account that man is very much shaped in the way he interacts with other people, by his culture, by the family he is in, and by the state of the universe at the moment. It's the interaction between the growing, changing individual and the environment which shapes the human being.

PROCTOR: The social system requires or expects certain things of the individual?

INSKIPP: Putting it simply, he is born into a family which shapes him, but he also shapes the family, so it's a two-way process, going on all the time between a growing individual and the environment. And it depends both on what the environment is and also on what stage he is in his growth, as to how he can respond to the environment. The environment needs to match his needs. If, for instance, when he's ready to crawl and explore, the environment doesn't provide an opportunity for him, he's not going to be able to develop the parts that are, at that moment, ready to develop. And, if he doesn't develop them then, it will later be much more difficult. So, I see it as important that the environment match the growing individual's needs which, of course, often it doesn't.

PROCTOR: What do you see as the purpose of all those growing human beings reacting and interacting with themselves and others in their environment?

INSKIPP: That's a very difficult philosophical question. On a very simple level, I see that the purpose is that the human being can respond to the environment and be part of it. On another level it's survival – plain survival – both in the situation and in the long-term. There presumably is a drive for the survival of the race somewhere within individuals. There seems also to me to be a drive in human beings for a personal identity survival. For this, human beings need to feel that they are part of a larger whole. Not that they survive in an identical form but some part of their energy system will go on surviving after the body ends. It may be that some people – perhaps people living on a high level – have their energy drive there. The basic energy drive is just for food and security – the Maslow concept – and as you get these lower needs supplied, there seems to be a higher level which seems to be self-actualisation. But presumably, self-actualisation is for a purpose of forming some essence of self which in some way will fit into some other system.

PROCTOR: How and when did this kind of approach to counselling originate?

INSKIPP: I've met it through writings of Leona Tyler and her book *The Work of the Counsellor*, published in 1961. It was developed very much more by Donald Blocher in his book *Developmental Counselling*. Much of the developmental work, I think, originates in Erickson's developmental psycho-social stages.

PROCTOR: Does it tie in with Piaget and the other type of developmental psychology?

INSKIPP: Certainly, Havinghurst and the developmental tasks which he states (I think he gives sixty-seven) does, but in general it doesn't seem to take an awful lot of account of Piaget, except as background. It's also tied in with Maslow's hierarchy of needs. And you've got the two themes – sequential development, and the hierarchy of needs and people moving through need systems.

PROCTOR: What processes or structures within British society today stand out as being helpful to the realisation of those appropriate or necessary uses of energy that you talk about?

INSKIPP: It seems to be in places where people become

committed to what they're doing – organisations or institutions which encourage people to form co-operative groups and small enough groups to be able to work in face-to-face interaction.

PROCTOR: Would you call families helpful?

INSKIPP: Families can be helpful structures. I think that now that the family has lost its economic purpose, it is considered that the family should be the emotional, social developer of people, and in this we are asking an awful lot of it. People expect to be able to get most of their emotional satisfaction from the marriage, from the family, and feel cheated if they haven't. Some families seem to manage that but a whole lot of families don't. A lot of people come into counselling because they are not getting the satisfaction from their families that they feel they ought to get. There's an assumption in society that families ought to be providing this emotional support and training in skills so that people can go forth into other things. A good school does this but it seems to me that small schools do it on the whole very much better than large schools. Big schools can be very difficult to deal with because there seems to be something in people that needs to feel committed, feel a part of a group.

PROCTOR: What is the damage a bad system can do?

INSKIPP: I think a bad system like a bad family and a bad school can make an individual feel unworthy. I suppose we all feel unworthy to an extent, but the more unworthy and inadequate people are made to feel, by the social system they're in, the more constricted they become as human beings and less able to cope effectively in a changing environment and cope with themselves changing. Highly competitive schools may be good for the people who come out at the top but the vast majority can be made to feel that they're not very adequate. It seems that, if those people are in a family situation or in a group situation in which they're valued, inadequate feelings can change. But often people are in schools and in families and in groups in which they feel devalued all the time.

PROCTOR: So people can't learn the skills they need or make the requisite responses until they have experienced being valued?

INSKIPP: It is important to set up structures where people can feel valued for being what they are and being unique. Not just valued for being academically or athletically able which are two of the constructs in schools.

PROCTOR: What do you see as the objective of the counselling task?

INSKIPP: I think the counselling task is to help people live as effectively as possible. That's a very broad outline.

PROCTOR: Effective for whom?

INSKIPP: Effective both for them and for the society in which they live. They are so much dependent on the society they live in, it must also be effective for that society. But it is primarily concentration on the unique human being and on there being thousands of different ways of being effective. There are situations in which people have a certain amount of freedom (more limited for some people than others). It's helping them use that freedom they've got, in their environment, to their own greater satisfaction I think.

PROCTOR: Your view of man, then, is that he won't be feeling as effective as he could unless he is getting some valued interaction with the other people that form his environment?

INSKIPP: Presumably, there are some people who get their satisfaction from living as hermits but they are few and far between. And many of them may be in communication with another bit of the universe and therefore don't need human interaction so much.

PROCTOR: What about aggression in that model?

INSKIPP: I think that a lot of aggression and destructiveness is through frustration, through people being under-valued or feeling worthless, feeling inadequate, feeling society has no use for them. I think that in a face-to-face co-operative group, conflict can be brought out and used constructively. But that's probably an idealistic view. If people are seen as individuals and unique even though we have a sequential pattern, everybody is different. Partly because of their reactions to their different environments, they will be different. It is helping people sort out what they really do value and what their attitudes are. I suppose people tend to be happiest, most effective, working in groups where they hold common values and common goals of some sort.

PROCTOR: What resources do you see yourself bringing to the counselling task?

INSKIPP: I find this a difficult question to answer. I see the most important thing as being able to communicate my under-standing and empathy to the other person, to be able to set up a relationship in which I am trying to communicate that I accept them as a person, and I'm suspending my judgement of them. Also that I am interested in them and value them, and that I try to communicate myself as a person who is open to them. These are personal qualities but they're personal qualities on which I am constantly working, in order to improve them.

PROCTOR: What do you mean by 'valuing' a person?

INSKIPP: I see it as a suspension of judgement. One of the ways in which I am better able to accept and value people now is that I have learned that, on first meeting people, I have a lot of feelings about them and that most of those feelings are irrational and tied up with all sorts of other things. When I get to know a person better by sitting down and listening to him and beginning to understand him, I can always begin to value something in him. I think there are some people whom I would find very difficult to value but the more experienced I become with a wider range of human beings, the more able I am to suspend judgement. I suppose I learned very early on to judge a person very quickly so that he won't attack me, and therefore I decide which part of myself I put out to him. If I can suspend that and feel that he is not going to attack me, I can be more open to him. The more I can work on my own self-acceptance and value myself as a person, the more able I am to be open to other people. It is important for me to develop these qualities in myself and to help other people to do this. However, they aren't any good as qualities in me unless I communicate them and that's the other thing I'm working on – improving my communication skills. I need to find out if my communication with others matches my intention. I need feedback from others, feedback from work, from video tapes, from clients.

PROCTOR: What other resources do you bring?

INSKIPP: Resources of increasingly trying to formulate in my mind a model of human beings that explains why people do what they do. As I listen to clients, I try to feel what it feels like to be them, what their motivations and attitudes and values are, so that I can communicate back to them that I'm under-standing what they're saying. My ability to help them explore themselves by techniques like reflection techniques, etc. Any understanding I've got of human nature and of a situation is important so that when the client is exploring his situation and when he is beginning to understand it, I am also able to add other frameworks which may help him understand the situation in different ways. It is almost like being able to give clients another pair of conceptual spectacles. They may be seeing the world in only one way and it is useful to have a variety of spectacles which I can say 'Try looking at it through these'. That's what I would see as the second stage. In the first stage they're exploring, and in the second stage we are together trying to understand them in their situation. And all this leads possibly to a third stage in which I would see as bringing resources to help them in problem-solving, decision making, behaviour change, or in helping them to further reduce confusion in their minds. Lots of people need help in sorting out their values and what they want from life.

PROCTOR: Is it important to you to have a knowledge of community resources that can be useful to your clients?

INSKIPP: Yes, I think I need a knowledge of the environment of the people I am counselling. It is very important that counsellors work in situations about which they know a lot and, if possible, are themselves active in and a part of that culture.

PROCTOR: But aren't there certain blind spots which develop when you are part of that organisation? Sometimes a complete outsider may not have the inside knowledge but he does have a greater objectivity and clarity about a situation.

INSKIPP: Yes, this is especially a problem for a counsellor in a school. Is it better to have somebody who is within the situation than somebody outside? On the whole, I think that the counsellor inside can be more useful as a resource to the pupils than somebody who comes from outside. I also see developmental counselling as anticipating the needs of clients and therefore working on the structure of the organisation as well, so that development is helped, not hindered, by the organisation. Because I see the interaction between the individual and the environment as something the counsellor is working on, I feel it's important to be part of the environment. I have to be seen as having some expertise in knowing what to do.

PROCTOR: So as well as showing your client a receptive face, you may have to show the system an active, effective face?

INSKIPP: Yes, I have to be seen as having expertise in knowing what to do and having the skills to act as a change agent, which means you can't be too aggressive or bull at a gate.

PROCTOR: What do you see as being the responsibilities of the client and the counsellor in a counselling interaction?

INSKIPP: The counsellor's responsibilities are to make it clear what the process is about, and to set up the structure within which the counselling interaction takes place. The counsellor structures the situation, although she allows the client freedom within the structure – the time, when it will take place and where it will take place. She makes it clear to the client that he is expected to talk about and explore what he's come about and to work with the counsellor towards helping himself live more effectively. She makes it clear, even when the client comes in for vocational counselling, that there is indeed a task to be performed.

PROCTOR: And the responsibility of the client?

INSKIPP: The responsibility of the client, as I see it, is to explore himself and what he's come about. I see the counsellor as setting up some sort of model of good human interaction. Part of the responsibility is to teach the client methods of exploring himself so that he doesn't always have to come back to the counsellor to do this. He begins to learn to know how to understand himself.

PROCTOR: Would you call that modelling?

INSKIPP: Yes, modelling. The longer I am in counselling, the more I believe that people learn from modelling.

PROCTOR: What is the difference between the counselling encounter and other encounters that you have?

INSKIPP: The counselling encounter is focused on helping, in contrast with teaching. You may be doing some teaching, but your teaching is to help the client to be more effective as a human being. If you are teaching in another area, your purpose may be to impart information or to teach a specific skill or it may be to put yourself over in some way to the other person. But I think the counsellor is specifically focused on helping the other person be more effective in the areas which *they* bring and in in which *they* want to be more effective. Counselling can be part of teaching. It is at one end, when you're helping people build new patterns within themselves because of the information that they've received. At the other end of the spectrum teaching is the imparting of information.

PROCTOR: Do you find that counselling is different from friendships?

INSKIPP: I think that many good friendships produce the same effects as counselling, but the difference in counselling is that there are limits and boundaries (for example, a time limit). Normally, you set your limits and your boundaries to what you will do with the client. The client may come to *you* for friendship but the counsellor is not dependent on the client for friendship. And if that is happening, there's usually something wrong with the counselling process. The counsellor needs to have, outside the counselling situation, good friendships of her own so that she's not dependent on the counselling situation. One of the problems with clients is that this may be the first time in their lives they've experienced this sort of friendly relationship, and, therefore, they expect much more from the counsellor than the counsellor is able or wanting to give. It is the counsellor's responsibility to try and make this clear to the client and that's very difficult if you are counselling in an unstructured situation. If you have a label as counsellor and a definite place where you work, then that's ok. But people can get very muddled otherwise. The counsellor may have to accept dependency from the client in the early stages to enable them to start working but the counsellor has to be aware of her own needs to create dependency and has to work gradually with the client to foster independence. If you are depending on the client for satisfaction then collusiveness starts to operate, as in a friendship. You dare not be as confronting as you want to be.

PROCTOR: Do you have ways of trying to ensure that your client and you have similar assumptions and objectives about the nature of the task and interaction?

INSKIPP: This is something I know is important and I am certainly trying to make the process visible to the client. It's not always easy. Making a contract may be one of the ways. Saying 'we've got one hour now', and giving him freedom, at the beginning, to start where he wants to start and gradually trying to put it within a structure of the time that is available, and trying to help him see the pattern of the way in which we're trying to work.

PROCTOR: But does your client have the chance to say 'No, that's not what I want to do'?

INSKIPP: Yes. I see counselling as a working together, not just a warm relationship. That may be all the clients need at the moment, a warm relationship in which they can just talk until they're talked out and shed off the emotion and say 'I feel better now. I can go'. But I see that as just 'stage one', which may be enough for some people. But if counsellors always work on that premise, they're of very limited use to clients. It may be enough for some clients but the majority need to go through the other stages into some form of action.

PROCTOR: So let's move on to tactics. Counsellors tend to focus on certain aspects of a client's total interaction to his environment. Where do you focus? Do you focus on any particular process or engage some faculties more than others?

INSKIPP: I think, as I said earlier, the focus is on helping people explore what they think about things and what they feel about things. I see both as being important – trying to keep the focus on them and their thoughts and feelings and not on the situation. I want to keep them focused on their thoughts and feelings *about* the situation. I try to get them to be very concrete in giving examples. If they say 'My mother's always on at me – she never stops,' I get them to focus down. 'Can you tell me what it was like? Give me an example of the last time she was on at you'. Most people are not able to explore the area of feelings as opposed to thoughts.

PROCTOR: What kind of climate do you seek to develop? And how do you see it being important for your joint task?

INSKIPP: I think that warmth and acceptance are the most important parts of the climate because I don't think people explore themselves and explore difficult areas, which are often what they need to explore, unless there is some degree of warmth and trust generated. But the climate mustn't be too cosy because it's got to be a working situation. It's not easy to get the balance between the warmth and the working because the warmth and acceptance may be very slow in a situation and the working situation may need to have more bite and briskness. Learning how to use time effectively is one of the skills in the counselling relationship.

PROCTOR: Does the idea that people tend to recreate old patterns of relating in a counselling relationship – transference – have any significance to your work and, if so, what do you do about it?

INSKIPP: I accept that people recreate relationships. I don't use transference in the counselling situation. I see counselling as taking place very much in the present and working on the present and the future. I would try to bring into the present what's happening now between the client and myself as something that is actually happening, not interpreting it as something from the past. I don't label the relationship as 'transference' but try to explore what's happening between us as it happens, reflecting the client's feelings to him and being open to my feelings and discussing them if it seems useful.

PROCTOR: But what do you do, for example, if a client is continuously looking to you for guidance, which may be his habit of relating to all authority figures?

INSKIPP: Again, I make use of concrete examples. You can get people to look at a concrete example, then another one, and then draw out patterns from those concrete examples. When they can perceive and acknowledge the pattern then I need skill to help them change, change their perception, or change their way of behaving, to alter their patterns. To be able to suggest to them ways they can work on changing and provide support needed while they are doing that. So not necessarily interpreting what's happening in the counselling relationship.

PROCTOR: Does human conflict and pain come into your framework? Do you think that people keep those patterns not just as anachronistic coping mechanism, but as ways of taking care of pain or fear?

INSKIPP: Yes, but I also look at it from a behavioural point as well. A particular way of interacting may be a way of avoiding pain in an actual situation. I often say, 'What is it that is being avoided? You may be gaining something by this way of doing it'. I try to help a client work out what the costs are. They may be gaining something all the time by this way of doing it and they may decide 'Well, the costs are too great to change', but I try to make the issues as explicit as possible.

And I think in those situations you can move on to other levels in their exploration, in which they are beginning to understand a bit more about their motivation, about their defences if you like. You can help them recognise defenses and recognise whether they're keeping defences which were very useful to them before but now might be usefully dismantled. You can work out with them little steps which they might try out with support. One of the skills and resources of counselling is helping people do things in little steps, and providing support and reinforcement for them. I also try to provide support and reinforcement in their environment (for example, talking to their teachers), because the counselling situation can be very limited. We can also work out things through role-play, so that they can build skills, because they are often very lacking in inter-personal skills.

PROCTOR: Returning to the question of modelling, do you regard yourself as a model for your clients and, if so, what do you model?

INSKIPP: Yes, I model for a client in being open and communicative, and exposing my feelings, attitudes, and values if it's useful to the client. I think it can be very difficult to decide what's useful and what's not. It is important to live my life as effectively as possible. Especially with my students I want to model somebody who is living effectively and who will go for help if I'm not coping. I see this working in physical, social, and emotional ways. If I set myself up to help somebody else, I ought to be making great efforts to be as effective as possible myself.

PROCTOR: Are you aware of positively conditioning certain communications and negatively conditioning others?

INSKIPP: Yes. I would positively condition exploration and understanding and talking about themselves and their feelings and their thoughts and I would negatively condition talking about situations and generalising. I positively condition people who are moving forward and I positively condition people's dynamic self-understanding, by which I mean 'now I understand and this is what I need to do about it'. One of the things that I'm trying to help people do in counselling is to pull out and look at the resources that they've got. Because people often come thinking they haven't got any resources at all and therefore I will condition them to explore their resources and to see what they can do and sometimes condition negatively to counteract the 'poor me' talk.

PROCTOR: Are there any other patterns of interaction which you would identify as a process which you habitually recognise and use?

INSKIPP: I see counselling in three stages. The first stage is an interaction, encouraging *exploration*, and using a certain set of skills, like asking for concrete examples. The second stage consists of a much more *dynamic understanding* and moving into deeper things, such as confrontation and much more immediacy. The third stage is the *action* stage. Although these stages may be intertwined, you can go back to stage one again, and that is still progressive interaction. I find it helpful to have a model of moving forward, and to have categories in my mind. Without actually pushing clients into them, I can sort the information that's coming in. I find Leona Tyler very useful. She says most people come for counselling either to *make choices*, or to *make changes*, or to *reduce confusion*. Often it starts off that people think they come to make choices but in fact they need to reduce their confusion before they're ready to go on to choices. Once they've made choices they then start to make changes. The other useful category is to separate three areas in people's lives which are important to them: their *work* areas, i.e., the way they spend their time; their *relationships*; and, thirdly, what Tyler calls *aloneness*, their personal identity and how they feel about themselves as a unique person with values. A lot of counselling is tied up with people looking for identity. Those are helpful categories to be able to use as filing compartments in your mind. It's also useful to look at those areas when you are setting up contracts about what you're going to work on. It's a method of sorting out this great welter of information that may come at you.

PROCTOR: Given the fairly limited number of ways you can respond to requests for personal help or seek to intervene in another's personal exploration, are there any other responses that you have found to be effective?

INSKIPP: Yes, I help people sort things out by use of sentence completion, questionnaires, file cards which can sort out 'this is how I'd like to be', 'this is how I am', etc. I have clients use felt tip pens and sheets of paper to put down diagrams – for example, a life space diagram with the client in the middle and significant people in his life in different spaces about him. I often have a non-verbal client draw matchstick figures with 'balloons' to fill in in order to encourage him to talk. I've worked on those concrete things, which help a client to be able to see a problem as a series of hurdles that have to be jumped over. I also try to teach social skills. Many people have no ability in forming friendships or forming relationships with other people. I do little bits of homework with them in that way. For example, I can say 'Would you like to try having a drink in the pub?'. I don't say it as a friend, but as a counsellor. Then, 'Practice walking up to the bar and asking for a drink without feeling everybody in the place is threatening'. I try to build a whole repertoire of skills which can be helpful.

PROCTOR: Are there any kind of responses that you deliberately soft-pedal?

INSKIPP: Yes, I try not to use interpretation because I think that people find this threatening. I don't like interpretations that imply that people are sick because I see counselling for the healthy as well. I try to keep people on the present and on the future and not on the past, though I'm often tempted to interpret. If that is encouraged, then people can put all the blame for what they are now on how they were brought up. 'Oh, I can't do that because my parents made me feel useless and I am stuck in this groove'. I believe that there are healthy parts to people and that people will move towards effective living if they're given enough support to hear inside themselves what is the effective way of living. These healthy parts may be very faint and very distorted because of things that have happened in the past. They may be very difficult to find in people but this belief that there are enough internal resources seems to me an optimistic one.

PROCTOR: Do you see a difference between counselling and therapy?

INSKIPP: Some people are stuck in a groove that they're not going to be able to get out of – possibly because of this internal pain we mentioned before. It somehow produces destructive behaviours. Such people may move forward to a certain extent but will continually return to some sort of destructive behaviour – frequently violence to themselves or to other people. I think it is an unconscious mechanism at levels which aren't easily accessible to them by self-exploration. It may become much more accessible to them through therapeutic techniques – some of the bodywork techniques are effective to help them bring, say, anger into awareness which surfaces as aggression in ordinary relationships and makes them destructive. The anger seems to be locked inside the body somewhere. I see some of the physical body therapies as helpful to some people and I see the therapist as working on that level. Counselling is often taking things out that have been deeply buried and rearranging them and putting them back in another package. I think perhaps therapy is that at a deeper level. There are no hard and fast boundaries, but I would see continual destructive and stuck behaviour as a need to move people on from counselling into therapy.

PROCTOR: Do you find that counselling is enough for most of the students that you train? If they, or you, find they are afraid of another person's fear or pain, do you suggest therapy?

INSKIPP: Most people are able to explore at a counselling level. Sometimes that's enough for them and sometimes they will decide they want to go into therapy. It's a matter of discussing with them what they really want to work on. What they are working on at the moment may be perfectly adequate, but they may later want to work a bit more. I see that students, during their counselling training, need to work on their own material with each other and with staff and in group situations. Being counselled themselves and working as clients is very useful. Some of them may want to work on a deeper level and we promote that as an idea: that if they go on developing skills that will need constant work. And modelling that, by myself being prepared to work as a client with my students.

PROCTOR: Are there dangers of the uninitiated going beyond the counselling level into the therapy level as workers?

INSKIPP: I think that this is one of the problems in counselling. You may stir up emotions in clients with which you're not able to cope in the time available. I think it's very important in school, when you have a limited counselling period, that not too much is stirred up when the students have to go on working in school and go home. But I think on the whole things are better out than in, so the dangers may be exaggerated.

PROCTOR: Clearly, the client group that you work with has influenced the way you work. Presumably you have arrived at developmental counselling because you are working with growing, developing human beings who are developing in a way that adults aren't necessarily encouraged to grow?

INSKIPP: Yes, although I would see my model as generally applicable because adults are changing and having to meet new roles as they go through life. But probably the greatest growing and developing time is during adolescence. The counsellor can help not only by working in the counselling situation but by working in an institution, helping people to see how to shape the environment and the school to the needs of the developing individual.

PROCTOR: Do you have any personal dilemmas in your counselling task?

INSKIPP: Yes, I'd like to work much more in a group situation, to try and produce the same effects as in one-to-one counselling. Another dilemma is whether it is better to spend energy on one-to-one counselling or whether to spend it on changing the environment. I think the main dilemma is where to focus my training energies in promoting counselling in schools. Most of my work is with teachers seconded for a year's Diploma Course in Counselling and Pastoral Care. The majority of them will return to work in some pastoral care role, very few as a full-time School Counsellor. I think the Course can make the greatest contribution to schools by sending back teachers with a good basic ability to counsel, and conceptual ability to demystify the process and impart the skills and attitudes to other staff (partly a training function). They should also have a sound knowledge of developmental needs and enough expertise to promote curriculum development and organisational change to meet those needs – to anticipate problems and plan courses and structures to prevent them. The dilemma is how to help teachers learn all this *and* give them room and time for their own personal growth and development which I see as the most important part of the course.

PROCTOR: Do you have any basic questions or doubts about counselling as an activity altogether?

INSKIPP: I don't like the word, 'counselling'. I would like to develop a word that sees the process as for everybody and not that one has to be 'sick'. I would like to see it very much more as growth promoting and would like counselling to be seen as a particular part of education and part of life. It could be provided as part of adult education.

PROCTOR: Do you have any dilemmas about the expert role of teaching people to be professional counsellors?

INSKIPP: Yes and no. What I'm teaching people is to increase their helping skills which can be used anywhere. I see them as going back and spreading their skills. I see counselling not as something that only a few people can do but as something that anyone who wants to and who is flexible and caring enough can learn to do. And I see myself as trying to spread those skills and to develop as many helping people as possible. Roger Carkhuff, who has very much influenced the way I work, suggests that 'Training is the preferred mode of treatment'. As you work with clients you teach them the helping skills you are using.

I see the professional part of counselling as working under a label which implies standards, a background of knowledge, skills, responsibility, and accountability.

PROCTOR: Are those trappings of the professional role, or are they necessary for being an effective counsellor?

INSKIPP: They are part of being effective. You need to keep enough records to be effective, plus you need to have enough knowledge of all your outside resources, and you need to know your boundaries pretty clearly.

PROCTOR: Do you think these questions have slanted the presentation of your practice and experience?

INSKIPP: I think they have, though I find it difficult to remember back to what I've said. I hope that what has come out of my answers explains that the developmental way of looking at man is as a healthy individual. It helps people move through life and learn new rules and new ways of behaving, to respond to a changing environment and to changes within themselves. This is a change from many counselling and therapeutic models which are based on having sick clients. It is important to look at this as healthy development and to learn how we can promote this healthy development in people. I also see one-to-one counselling as a very inefficient but necessary way; we ought to be working very much more in groups. I see that to teach people counselling skills is a very good way of teaching them to be more effective human beings because you're helping to develop qualities in them which are very important in human interaction.

Michael Reddy

5 Transactional Analysis

Michael Reddy's over-riding interest is in the whole scope of psychotherapy. He has a Doctorate in Counselling Psychology, and spends most of his time training psychotherapists, counsellors and people whose jobs are connected with human relations. He is currently President of the European Association for Transactional Analysis.

Transactional Analysis was developed during the 1950's in the United States by Eric Berne, a trained psychiatrist who was dissatisfied with orthodox psychoanalytic practice. T.A. is expressed in a language which opens up the concepts of psychoanalysis, and of T.A. itself, to the layman. It uses four major methods of looking at human behaviour: *Structural Analysis* looks at what is happening within an individual and sees each person as having three ego states; the Parent, the Adult, and the Child. *Transactional Analysis* is used to understand the transactions that go on between two or three people. *Game and Racket Analysis* look at particular kinds of transactions which people engage in an order to feel 'not ok'. *Script Analysis* helps to understand the life plans that people make as a result of early parental messages.

SUGGESTED READING:
Berne, Eric, *Games People Play*, Harmondsworth: Penguin, 1966.
Berne, Eric, *What Do You Say After You Say Hello?* London: Corgi, 1975.
Harris, T., *I'm OK, You're OK*, London: Pan, 1973.
Schiff, Jacqui, *All My Children*, Philadelphia, Penn.: M. Evans & Co., Inc., 1970.
Woollams, Stanley; Brown, Michael; Huige, Kristyn; *Transactional Analysis in Brief*, Ann Arbor, Michigan: Huron Valley Institute, 1976.

PROCTOR: I'd like us to focus on just one thing and ask you to wear only your Transactional Analysis spectacles.

REDDY: O.K. The first thing, if I'm wearing Transactional Analysis spectacles, there are values built into the system. For example, awareness in itself is a good thing, spontaneity is a good thing, autonomy is a good thing, intimacy is a good thing. Those four values are built into the kind of work that a Transactional Analyst would do.

PROCTOR: Those being good things in terms of what? What do you see as the purpose of human energy?

REDDY: I'd like to separate those two because I don't think the question about the purpose of human energy is in play. I'm even hesitant about rhyming off four things like that, because they are part of the humanistic framework, and I feel them as flags which we automatically run up these days and salute. But, it means that individual people can be more autonomous and free to be more intimate with each other, be candid, be game-free, be non-exploitative. And that is assumed to be 'good'. 'Good' in terms of what, or in terms of some ultimate purpose, is a question that isn't asked. Transactional Analysis is about what is happening in a particular relationship rather than what the particular relationship is about, or *for*. I don't really think that T.A. says very much at all about political, cultural, ecological and social systems. And my reading of Berne is that his understanding of more systematic approaches, like group dynamics or group analysis was not really very much in touch. Group phenomena are almost absent except so far as they relate to what an individual is doing. How is it the individual is replaying his script? Within a game he may be playing a particular role and therefore other people in a group would be identified as victim or rescuer. That is characteristic T.A. language. The focus is very much on: How come the individual is doing what he doesn't need to do? How come he is making somebody else not o.k., when he need not make that other person not o.k.? How come he's feeling not o.k. about himself when he need not be feeling not o.k. about himself?

PROCTOR: So basically a T.A. analyst is interested in finding out how people can help themselves feel good all the time?

REDDY: Yes, I would accept that as a basic overall statement, or at least *more* of the time. I would also like to put in something else. Much of the talk within the T.A. language is of the negative kind. For example, Berne in his last book said that what stops people being autonomous, aware, spontaneous and intimate is the trash in their heads. If people get rid of the trash in their heads then they will be free to be all of those things. So the book is in fact about the trash in people's heads, and there is very little about what autonomy or these other values are. They are there and they have been in some way distorted, minimised, washed out of existence by people's previous experience and what therapy can do for somebody is to free them again to be what they naturally are.

PROCTOR: So that says something about how you see people interacting with the groups and systems of which they are a part?

REDDY: In a sense, the way a person is now will be very much connected with the way he learnt to relate to his original group, largely mother and father and older brothers and sisters and other relatives, neighbours, and children who had a powerful influence on him.

What happened in that group will determine to a great extent how he will function in life in general. If it was a group that exploited him, or oppressed him, then he's likely to come out of his childhood over-responding to alienation and oppression, and exploitation. Whereas if he is relatively free from that in his early childhood, then he is relatively free in his response later on.

PROCTOR: In order to cope, kids have to make negotiations about power because of their dependent position?

REDDY: Yes, that is true. I want to go on to add a Groucho Marx saying, 'However, the contrary is also true'. Namely, that the child has some part in the decisions that he took in response to childhood pressure, and one of the things I like about T.A. is that it doesn't have a deterministic philosophy. It says 'sure enough, the influences were powerful, and maybe from the child's perspective, too powerful to be contested. Maybe there was a survival issue there, he would have got beaten to death in a real or metaphorical way, if he had not adapted in the way that he did'. But none the less, there was a decision involved and, where there is a decision, re-decision is possible.

PROCTOR: And if they make a re-decision and choose to be

freed to be what they naturally are, that is bound to be a good thing?

REDDY: That's bound to be a good thing for the human species, yes.

PROCTOR: So what is the purpose of human energy?

REDDY: I'll say something about that personally because Berne simply doesn't look at the question. As far as I'm concerned, I don't know where I am at the moment. I've moved within the last few years from a radically religious perspective, which says that the purpose of human energy is to be in a relation with a divine energy personalised in a personal God. I grew up with that from the very beginning and explored it very fully, really committed myself to that point of view in my life-style and my thinking and my philosophy. Having had such a total commitment to that point of view and only quite recently having explicitly broken away from it, I am somewhat at a loss. I really don't know. Human energy may be radically purpose-less, in some total way – I find that hard to stomach, but I think I need to face that as a possibility.

PROCTOR: And you can sit quite comfortably with a framework like T.A. which doesn't question why?

REDDY: You made a connection there that I wouldn't make. As a language system, T.A. can be translated both within and without a transcendental philosophy and from the beginning a great number of clergy had no difficulty using it within their over-arching system, and others who are agnostic also have no difficulties.

PROCTOR: Perhaps you can tell me briefly how and where and when that T.A. approach originated? Why did it need to originate?

REDDY: I was doing a very similar project to the project you are working on here. I wanted to know what goes on in a counselling relationship? I set out to interview people as you are doing. It was recommended that I would need a chapter on T.A. since it covers such a large slice of practitioners in the United States. Then I came up against a language which all of a sudden said a great deal to me about human behaviour, including my own, especially my own. I have made a great number of changes for myself on the basis of what I have understood about T.A. I was at a point when I decided that I would abandon a cool eclecticism and commit myself intellectually to one language, to explore it fully, to find out what its limitations and its strengths were. It's as if I decided I would learn Chinese, and I would learn it fully. It seemed, from what I saw of T.A. in action, to be a faster tool than any other and I was able to use it and give the tool to other people. The language, if not common, could be quickly taught. It seemed to demystify the therapeutic process, and make the person part of it.

PROCTOR: Are those the same answers for why it arose historically in the States?

REDDY: It arose in the States in a psychiatric context with very seriously disturbed people. After it was initiated, there was a lot of excitement and enthusiasm as to how people who had been stuck for years or for months in an institution suddenly were re-assuming social control. What excited them originally was that by being able to distinguish between ego states, some quite seriously disturbed patients got sufficiently de-confused in a hurry to be able to make more autonomous decisions about what they wanted. Here was something that very quickly got people to a place where you can deal with them.

PROCTOR: And where does it stand in relation to classical psychoanalysis?

REDDY: It stands, I think, in a closer relationship than one would normally imagine. Berne was a psychoanalyst and that was what made the most sense for him for many years. He wanted people to say, 'He's an Analyst', but as his system evolved, it was clear that it was different. He failed his exams for the third time in 1956 with the Psychoanalytic Institute of San Francisco. He decided to read the writing on the wall and be more explicit, to articulate his own thinking. Interestingly enough, the earliest implications of Berne's writing were that if you want somebody to get control of himself quickly, T.A. is excellent. If you want to cure him, send him to the psychoanalyst. It wasn't long before that particular bashfulness gave way to something more like transactional analysis as the over-arching system, of which psychoanalysis was a very interesting branch. Just as Freud had underlined the Oedipus complex, Berne stressed there were many other complexes. There was the Sisyphus complex, pushing the stone up the hill. There was the Odysseus complex, and one could go through history and Greek mythology and separate other scripts. So Freud only touched one corner and only underlined one aspect of transference. A much wider aspect of transference is the way people cast other people in any group for different roles, not merely work out an unfinished relationship with mother and father.

PROCTOR: What processes and structures in British society stand out, to you, as assisting people to be aware, spontaneous, intimate and autonomous?

REDDY: I personally don't have any particular axe to grind about the system. Nothing is stopping me from being all of those things within the society's structure because I learned very young to figure out the rules of any game that was being played and, at the partly aware and partly unaware level, what the system is all about. I'd come up much worse in a totalitarian system or a fascist or concentration camp type of political system where I don't think it is possible to figure out rules. So this society leaves me enough liberty to figure out and capitalise on its rules and to be as autonomous as I want to be. Now where I am at the moment is saying to myself 'maybe there are some people who are not able to do that' and that one of the things I ought to be invested in is looking at how come people are not viable within the system. I've sensed in some of my own clients, who have had a psychiatric history, the panic about being labelled. I have a lot of sympathy with the radical psychiatry movement in the thesis that fortunate people with relative freedom are able to label the less fortunate and therefore not have to do anything with them.

PROCTOR: Maybe it is a system which, in the T.A. language, gives 'strokes' to people who play games rather than to people who are spontaneous?

REDDY: I would balk at that. I don't think of what I am doing as games in the T.A. sense, which are un-straight procedures. I think games can be used in the larger sense. For example, – Boddhisatvas, who leave the society in which they belong, may spend three years in the desert, and then come back to it as outsiders, as Martians. They are able to pick up what the whole structure is about and maybe it can be called a game, because they treat it as a game from thereon, and play it in whatever way they choose. I would like to be both part of my culture and to be sufficiently free that I can comment as an outsider, and take up a stance against it, or for it, from a position of personal freedom. I admire people who can play *that* game and I am all for teaching as many people as possible to acquire that detachment. But that is not a game in the T.A. sense.

PROCTOR: Are there things in day-to-day life as it is lived in schools, in families, in work situations, that militate against people being able to be autonomous, spontaneous, etc?

REDDY: There again, you've caught me moving towards saying 'there must be and there are'. I read that Ivan Illich stuff and I'm fascinated to see how he can show that the education system is based on the premise that more than fifty per cent will feel bad about themselves. It's based on a meritocracy system, and within a competitive frame of reference. I don't see how people can want to cooperate without feeling that they are losing in the process. So, there is competitiveness in the structure which makes it difficult to realise those individual values. I want to investigate more about the structure of medicine, and psychiatry, and psychology and social work, to see how they are structured into the so-called helpers and the so-called helpees. The helpers need the helpees to be there every bit as much as the helpees need the helpers. I don't want to be a part of that kind of a system. Internationally, in T.A., I do not want to get into a competitive structure with people who want to professionalise their work, but who at the same time are protesting about the way professionalism is set up.

PROCTOR: What do you see as the objective of the counselling task?

REDDY: The point of the counselling task for me is to release people from the kind of internal prison in which they currently are. I know that some people come to counsellors with anything but that in mind. They may simply want to get some justification to do something they have decided to do anyway, like a divorce. They want some external validation of the decision that they have made. I would rather not be involved in that. They may only want support. A lot of people don't have the opportunity to explore what goes on inside of themselves – feeling and thinking – with somebody who has relative objectivity, who has no particular investment in them, and with whom they can do that confidentially. It is often a tremendous release, to be able to do that. So a counsellor who is doing nothing much more than that would get my vote as a counsellor. But that's not what I'm usually doing when I'm counselling.

I'm looking for people to free themselves from their script.

PROCTOR: Do you have ways of trying to ensure that the client and you have similar assumptions and objectives about the nature of the task?

REDDY: Yes. T.A. clearly underlines the necessity of a therapeutic contract. So one of the characteristic questions will be: 'When we've finished our work together, what will be different for you? How will you have changed? How will you know that you've changed?' If it's appropriate, 'how will I know that you've changed?' For example, the most concrete contract I ever had was with a woman who wanted to be pregnant. It turned out in the course of the counselling that she really did not want to be pregnant, and that I had bought into an 'ought' contract. She felt she *ought* to be pregnant and it took a while to elucidate that. If I had been more experienced at that time, I would have discovered it that much earlier. Somebody else whom I saw for quite a number of months, probably over two or three years altogether, didn't want to buy into the T.A. stuff. She was into a great deal of interesting oriental and mystical exploration of her own at that time, and it was taking her further than the kind of therapy I was doing would take her. There I adopted not much more than a Rogerian stance and allowed her to explore with me what she was up to. I think it was a valid thing for me to do. That was what I saw her as needing. In that way I'm thinking still in T.A. terms, but I'm approaching her from a Rogerian point of view, and also doing things a strict Rogerian might not do, which is telling her what I thought and what my value system is.

PROCTOR: Do you always make a contract at the beginning or does it emerge?

REDDY: Not always. It can be quite frightening. A wife might come here and be very upset about what seems to be happening in the marriage. She may well wind up after a few sessions saying 'Look I have to decide whether to split or not, that is the real question'. So we might not get to a contract for a while. I don't mind doing that. I think some T.A. people want to move into a contract phase immediately. It is ok for me to give people time to shape the contract, and maybe when they find out what the thing is about, they are frightened. They don't want any more counselling. That's too frightening to be considered. They've made their decision. They may come back a little later, but at that point there's nowhere to go forward.

PROCTOR: What resources do you see yourself bringing to the counselling task? What gives you the right to be a counsellor?

REDDY: I'd rather take them as two different questions. In the back of my mind one of the images that I think of is a sculptor. There is a statement by Michaelangelo, that the David was already in the marble. All he had to do was chip away the superfluous marble because the David was there. To some extent I like that image as an image of therapy, one's chipping away the superfluous which doesn't allow the beauty of the individual to be seen. That sounds grandiose, but in a pragmatic way the image still satisfies me. I think of myself as a journeyman. I've served an apprenticeship, I may get to the place of being a master craftsman sometime.

The image breaks down because in sculpting you use a tool, and it seems to me that the therapeutic process is highly interactive. So what I bring to the counselling situation is basically myself, and to do that I have to know myself well. If people are going to cast me in a role for their script, I need to be fairly sure that the surface I'm offering them isn't inviting them to do that. If they do it to me, I can have some security that they are doing it on the basis of *their* internal process. But it is an interactive process. This is also connected with contracts, because one of the first things I have to do is to tap here and there, with a mild mannered tool to test where the grain goes, and to respect the material that I am working with. One of the dangers of Transactional Analysis is that it can appear to be a box of tools, and all you need to do is get some permission to use them, or find out what they are and waltz in and start applying them on people. So it is more important for me at the beginning to use a tool that is a gentle one. Maybe at some stage I will want to put in a harder chisel and with a good thump crack off a large lump; maybe somebody has some unfinished business, has not said 'goodbye' to their mother or father, and until he does that, he is going to be for ever in the same pickle. But that might be a strong and heavy and difficult piece of work. Before I do that, I want to be sure that that is where he is at and that this is the moment to do it.

PROCTOR: That implies that you see yourself bringing a greater awareness about a client's own needs and situation than he has himself?

REDDY: I want to be clear that I don't think my main business is to know more about him than he knows about himself, or that the main skill of the therapist is to be able to sit back and analyse somebody else and tell them about themselves. I may be a whole jump ahead, but that is not the essence of being a therapist. I would much rather think that I am a quarter step ahead of the time but that a good part of the time the awareness in the client comes before my awareness. I may never catch him up. So I would be very much against the impression coming across that I think that my sharpness and my awareness, my analytical ability needs to be greater than the client's. In some cases yes; in others it needs to be pretty well written up on the screen and in front of both of us, to the extent that the client would find it difficult not to agree.

PROCTOR: So what is it you bring? Is it just experience, just self-awareness?

REDDY: I expect the client's awareness to expand considerably over a period of time with my prompting and with my second guessing and with my listening with a third ear, to pick up what he is not yet aware of. So, I think that my listening skill is one of the major things that I bring.

PROCTOR: And how does that develop?

REDDY: I have a strong Rogerian background. I developed it by doing it.

PROCTOR: By being trained?

REDDY: By being trained and doing exercises in listening and by giving courses. I'm particularly good at listening and I think people can be taught to listen. It's not intuitive. With the help of a tape recorder, I can say where I heard something even though the person has not picked out anything special.

PROCTOR: What about cognitive skills? Do you think that you bring a mind which is important to the situation?

REDDY: No. I happen to be a cognitive, intellectual kind of person. That's a strength in me which I have been developing since I was very little. I think it may be useful but I think one can equally well do without a highly developed conceptual ability. If I'm training people to be counsellors I want them to be able first of all to listen. If I find they are not able to listen, if I find that the noise that is going on in their own head, is of such a volume that they are not really hearing what the person is saying, I'm not going to give them anything else until they are able to do that. The second thing I want them to be able to do is to be aware of themselves. Rogers, who started out with empathy as the most important quality of a counsellor, wound up by saying that genuiness is the most important - genuine as being in contact with himself, to be able to express what was going on in himself in a congruent way. And only in the third place, would I say 'ok, now it's a good time to go out and read Fenichel and read Leon Salzman on the obsessive compulsive personality, and so on, to get some conceptual skill'. It's only at that point they can use that kind of thing.

PROCTOR: What do you see as being the responsibilities of the client in the counselling interaction?

REDDY: I'm not sure. I usually put very little responsibility on the client in theory. In practice I want the client to be straight with me; but I don't see it necessarily as his responsibility to walk in with the determination to be straight. If I find him not answering my questions, I confront him with the fact that he's not answering my questions and put some responsibility on him to be straight with me if we are going to work together. If he is making other people responsible for the way he feels, I'm going to confront him sooner or later and ask him to take responsibility for the way he feels. Part of the conceptual framework of T.A. puts responsibility for his feelings on the client, and for his decisions, and his attitudes, and does not merely attribute them to his past experience or to his present experience.

PROCTOR: Is there a time, ever, when you feel a client isn't able to be fully responsible for himself, or that you worry about their ability to be responsible for themselves?

REDDY: Oh, yes. My own defence structures are so well in place that there is very little likelihood of my ever needing to make myself helpless in order to be taken care of. (That is what I see as a 'good' part of what happens when people become what is usually called psychotic – they now have to be taken care of.) Where I'm still weak in my own theoretical background is in developmental psychology, particularly in infant psychology. I'm not always in touch with how the attempt to repeat an early phase, to regress to that phase, to be taken care of again, and to grow up successfully, can be a healthy mechanism, and how I need to support it rather than to confront it.

PROCTOR: And the counsellor's responsibilities?

REDDY: I do think a counsellor has responsibilities to take care of himself. It may sound odd, but if he isn't able to take care of himself or protect himself, to get his own needs met outside of the therapeutic counselling context, then he is more likely to do a disservice to the other person. He also has a responsibility to take care of himself healthwise so that he is functioning well in interviews. I think he should have all of the professional responsibilities that are associated with other professions like the law, and medicine – to keep himself acquainted with thinking, and with the safeguards that need to be built into a profession.

PROCTOR: Confidentially comes into that of course?

REDDY: Confidentiality of course plays a big part in that. I'm not thinking just of confidentiality though. If I go to a lawyer I want to have some way of knowing whether he is likely to serve my interests or not. It is hard enough to know whether a counsellor is particularly good let alone whether a counsellor is particularly ethical, is willing to take confidentiality as a prime value. Whether he is likely – this is the worst thing for me – to be working out his own difficulties through a client, and getting them to go through the mine-fields of his own problems to see where they blow up. I don't think a client can know about a counsellor ahead of time sufficiently to protect himself, and therefore I think that the counsellor has a responsibility to professionalise himself and to submit himself to the scrutiny of his peers, to determine if he is strong enough and competent to do his job. You know, the first principle of medicine is don't do any damage – that's absolutely right. And I think the counsellor certainly has an at least equal responsibility to make sure he's not a damaging person.

PROCTOR: New ideas often means breaking new ground. Isn't there a grey area, where it is hard to get validation?

REDDY: I don't go with that, Brigid. To be a member of a profession one has to be pretty careful. For example, one wouldn't get involved in a sexual relationship with a client or exploit a client financially in a way that, if it became public, one would be disbarred. There are professional safeguards that Berne, for example, was willing to put himself within, even while he was trying something new. There may be counsellors in that position, but then I think they have a responsibility to get supervision. And quick. To consult with colleagues, not just one's best friend who will tell you that you're doing a terrific job, but to check with people who may have a more objective view.

PROCTOR: Is the counselling encounter different from encounters you have in other roles?

REDDY: I feel it to be different. If I want to work out some problem of my own, I will go to somebody who I think will not treat me just as a friend, but will be able to be dispassionate as well. And that makes it different from friendship encounters. It is not a hard and fast distinction. I can get in one sentence from a friend or a relation, a powerful therapeutic kick in the pants, or a powerful piece of loving, which is therapeutic.

PROCTOR: And what about teaching? Is there a basic difference between the teaching relationship and the counselling relationship?

REDDY: Yes. The teaching relationship I think of as so heavily focused on the transfer of information that there is very little else involved. In the counselling relationship you may well be conveying quite a bit of information. But there is another aspect to the counselling relationship we haven't even touched on so far because we stopped somewhere when I was talking about my being cognitive, and about my expecting that the person's awareness is expanding. I bring other things to bear in the counselling situation. One of them is protection. I know that when I am doing a piece of work on myself, I need *protection*, to have some sense of safety, so that it is ok for me to explore this, even though I don't know where it might lead me.

Another thing – as a counsellor, I'm not only going to be confronting the client with another frame of reference, which may say 'hey, your problem might not be like this, it might be like that, and if it's like that, then it is solvable'. When I'm doing that kind of confrontation, or if the person is confronting themselves (and I think a skilled Rogerian can make someone do it themselves), that's scary. At that point I have to be able to offer two things. Again one is protection and the other is *permission*. I use the word in the technical sense that it is used in T.A., which means that I am giving full permission *to disobey the injunctions* – messages which were built into an original script. For example, a person may have had a message in his original script not to be close with people, not to be affectionate, not to be warm, not to touch, and it is clear from the way he is talking and what he himself has said, that he needs to be able to be and do these things. Somebody may come who cannot cry and wants to be able to be in touch with sadness again, but one of the reasons why he is not is because there is a strong prohibition in the parental script messages. Now I have to be able to give permission which has at least that power to the contrary, and when the person is willing, he gives me power to do that. I don't have the power myself, but I need to be able to take the power from him, the client, when he offers me that power – to use the power to give him permission to change. Then I need to be able to *protect* him while he is *changing basic script decisions*. That's a matter of months. An organic development goes on in that time – when he is experimenting with behaviour for example, and phantasising, as when he was very small, what the catastrophe would be if he were close.

PROCTOR: Could you talk about the particular processes you focus on, the faculties you are engaging, when you are in an interaction with a client?

REDDY: There are two processes that I use. The first one is that I want to engage the *Child ego state*, speaking within the conceptual framework. The Child ego state, for me, is an archaic throw back. By an ego state I mean a complex of behaviours, of feelings, the way one thinks, all this probably connected with neurological and biochemical loops and links and systems. If I suddenly burst into tears in front of you right now, the chances are that I have 'rubber-banded' back into a Child ego state and I am responding to you on the basis of something that happened to me a long time ago. You've hit my Child ego state. And from there I'm likely to be mostly determined by my feelings. It's very characteristic of the Child ego state for feelings to prompt thinking. What you did just then was, say, to criticise me or do something that was particularly hurtful

to me when I was little. Maybe there were two or three traumatic incidents around that or maybe it was my general
experience as a child. My general response to criticism as a
child was to cry instead of to get angry, to get sad or to withdraw or do something else. So I would rubber-band into my
Child ego state which is the way I was when I was a little boy.
So the Child ego state isn't an abstract concept. If somebody
erupts in a group and starts throwing things around, it is
because that's what *he* did when he was little, not because
Child ego states do that.

PROCTOR: You're trying to engage the Child ego state?

REDDY: That's right, as opposed to the Adult ego state which
is here and now, up-to-date, data processing. Most of the
problems that a person has have to do with confusion and
contamination with their feelings and their thinking, related to
the same kinds of contamination that were true of them when
they were small people. I find that a good way of getting to the
Child ego state is to ask someone to relate their favourite fairy
story, and to identify with the characters in it, to feel themselves
in it.

Other kinds of Gestalt are excellent for that, too. Two chair
work, for example. I think Rogerian counselling, when it's
done skillfully, gets the person into a trance state, where they
are effectively in a Child ego state. They come out with the
most absurd things, then jolt themselves out of it, and say
'That's ridiculous, isn't it'? I'll constantly be saying 'What are
you feeling now'? Rather than follow the logic of the head, as a
thread, I'll be wanting to follow the logic of the feeling because
it is probably much more reliable for getting to an emotional
impasse.

PROCTOR: And basically, emotional impasse is where you want
to focus?

REDDY: Yes. In T.A. language I'm looking for what are called
'racket feelings' that an individual characteristically chooses
to have, in response to a wide range of situations, not all of
which appropriately prompt that feeling. I'm checking for
feelings which a person brings on himself. The reason why
people bring feelings on themselves usually arise out of decisions that they have made in the past, so my focus is on
decisions that were made in the past, maybe when they were
four, when the information that they had was inadequate, like

'I'll never, ever trust a man again'. This most important person, the one that they needed all of their male support and love from, proved unreliable – he may have died, or he may have been very cruel to them. So they made a decision on insufficient evidence and under a lot of powerful pressure when they were four, because this is the little world they live in. They have to accommodate to this world and not to some other world, and they assume that every world is like this little world. What I am hunting for is decisions in the Child, and I'll go to them through behaviours – the person's way of talking, for example – or through feelings which seem to be characteristic and inappropriate. I'm looking for myths that people have, like 'All men are X' and 'All women are Y', or 'If people know what you want, then they'll stop you getting it', or 'It'll all come right if you don't think about it'. There are ways of solving problems in an up-to-date reality which are impeded by old patterns, the patterns related to old decisions, old feelings, old myths, old behaviours.

PROCTOR: People are not satisfied until they've got the fresh experience they are having today to fit the old pattern? It wasn't even satisfactory then and certainly isn't appropriate now?

REDDY: That's right, yes. Most of that is not in awareness.

PROCTOR: Is some of your work just bringing it into awareness?

REDDY: Yes, but I don't want to get stuck with being an insight therapist because I think that the protection, the potency that I talked about before, the permission, having fun in therapy, laughing, getting people to actually change behaviour is all important.

PROCTOR: So you are quite likely to actually ask someone if their behaviour is how they want it to be?

REDDY: Absolutely. In the group and outside of the group and doing homework. I am quite specific about what it is they need to do. Someone whose behaviour up to date has said 'I'm not important, please don't take any notice of me', I'll get to go to other people in the group and ask them to be quite explicit about it. And then to find some exercise they can do that will regain their importance for them. I'll use role play to find out how come a person doesn't have a particular behaviour in his repertoire. For example, being able to speak clearly and able to finish a sentence, if that's what it's about. Never actually getting around to asking a girl for a date.

You can saddle a horse from two sides – either from understanding and then doing differently or doing differently and then understanding, feeling differently afterwards. I don't care which side, if they get on the horse.

PROCTOR : What sort of climate do you seek to develop, and how do you see it as being important for your joint task? You've said a climate where people can have permission to do things. . . .

REDDY : Yes. And ask for what they want and explore that kind of 'Getting-one's-needs-met-behaviour' in a different context. This may be laboratory and artificial but.

PROCTOR : Do you just respond as you feel is right for a person, or do you have different ideas about the set up for each client?

REDDY : There are some ideas that are not definite and I would like to get definite. It's quite clear from my work that people find a safety in working with me. Sometimes it's a safety of my dispassionateness and my non-emotional outlook. So in some ways I think I'm at the cool end of the spectrum. Yet in other ways I'm not, and there is more physical contact in my groups now than there was two years ago, and that must represent a change in me. Secondly, I have worked with other therapists where a back rub, or a foot massage, or to be held, is absolutely permissible and in that context, I've seen some people do some *very* good work. So I have no theoretical position that, for example, if people are warmly held, they will retreat into not-thinking, because I've seen the opposite. And on that basis the direction I am moving is towards the warm end of the spectrum.

PROCTOR : Does the idea that people tend to recreate old patterns of relating in counselling relationships have much significance for you, and if so, what do you do about that?

REDDY : I've talked about that to a certain extent already. I am constantly *chasing script*. Chasing scripts in T.A. terms means chasing the messages that people got from important figures in their early environment, which usually are mother and father. There is often unfinished business with mother and father, and people in the counselling situation are wanting to re-create that. And I know that counter-transference too – my own unfinished business – may well be in the way of

working with people. If any counsellor chooses to ignore that –
the transference phenomenon, to use the Freudian language,
or the recreation of script, in T.A. language – if he chooses to
ignore that, I think he is turning a blind eye on something
that's there.

PROCTOR: Do you invite it and use it, reflect it back or what?

REDDY: There's a third thing which I think would be more
characteristic of T.A. I'm beginning to take what I call
'*parenting contracts*' with people, and not merely therapeutic
contracts. In those contracts, I am willing for the person to
have the feelings again on a permanent basis, as long as it
lasts. I have a contract to give new parent messages. Now that's
a direct invitation to transference. It's clearly an invitation to
re-run the old relationship and then make it come out better.
So there is one way in which, even more explicitly than the
analysts, I'm inviting the transference relationship, with an
understanding, on both sides, that what we are about is to make
it come better. The fourth thing that would be more characteristic of T.A. is to do what's called a '*script matrix*' which is an
analysis of script. It highlights the messages that were given
by the original parents and significant people in the early
environment – the decisions that the person made on the basis
of those messages and the rackets, the myths and the behaviours that followed from there. There would be an attempt
at the back of one's mind, as though there were a permanent
blackboard in the room, to map what are the likely manoeuvres
of this person. Part of the contract might well be to change
those manoeuvres to a different message and behave as though
one now had a new message.

PROCTOR: Do you regard yourself as a model for the client in
any way, and if so, what do you see yourself as modelling?

REDDY: My immediate reaction is to run away and hide at the
idea of being a model for anyone else. If I turned a blind eye
to the fact that I will be taken as a model of behaviour and
attitudes, again, I'm in cloud cuckoo land. My teaching
experience, when I was a teacher, was that many times kids
would take me for a model and I wasn't even aware of them.
And kids that I had a particular therapeutic intent for seem
to have been no better off, and to have forgotten me when I
came back. And so I know that the modelling goes on. It will
certainly go on in any contract that I have which veers to the

parenting end of the spectrum, rather than the therapy end of the spectrum, because I'm setting myself up as a parent figure from whom the parented person will pick up values and attitudes. When she is feeling like an eight year old girl, she's going to be overhearing me talking with other adults, as it were, or talking with her about what I think is important. And if she sees me being sloppy with money, she will take me for a model for how to handle money. If I'm honest and don't get embarrassed about things, or if I get embarrassed about things and say 'I'm too embarrassed to talk to you about that', she gets the message about honesty, and about it being possible to tell people how you are feeling. If I don't do that, she'll get a message that maybe it's not ok to tell people how you feel, so she won't do that. That's a very clear case of modelling. I think the same thing is true with patients in so far as they give me what I've been calling 'potency' and effectively put me in a parent role, and put themselves in a vulnerable open position viz-a-viz my Parent ego state. So yes, that's going on all the time. The modelling still has that element of shyness about it, in that it's the way I am that people model, not a model that I put on for their benefit.

PROCTOR: You're obviously as aware that you are conditioning people, whether you want to or not?

REDDY: One of the things that I must as a Transactional analyst do, is to pick up on what are called cop-out words, like 'can't' instead of 'won't', or like switches of pronoun which say 'So I was walking along the road and I decided I would do this, well what can you expect when people treat you like that'? That switch – from 'I' to 'you' – for me represents a switch of ego states and the probable copping out of responsibilities. So I pick up on a word like 'you' when there's a switch – pick up words like 'can't', words like 'it' suddenly came over me and I panicked. If somebody says 'guess what happened, my pants fell down in the middle of the street, ha, ha, ha, if that isn't typical of my life, that's me all over, that's the history of my life, ha, ha, ha,' and I say 'ha, ha, ha', I'm reinforcing what I think of as scripty behaviour. I'm very conscious about not positively reinforcing scripty behaviour. That would be one important way the T.A. people are conscious of negatively reinforcing unproductive patterns.

PROCTOR: Are there any other patterns of interaction which

you would identify as a process that you habitually recognise or make use of?

REDDY: That gallows laugh is an important aspect of T.A. therapy – the so-called gallows laugh – when somebody is being self-destructive or recounting some self-destructive behaviour of their own, with a strong invitation to the audience to laugh at them, and not to be in touch with their destructiveness. I pick up a lot of other kinds of interaction between people which I think are not straight. So one of the things that I do a great deal about, in groups, is to try to get the communication straight. If somebody is making demands on somebody else without being clear what their feeling is, I'm going to say 'Will you clean up that piece of interaction you've just had?' I'm asking them three things: what were your feelings, how did you construe the situation out of that feeling, what is it you actually want? Sometimes somebody has been to other kinds of humanistic psychology groups, and has got the idea that the big thing is to tell people what you feel. So they come along, and they say, 'I'm really furious with you' and they sit back – message – it's now up to you to do something because I'm furious, or I'm crying. As though a baby, for example, would have a tantrum and then would sit back and say 'well, that was a great experience, and I must have another of those' – as though that's what feelings are about. I'll watch for those kinds of interaction and say 'how can you think that all you need is to tell someone you're devastated by what they've said, without making it clear what it is you want from them? The baby makes it clear that it wants something. The baby uses yowling usually, because it is the only system it has; if you are in a group, you've got a better system'. If I see somebody who seems from their posture or their silence, or the way they talk, to have been *collecting stamps*, I'll challenge that. And I watch for people making statements disguised as questions, and people redefining the content of questions asked them, and so on.

PROCTOR: Perhaps you'll explain 'collecting stamps'.

REDDY: It is when somebody has been collecting feelings in a group, feelings of withdrawal, feelings of having been misunderstood, of having been put down, feelings of having been ignored and discounted. The person will continue to collect the same kind of stamps and maybe will have sat silent for two and a half hours doing this, just like you collect Green

Shield stamps in order to trade them in for a prize. The prize may be quitting the group, or the prize might be so that they can come back after three quarters of an hour, when they have collected enough, to really dump them on somebody else. I see that again, as an unstraight interactive process. I'll want to challenge and confront that. 'Are you collecting stamps, and if you are collecting stamps, do you know what you are going to do? And if it is to have a good "put down" on somebody else, how about doing it now and not bothering collecting the stamps? How about making the "put down" straight?'

PROCTOR: Are you talking about 'games people play'?

REDDY: Yes. One of the most important elements in a game is the unstraightness of the communication. It's a communication at two levels, where people buy into one level as though that's what it's about, whereas just outside awareness, they know that it is really at another level. Neither of them are willing to deal with it. So in moving in quickly to confront unstraight communications, I'm breaking a game up before it starts. What is also characteristic of the game is that at the end of the game, people cash in their stamps. So I am trying to short circuit that process. I'm more likely to confront games before they've flowered fully than to let a game go and then to say 'I just caught you playing X, or caught you playing Y'. Sometimes in T.A. groups it becomes a T.A. game, being able to name a game that other people are playing, or even the game I am playing, to show them I am clever enough to play the game and know the game that I'm playing.

PROCTOR: Which reminds me, we haven't mentioned the little professor.

REDDY: The little professor does the thinking for the Child ego state. Hence he's likely to be as shrewd and as sharp as the original little child was in spotting what's going on. But it is also the little professor that at the age of four says 'I will never get married because I know that you can never trust women – quite dangerous in the premature conclusions that he can come to. But when given free rein and when as it were, attached to the Free Child, rather than the Adapted Child, he is still the source of a person's creativity, ingenuity and sharpness.

PROCTOR: I'm going to have to ask you about Free and Adapted Child too.

REDDY: Well, take the new born baby – he has very little capacity at the beginning to put one and one together. In T.A. language, we would describe that as the *Free Child ego state*. That is distinguished from the *Adapted Child*. What the baby has to do sooner or later is begin to do a trade off with mother and father, especially around 18 months to 2½. The trade off is fierce. The baby gives up the immediate gratification of his wants because he comes to fear that the only way he is going to get his needs met in the end is to meet somebody else's first. So you get into the socialisation, civilisation part of a young person's development. And what emerges out of that is an Adapted Child because a lot of the conclusions he comes to in that trade off, are programmed by his feelings. And some people will trade off so much that there is little Free Child left. Others will be lucky and not have to get into such a hard bargain, in order to build the Adapted Child to the place where they will be able to negotiate with the big people.

PROCTOR : Are there responses you've worked on using effectively?

REDDY : Well, what's characteristic of T.A. people and probably less characteristic of me is confronting with the language. 'So you've been collecting angry stamps.' My confrontations tend to be more indirect.

PROCTOR : Are there any responses that you deliberately soft-pedal?

REDDY : One that I am working on is using my own feelings in a situation. I'm still not as likely as I would like to be to use any discomfort I feel, to make it public and explore what the discomfort is about instead of suppressing it. To say 'I'm uncomfortable about what is going on here, and the way I see it, my uncomfortableness is that you are trying to snow me with words, so that I'm ineffective, and I am seeing you as having some part in that ineffectiveness, by the way that you are presenting yourself. What I'd like you to do is to tell me clearly what it is that you want from me'.

As far as soft-pedalling goes, I think I'll lean over backwards not to let people regress into highly emotional states until I'm fairly sure I know why they want to do it. And whether I'm going to be comfortable supporting them while they do it. If I have someone who wants to have a beserk rage, I'm scared of that; somebody who wants to just about melt into helpless hysterical tears, I'm afraid of that, because I don't know how to respond to it, unless I'm sure what it's about and unless we have some contract about it.

PROCTOR: So you don't want to use cathartic techniques?

REDDY: Not just like that, not until I'm sure that that in itself isn't a racket manoeuvre that I'm reinforcing. And until I know what they want to get out of that.

PROCTOR: Do you see any demarcation between counselling and therapy? And if so, what are the dangers of the uninitiated going beyond it?

REDDY: This is one of the questions that I'm enraged each year at what I was saying about it the year before – so I expect to be enraged again. Re-parenting quite definitely nails down one end of the spectrum, and that's where I would encourage regression techniques. I can see myself evolving to where I would be willing to bottle-feed somebody, and even change them and bathe them and give them the sort of messages that one gives a very small boy or girl – that they're ok, that they can think for themselves, it's ok to solve problems, that I don't want to hurt them, that I am willing to provide a particular environment for them. Therapy I see as something quite different. I wouldn't invite regression, I would invite exploration of the Child ego state. The aim is to get the Child ego state and the Adult ego state to eye-ball each other. I think of that as a basic element of therapy.

Now when you talk about counselling, I think of a process where responsibility lies wholly with the client. Here the counsellor is reactive, rather than proactive as the therapist might be, or perhaps the giver of straight information. In what I consider the counsellee seat, I'm very much more in charge than if I go to a therapist or somebody who works in a T.A. or Gestalt modality, or psychodrama – what I would think of as an aggressive modality. With either of those two people working with what I consider an aggressive modality, I put myself in the patient role, and I give them the power to do things to me. If I go to somebody because I want some counselling, it's because I'm in charge. I don't want them to do anything more than help me sort out what I'm actually thinking and feeling. That's this year's version!

PROCTOR: It's interesting as a version, because you define it by the contract the client gives to the helping person, rather than by the qualifications or experience or skill of that person.

Are there dangers of people allowing clients to make therapy contracts?

REDDY: I think that I can take care of myself and can protect myself when I go to a therapist, or to a counsellor, by knowing when to pull out. A lot of people will still go, even to the most mild mannered counsellors, with the expectation of being sorted-out, and leave themselves quite vulnerable to anything the other person might be doing. They would allow themselves to accept an invitation to go into a regression, for example, or to become violently angry because the other person has suggested that that's what they need to do. They will allow the other person a lot of power that the other person may or may not be able to use to their good.

For example, two or three weeks ago, in another country, there was a woman in the group who had recently divorced. She wanted to finish with her husband, as she had a sense that she was still married to him in her head. I worked with her on that contract. There were actually three groups – group A ran for three days and I was running it, group B ran for four days and somebody else was running it, and group C for another six days, with somebody else. She stayed from one to the other. Now in group B she was invited into a regressive state which she apparently couldn't get out of. She had a two hundred mile drive at the end of it and she was unable to drive. Alternative arrangements had to be made to get her and her car back to where she came from – there was no follow-up protection for her. She had de-commissioned her own Adult and her own Parent, maybe in the service of her own finally getting better – but the uninitiated therapist had invited her to make herself helpless when the help that she needed, in that position, was not available. She was committed to a psychiatric institution in her home town the day after, where she still is. And I see that as an unethical and unprofessional use of power on the part of a counsellor who didn't know enough about human beings, or enough about her, to know that when people get themselves into certain places, they are not always able to get themselves out.

PROCTOR: If you are training people for whom counselling is only one part of their work and they are never going to be able to be, or want to be, full-time therapists, what are the words of wisdom about when to be wary in what they are doing?

REDDY: I don't see it being possible to give prescriptions in counselling. I do supervise quite a number of counsellors, by hearing the tapes of their counselling sessions afterwards. The things that I'm after them for most are not listening, not having a clear contract with the person as to what that person is going to do, how he is going to be different afterwards, not being in touch. Maybe this, more than anything else – not being in touch with what is going on in themselves. So that if I hear somebody say 'O.K., I'd like you to do a two chair exercise' and I hear chairs being dragged around, when I am listening to the tape, I say 'why did you do that? How come you thought that was an appropriate moment – what were you feeling', and if they say 'I was stuck, I didn't know what to do', I'll say 'that's not a good reason for doing the two chair exercise'. If they say 'well, they were practically talking to their mother or father, so I put it out in the open', I'll say: 'What did you think might happen'? So I'm wanting them to be in touch with themselves, to do things for a reason, and not to do things without a reason, not to do things which discount their own anxiety or their own fear, or their own anger, their own resentment of a patient. Counselling is a very aggressive activity – it's an invitation to be quite aggressive in getting inside another person and being in touch with things in the other person that are very tender and very sore. Given that, I think they need to know a great deal about how they would like to use their aggressivity, which I use in a neutral sense there. What do they get out of it? So that if somebody is angry with a client but not willing to acknowledge that they are angry with them, they are likely to open up aggressively areas that the person doesn't want to have opened and doesn't need to deal with at that time.

PROCTOR: Do you perceive one-to-one counselling as the same activity as group work?

REDDY: No. I think in script terms it is much more difficult for the client to cast me in all of the necessary roles. In a group, there are several people to take up several roles so I think it is a different animal. But much of the same dynamics will be going on and I will be looking for the same kinds of things. I will be doing some teaching, explaining what I mean by racket and Free Child, the Little Professor, Games and so-forth. I'll be doing the same translating to the T.A. language as a form of confrontation. I'll be tracking the feelings, and the way the feelings meander, shift direction; rather than the head logic, I'll be following that weird child logic that underlies problem behaviours.

PROCTOR: Does the kind of client or group with which you largely work influence you in counselling?

REDDY: It has to influence me enormously, because I've changed.

PROCTOR: Perhaps I should ask first of all, what kind of client have you worked with? Are they middle class, articulate or. . .?

REDDY: I haven't worked with children at all. Many of the people I've worked with are in fact professional counsellors, social workers, psychiatrists, psychologists and so forth. They are the groups I'm most familiar with. But I want to put in one qualification there. Professionals I've worked with can well be encounter group leaders who are very free with their emotional equipment and I am quite likely to be of use to them with T.A. I have, through the counsellors I supervise, seen a great deal of work done with people who are relatively inarticulate, working class people, for whom this is a first time experience. I've seen it work very well.

There is one conclusion that T.A. people who work in prisons have come to. That is that prisoners themselves must be their own therapists and all they can do is teach prisoners to be therapists and not be therapists to prisoners in prison. It has a very cognitive aspect to it. It is called, after all, Transactional Analysis and it sprang from the Freudian analytic background. It is always likely to be a highly verbal therapy. Nonetheless, because there is an emphasis put on pursuing the Child ego state, there is also emphasis put on what is going on in the feelings. Most Transactional analysts do not discount feelings, and many of them are trying to add to their repertoire a good grasp of the practice of bio-energetics or Gestalt or psychodrama or massage – or techniques which have more body and non-verbal orientation – to combine them.

PROCTOR: What about T.A. in organisations or T.A. for managers? Once you have got the insight that T.A. gives you, it *can* be used to help people fulfill their own objectives or it *can* help them to be more comfortable in fulfilling yours. Would you say that was fair?

REDDY: No. It is not fair in my experience, because the people who ask about the ethical use of the tool are invariably managers. Doctors and psychiatrists, psychologists and social workers, never seem to ask the question 'can I use this for ill'. They assume they are using it for good, non-manipulatively; in the very context (organisations) where manipulation would appear most likely, managers seem to be the most immediately aware, and they ask that question. It could enhance people's abilities to manipulate others by, in a cynical way, stroking them, to obtain the behaviour that they want. People do that all the time anyhow, out of their awareness. T.A. can't teach managers very much, in that respect, except perhaps invite them to do it less.

PROCTOR: Do you have any personal dilemmas in the counselling task?

REDDY: My dilemma is about recognising how much I don't know, recognising more and more how my own script issues come into the work of therapy, and making a decision about whether in fact I will continue to do that. Or whether I'll play the piano in a bar, or paint, or write books, or take over from Percy Thrower – something else instead.

PROCTOR: Do you feel the framework of these questions has slanted your experience, and if so, is there anything you want to add?

REDDY: While I've been talking I've been able to say a good part of what I feel. I thought when I read the questions at the beginning that you wouldn't get at more than a cross section of the way I think and act, and that if you saw me working in a group, you might say 'Was that the same fellow I talked to?' I also guess that if you came back in six months' time you'd get different answers. Also, when I first read the questions, I had a sense that there was a political aim, or axe to grind, behind your questions, which I didn't particularly want to grind or to refute, because I hadn't thought about it enough. I think too my first reaction on reading your questions was something like 'shame!' – that I hadn't thought of those questions to ask myself before. So I'm not quite sure what will come out here, or whether reading it six months later, what I've said now might be different.

PROCTOR: Is there anything if I were to see you in a group or with an individual, that you imagine might look different from the fantasy of your working you now expect me to have?

REDDY: I think you might see somebody who was less confronting than he sounds, and also using his own feelings less than he says he likes his own trainees to do. Those are the two things that come immediately.

Gaie Houston

6 Gestalt Therapy

Gaie Houston began her formal training in the
behavioural sciences in the late 1960's in this country and
in America at the National Training Laboratories. An
accomplished playwright, she wrote the book *All in the
Mind* in 1975 after working as facilitator of a small group
in an eleven-episode BBC television series. She now works
as a TV presenter, as well as in Gestalt group and
individual work.

Fritz Perls, who was born in Berlin in 1893 and who died
in America in 1970, is generally acknowledged as the
father of Gestalt psychotherapy. Trained as an analyst
under Karen Horney and Wilhelm Reich, he set up his
first Gestalt Institute in 1933 in South Africa after
fleeing from the Nazis; in 1946 he became a US citizen
and in 1966 he founded Esalen in California.

Gestalt philosophy had only a minimal impact on
Perls, and he was never accepted by the academics. To
quote Perls, 'A gestalt is a pattern, a configuration, the
particular form of organization of the individual parts
that go into its make up'. He developed this concept
into a form of psychotherapy which shifted the emphasis
of psychiatry from the 'adoration of the unconscious'
into the phenomenology of awareness, of here and now
reality. He believed people to be functioning healthily when
they form clear gestalts or configurations of their needs,
and are free to contact and agress, rather than avoid,
their surroundings.

SUGGESTED READING:
Perls, F. S., *Ego, Hunger and Agression*, New York:
    Vintage Books, 1969.
Perls, F. S., Hefferline, Ralph, and Goodman, Paul,
    Gestalt Therapy, Harmondsworth: Penguin, 1973.
Perls, F. S., *Gestalt Verbatim*, New York: Bantam Books,
    1972.
Perls, F. S., *The Gestalt Approach & Eye Witness to
    Therapy*, New York: Bantam, 1973.

PROCTOR: What pair of spectacles are you going to wear for the purpose of this interview?

HOUSTON: Gestalt. That's not the only way I work; but it's the way that interests me most.

PROCTOR: How do you usually use it in your counselling?

HOUSTON: Lately, I have done a lot of training workshops in Gestalt with between 7 and 18 in a group; and every week I've been using it with individuals as well – probably for two or three hours per week – so it's both one-to-one and with groups.

PROCTOR: Looking through that pair of spectacles, what comes into relief as to the nature of human beings and their relationship with groups, social systems, and the total ecological systems of which they are a part?

HOUSTON: I believe that the conflict, the apparent dualism within and between people, within and between systems, is only superficial. Integration and harmony are the beginning. And they are the end about which all our struggles revolve, often tragically. Until we've worked on these conflicts, the underlying integration cannot emerge into awareness.

PROCTOR: What is that saying about individuals, groups and systems?

HOUSTON: We've got some social systems – some parts of social systems – which produce separation, alienation, compartmentalisation, specialisation. We very often employ people, as if they are functioning in only one or two dimensions rather than all their dimensions. People then perceive themselves that way and that helps them to imagine and make conflict between themselves and what they don't know about in other people or in other systems. Gestalt is one way of moving towards political and systems awareness and intervention, as well as personal insight.

PROCTOR: Is there a purpose in the way things are and the way you perceive people?

HOUSTON: I don't know if there is any purpose but what I perceive is my own right-mindedness and the right-mindedness of the people I work with. By using that word right-mindedness I'm trying to describe that innate monitoring that I see in everybody. It is a way for each person to tell themselves if what they're doing is right for them at any moment. I see that as a strong system, independent from the guilt and anxieties which are put in by the programming we get in early life from other people. It is probably a species preservation device that's in us. I believe that it's more than that – that it's a device inside us which allows us to transcend ourselves and allows a more exciting, more coloured, a richer and a more fulfilled meeting between us and our environment and us and each other. It's very unfashionable to believe in the perfectability of man – that Victorian concept – but I think I do believe in that. The phrase is 'It's not choosing the right path, it's choosing the right fights'.

PROCTOR: So the human race as a whole is meant to use energy to somehow break out of its current constraints and modes and find fresh and new ways of living?

HOUSTON: Yes. Anything that is capable of imagination is a part of truth. The image with me at the moment is of the prodigality of nature. Thousands and millions of spores will come out of one fungus, for example, and they might have to wait seventeen years for one of them to make a new fruit. I see people like that. We are all compact with possibility, so the possibility is there in anyone if you can touch them; but the chances are a lot of people are going to live dead and die without living, in my terms.

PROCTOR: How, when, and where did your approach to counselling originate?

HOUSTON: My direct learning about this approach came in the States in the late sixties. I went to what was called a 'T' group. The methods that we used in that group were a mixture of Rogerian and Gestalt, with dashes of this and that. All the ideas that I'd had, that I'd written into plays, and which had not been accepted as having any sense in them, were the common currency of accepted ideas of the people who were working with these 'T' groups. It was like coming home to be there and to be with people who understood my meanings. That group was an extremely strong experience. The psychiatrists who were running it encouraged me to take some training of working in those ways and so I did, and that was the beginning for me.

PROCTOR: What processes or structures within British society today stand out as being helpful to what you have described as the proper purpose of human energy?

HOUSTON: I am often very angry with almost every part of our educational system but, as well, it in some ways helps people along a path that I'm talking about. I went to a State school in a small town in the Midlands and I got a State Scholarship. Without that, I suppose I would have been a typist or worked in a shop.

Our Health Service is a very bad health service but it does take preoccupation with illness away from most of us most of the time. We can contemplate things beyond being terrified about whether we will be able to pay for operations or to have a tooth out. Then there are some conflict devices – the grotesque example is of the T.U.C. and the C.B.I. I don't think they fight the real issues, but at least they are allowed in this society to fight. I don't believe that this fighting is merely as some thinkers would say, repressive tolerance. The fight is growing more even-handed as times goes by. And, having just come back from China and Russia where that sort of conflict is not allowed to surface much, I feel grateful that in this society it can.

PROCTOR: And what processes or structures appear to impede their realisation?

HOUSTON: The first word that comes to my mind is 'property'. Property is a wicked fiction and it's one we've made into reality and which dominates how we live. It is specially translated architecturally into separate dwellings, crammed up with possessions, kept behind lock and key. And so people begin to be seen in terms of property as well and are kept locked up by doors and the institution of marriage. I remember Bion's interpretation that pairing is flight from the group. It is quite frightening to look at a whole nation which more or less universally has made an institution of that flight. That little tiny isolated unit is encouraged to stay separate from the time of marriage until death and habit seems to dictate that the widowed live alone, mourning. That seems to me a really destructive institution. China reinforced my feelings about that clearly. People don't just have their family, or even extended family, as their reference group there. They have a work group, neighbourhood group, study group and that means there is much more flexibility and interchange of role.

I see a lot of value given in this society to processes which are alienating. For instance, reading is considered an educated and good thing, yet much reading is a weird substitute for living and being and relating. Watching television causes a one-way flow from a machine into each person who is looking at the machine and, by and large, stops any dialogue between the two or three people who might be in the same room. I dislike too the parts of our education system which are saying 'The instructor is the holder of all wisdom. Other people have no right to, and will be stupid if they do, question. They have a duty of total attention, total comprehension and no rights to interact with each other while the teaching is going on.'

There are a lot of structures that simply prevent communication within each person and between people and between them and the environment. For a lot of the time we are maintained in a very curious and isolated world – what Perls might call a mid-zone – a zone of fantasy which is in newspapers and tapes and radio and books and television. Our heads are stuffed with phantasy like great larders of goods which are never going to be used, never going to be changed into energy and made available for anybody else.

PROCTOR: So what do you see as the objective of the counselling task?

HOUSTON: My first objective in counselling is to help the person who is being counselled to become more aware. I try to be very overt about that being my task.

PROCTOR: Is the underlying belief that if you can help them become more aware, they will find their own paths – their own ways and realisations?

HOUSTON: Yes. I have never heard of Perls going as far as I would about that, but when I begin a training workshop, I explain that my short goal is to raise consciousness, to raise awareness. My underlying assumption is that if people raise their awareness, in the framework we have there, they will only do themselves good. They will move step by step closer to what I call their right-mindedness. They may cause themselves amazing pain in the beginning in doing that, but my belief is that they are inevitably going to move themselves towards their own centre and the integration that is there. There is only themself to find and they are a friend.

PROCTOR: And what resources do you see yourself bringing to the counselling task?

HOUSTON: My familiarity with some methods of Gestalt work. Considerable stubbornness about not being seduced from the task by the other person, and some courage about staying open about what's going on for me and for them. The awareness, and communicating the awareness, is probably the major resource. I have a capacity, when I'm working, to feel respect and often love for other persons and to help them to respect and love themselves, so their esteem is high enough that they dare to be irrational, whiny, mean-minded: whatever they need to be at that moment in order to begin to heal themselves.

PROCTOR: What do you see as being the responsibilities of the client and the counsellor in the counselling interaction?

HOUSTON: I think that the clients' responsibility is to want to change. If they don't, then the whole relationship isn't a counselling relationship and we might as well do something else. My responsibilities as a counsellor are to be as clear as I can be about what I'm going to do, in so far as I know what I'm going to do, and to help the other person to stay with the task. And I have got a very clear responsibility to not do more than half of the work. Otherwise, what are they bothering to come for?

PROCTOR: What about the more mundane responsibilities, such as confidentiality?

HOUSTON: Gestalt as a general philosophy doesn't care a rap for confidentiality. Perls and other trainers provoke people into gossiping and then go and confront the third person with the gossip as a means of moving people on. Though I don't have a strong pre-occupation about confidentiality, I'm very little inclined to gossip about what goes on in groups or with a person who is in counselling with me. But if I judge it useful to violate confidence, I'll violate it. If somebody is talking about suicide and I have a guess that they are really going to do something about it that evening, I most certainly will tell the person they are going to be with that evening. Confidentiality depends on where and when. Yet I would imagine that I'm trustworthy for anybody, that I don't violate confidence.

PROCTOR: Then how do you ensure that your client shares your assumptions and objectives about the counselling task?

HOUSTON: Just by open discussion at the beginning about what I'm seeing as my responsibilities and needs and rights, and what the other person's demands and needs are and what we can do about those.

PROCTOR: Do you let people in on your assumptions and

objectives by straight teaching?

HOUSTON: The way I choose is straight teaching and as clear information as I can give. Perls uses the world 'mystifying' as a bad word and disapproves of mystifying, but it seems to me that a lot of the ways that he used the Gestalt method, and certainly the ways I've seen other trainers use it, can sometimes be very mystifying to people. I don't see the long-term useful-ness of that. Gestalt is dealing with the present. Much of the Gestalt therapist's task is to maintain clients in the present so that they can discover from the present whatever they need to. The way that I gesture with my hand, the way that I hold my breath – all the little minute habits and patterns that I have – are repeated over and over again. They all have a meaning that is probably very useful to me. If I really notice it, the chances are that I can discover what the meaning is and then move on. Until I have made that discovery I'm stuck with the unfinished pattern that I'm forever dramatising and acting. After I've taught someone to notice themselves more, and when we have some sort of agreement about what we are doing, I feel free to say 'what's your hand doing at the moment?' or, 'you seem to have stopped breathing'. These seem quite unthreatening things to say when there's an understanding between both of us as to what my task is. I have been in Gestalt workshops where there are people who don't know anything beyond the word Gestalt, who have suddenly been asked to say what their foot is saying or something of this kind. It frightens people, it turns them off, and sometimes they defend themselves by trying to annihilate communication altogether. It doesn't seem to me that's useful to them. The trainer is wasting his time waiting for something to happen and sometimes he's actually reduced to a sort of analytic position of making some interpretations of what's going on, because there's nothing else to do. So it suits me to explain at the beginning, so that the other person feels ok with what I am doing.

I will take an apparently intrusive role quite often, but I make it very clear that my intrusions are attempted intrusions, and that the other person has the responsibility if they wish to tell me not to intrude, and to stop me in what I am doing. What I'm trying to do is to create, from the beginning, a climate of such safety that the person feels free to explore themselves. I often succeed.

PROCTOR: Is the counselling encounter different from other encounters you have in other roles?

HOUSTON: Yes. The difference that comes to my mind is that I do feel myself to be more fully present when I'm working in Gestalt than in many other roles. I feel freer, I give myself more permission, and I confront from where I am. I am very aware and I find it exciting to be in that mode. I don't permit myself as much freedom in a lot of other roles and then often will feel irritated or put down by people, but won't do anything about it.

PROCTOR: In what ways do you see it as different from teaching or training roles?

HOUSTON: There's a difference of method, but I don't think I really have a difference of stance in other professional roles. I feel very responsible, and, as Perls would put it 'very response-able' – I'm aware of what my responses are and feel I have got quite clear choices of what I do with them when I'm working professionally with people. In a way, counselling is very like teaching; it's giving a framework for the person to learn themselves. And most of the formal teaching I do is about our selves and our interactions.

PROCTOR: Counsellors tend to focus on certain aspects of a client's total interaction with the environment. What particular processes do you focus on and what faculties do you engage?

HOUSTON: My focus is on what is going on in the present. I do spell out to people that I see my task as keeping them in the present tense and frustrating all their devices for escaping from the present. That means reporting to them whatever comes into my awareness about what is present for them, and which I guess is probably out of their awareness at the time. A lot of that will be seeing things that they are doing, hearing their voice tone, noticing my response to the other person and reporting that. I'll find tears are coming to my eyes, or that my throat is closing or I'm stopping breathing, or tensing in some way, and I'll try to be aware of that in myself and offer it to the person to see if I have picked up from them or whether I'm responding to myself. The chances are I've picked up from them because I find that I work like that. I often mirror what's going on.

PROCTOR: How is that different from interpreting what's going on?

HOUSTON: I'm not offering *my meaning* of what is happening – I'm offering my *observation* of what is happening. To me, that's qualitatively different. If I notice that somebody freezes their hand while at the same time rotating their ankle, I might say, 'Are you aware of your ankle'? I remind them of some of their own behaviour. Less and less, do I make private guesses because I find that those guesses are often way off and it is more useful just to find out from the client what is happening.

PROCTOR: It sounds as if you focus quite a lot on what's happening to them physically?

HOUSTON: Yes, and not only on physical things, though very often it's such an obvious place to start. There's something so undeniable about the fact that someone's shoulders are hunched up, or they are gripping the arms of the chair. I often also work with repetitive patterns that set up over and over again in the interview.

PROCTOR: Do you discuss what happened in the past or plan what your clients are going to do in the future?

HOUSTON: The present is the point of departure and, in the early stages, I find it useful for it to be the total focus. It's such a different way for people to be perceiving that they really need the training of staying with being aware of what they are doing at the moment. They need to realize that they are not dangerous animals who have to be ignored or punished because they grip their hands or pull their hair or whatever. If a person is moving into awareness of other times, of other people, we maintain clarity about what's happening. I might say, 'Now you're going into a fantasy about next week. Don't talk about it. Imagine you're there'. I use the device of asking people to retell things in the present tense. I discourage them very strongly from talking *about* anything. I ask them to dramatize what's going on, as a way of making it vivid so that, again, it becomes present. In the present, you can move on, instead of being encapsulated in an anecdote which you could tell to every therapist from here to eternity.

PROCTOR: If it's fighting the right fights, do you focus on points of tension and conflict?

HOUSTON: Yes, I do. Much of the time, what comes to my attention is tension in the other person, and awareness of polarities in what someone is doing or saying. Often in their metaphors or vocabulary, there is a choice of words which has to do with two sides of a person or two sides of a conflict. The Gestalt method is to invite the client to dramatize that conflict, whatever it is. If they say, 'somehow my legs just want to run away but my heart tells me I should stay here' – I invite them to set up the dialogue, ridiculous as it may sound, between those running legs and steadfast heart. I don't interpret with another word about this heart and those legs, I use their words – very purely returning them to the speaker. Very often, that fight isn't really the right fight. Listening how they speak from the two sides of that conflict, I'll hear that they are using some new words, that they are suggesting that there is another fight. So the dramatis personae can change constantly between the two chairs between which they are working, until they get to their honest fight.

PROCTOR: That reminds me of Perls talking about going through the Games layer on which T.A. focuses, to the 'impasse': is that the real conflict?

HOUSTON: Fritz talked about the impasse and the heavy resistance place and Gestalt is a very handy tool for dealing with these two levels: with what the real conflicts are and also with pointing very quickly to the manner of the resistance. It's a way of letting people familiarise themselves with their trick for stopping themselves from dealing with their real conflicts. When I'm working with someone, I'm dealing with the *person*. I'm not separating a person into those fragments which are in the body or the memory or the imagination, though the person is very likely to be doing that with himself – to be seeing himself as disintegrated, warring fragments.

PROCTOR: Talk about how you work with dreams.

HOUSTON: In the way Perls developed this dream work, you and the person who had the dream approach it with respect, with the belief that it has perfectly coherent meanings which are somewhat obscure and which are available to the person who dreamed the dream in whatever way they want to make those meanings available to themselves: There is a poetic faculty in people which produces dreams and, very curiously, the Gestalt way of working often allows people to return to the dream mode while they are awake. They continue that poetic process, but not in a schizophrenic way, by which I mean a way that separates them from mundane sense. Again, the method is to return to the present. Somebody arrives, preoccupied with this terrible dream they had last night, or this exciting or recurrent dream. I let them tell it in their own way. Then I ask them to tell it again as though it is happening in the present tense, to go back into the dream, be the dream, go through it in the present tense. As they are doing that, I'm learning the elements of that dream, and they are probably noticing more about the dream than they did when they first told it in a general anecdotal way. I usually ask them what part of the dream is most clearly with them now when they have finished telling it; then I ask them to be whatever that is. It might be a person in the dream or it might be some in-animate object. I ask them to describe themselves as if they really are that, whatever it is. My assumption is that they are dealing with a part of their energy which they have locked into something, alienated from themselves. If they are noticing a rug, say, they might describe themselves as warm and richly-coloured, or as worn-out, trodden on, ignored. When they have described themselves as whatever it is, they often get quite an insight just from doing that.

Very often, there will be two opposing elements in the dream which the person can separately own. These two elements can engage in a dialogue, which may grow into some kind of fight with some sort of resolution. That doesn't necessarily happen but it's quite likely to. Often, they find the dream is changing as they begin to be a part of it. By the end, they have made their own meaning of what was only a garbled experience in the dream they had in the night. They may tell me their meaning excitedly afterwards, or, maybe not – part of my responsibility as a therapist is to keep my mouth shut about my meaning for their dream.

PROCTOR: What kind of climate do you seek to develop for your task?

HOUSTON: I don't believe that many Gestalt therapists would give my answer, of safety. Quite a number I know actually value the anxiety they can produce. I don't want to produce a collusive safety where we all pretend to feel comfortable and like each other. I want there to be enough respect around for the person working to respect himself. What I'm wanting is for people to achieve their independence, in so far as that is a reality – and to be able to make a choice which is right for them even if I and everyone else around them disapproves and punishes them for that. So I am at pains not to collude with people over giving them permission to do things – I violate a lot of the ordinary politeness of society. I won't always answer if people ask me questions that I don't want to answer; I may do things which in the short term make them very angry. But where I feel I differ from other therapists is that I'm at pains to establish first what my expectations are. I believe there is a functional amount of anxiety to maintain in therapy. Beyond a certain point, paralysis sets in. I don't see that as useful.

PROCTOR: So, unlike if you are working in a Rogerian mode, you give yourself permission to play some tricks?

HOUSTON: I don't see the things I spoke of as tricks; I see them as responses to myself rather than to social correctness. I feel that excitement is one of the best possibilities in Gestalt therapy. We are not structuring our time in such a way that we kill it before it happens. We are allowing the possibility that the next part of the future is new for everybody. That is frightening as well as exciting. It's a paradox. I feel that I make a climate of safety, in which people can let themselves take risks to be unsafe.

PROCTOR: Do you view yourself as a model for your clients?

HOUSTON: I model being fairly painstaking about communicating what's going on for me. One level of that is being open about all those subtleties that there are in awareness if you stop to notice. The other level of modelling is that I'm giving myself space to use group time or client time to say what's going on for me. That gives permission to the other person to give themselves space. And I think I probably get stronger as times goes by, at just *being what I am at any moment*, and that puts in the unsafety I've talked about. There are moments when I absolutely loathe the sight of the person sitting in front of me and I hope that we get enough safety that I show that loathing or express that irritation. In that way, I give them permission to own their own negative feelings and to find that the world does not disintegrate when you do; instead, it gets more exciting. I hope that I model *making clear choices and staying with them*, even though it's obviously getting me disliked at the time. I am talking in terms of negatives. Positives can happen but I think the fears are around the negatives so that's what I find I'm concentrating on at the moment.

PROCTOR: Does 'transference' have much significance for you? If so, what do you do about it?

HOUSTON: It may have a lot of significance for me if it seems to for the person who is with me. Transference is not high up in my awareness, as a concept, but, nevertheless, I often am dealing with it. Usually, my attention tends to be on very small processes in what's going on between me and the client or what's going between the client and himself. I see those parts, often, as minute looped tapes of old patterns of behaviour which could be labelled transference. One I can think of is someone in her first interview with me. Four or five times, I noticed that I had a kind of sad clutch of the stomach and I felt quite let down, somehow. She wasn't apparently even relating directly to me; she was working on things with herself. But I got this let-down feeling. I reported it to her and we worked on that. It was certainly a transference because she produced in me, and produced in herself, feelings which she had been used to produce in herself and produce in her mother. She gave herself a confused and let-down feeling but she also apparently gave it to her mother, we suppose, just as she gave it to me. It took considerable work to get to, by plotting what she did and what I felt. She had a way of suddenly sighing, her shoulders sinking, and she looked out the window, looking terribly wistful and sad. She actually at that moment was confused and had forgotten what she was talking about but she felt terrible and it was a recurrent feeling with her. That turned out to be about transference.

PROCTOR: Do you induce transference?

HOUSTON: No. I'm not in any way, I think, trying to set up what is going to happen below the overt level of how I'm going to work.

PROCTOR: If they are angry with you, do you, like Perls, get them to 'put Gaie in the empty chair'?

HOUSTON: That's projection to me, rather than transference. Perls was refusing to own an aspect of someone else which they were highly aware of in other people. 'You deal with that within yourself'. It differs from transference, which for me, is an attempt to reproduce some part of a former relationship with me as stand-in for the original character.

PROCTOR: Conditioning. Are you aware of it and what do you do about it?

HOUSTON: I am aware of conditioning. In a very obvious way. I am attempting to condition people to perceive in other modes from ones that are socially conditioned. I'm not doing it covertly. Sometimes I've done something which is a little nearer covert. If somebody is immensely obliging and always goes along with what I say, occasionally, I've suggested that they do something more outrageous – until they realise that they are simply concurring with what I say and that they are not making independent choices. I'm covertly conditioning them to know where their boundaries are, and of where they are pushed around by other people.

PROCTOR: Are there any other patterns of interaction which you would identify as a process which you habitually recognise or make use of?

HOUSTON: There are three that come up time and time again that Perls talked about. I've talked about projection a little already. Then there are introjection and retroflection – those are Gestalt concepts that I respect. *Introjection* comes down to swallowing whole; what Perls suggests as a better process is to chew thoroughly and to assimilate and or eliminate. He makes a clear comparison between the way people approach their food and approach experience – whether they take tearing bites or hang on or nibble or suck, for example. Most of us are walking around with some very large undigested lumps which need to be either vomited out or assimilated, re-chewed. That will show, if we are dealing with awareness of what's going on in the present. *Retroflections* are doing to yourself what you would like to do to others. That shows up time and again, as someone sits in the client's chair, tugging away at their own hair or stroking their own face, kicking their own ankles – somehow turning on themselves some feelings that they've not dared to turn on to the appropriate object. *Projection* is putting onto the other people the things which actually belong to yourself but which you are not prepared to own for one reason or another. So those are ideas in me, which I will try out by one means or another, as possibilities of what somebody's doing.

There is also the concept of the top dog and the underdog, the Aristotelian false concept that all relationships are power relationships. That seems to be internalised into masses of people, so that they are behaving as if they are at the same time the master and the slave, or the top dog and the underdog. Though the top dog appears, usually, to be the one who is in control, it's the devious slave or underdog who is really in control. It is very confusing for the person who has first chosen to conceptualise himself in those terms and then act out this concept. Both sides of that conflict are holding energy in very dysfunctional ways. Until they have released the energy at each other and made an integration, the energy doesn't seem to flow back to the centre.

PROCTOR: What does it look like in your therapeutic session when someone is allowing himself to fight between two lots of locked energy?

HOUSTON: The convention is to set up two chairs and to ask the person working to define which part of herself she is when she is in one chair or the other. She passes back and forth between the chairs as she finds she is in touch with one side, or the other, of the dialogue. A lot of my task is to keep her clear about what she is talking about and to whom at any time. That dialogue may remain verbal, or it may go to something pre-verbal – crying or moaning or whatever. It may become physical, one side may want to trounce the other. It works very well for some people to be able to punish a cushion or something inanimate, as a symbol of one part of themselves. What tends to happen is that after having done their level best to annihilate one part of themselves, they end up embracing that part. It's as if they owned and integrated it, and that is not because I have pre-empted that dialogue in any way.

PROCTOR: Are there other responses you have worked on being able to use effectively?

HOUSTON: The reponses that I find myself using the most commonly are those that give the ownership of what is happening firmly back to the person who is speaking. I constantly remind the person who is working that it is that person who is working, and not me. Now I *am* working, very hard, but a major part of my work is to show the clarity of where the boundary of the other person's system has got to be. They are working within their confines, and there is no way I can be there before them.

PROCTOR: Are there any responses that you deliberately soft-pedal?

HOUSTON: I am very strict with people in that I don't let them interpret themselves, because I distrust that sort of intellectual process. I think that it limits meaning more often than enhances it.

I'm encouraging them to be so aware of the moment that they dare flow or fight into the next moment of the unknown. I encourage living, not theorising.

PROCTOR: How does that relate to your being able to conceptualise very clearly and answer my questions in conceptual terms?

HOUSTON: I don't feel conflict between being clear in these sort of words and working in Gestalt. I see Gestalt work as the most beautifully intelligent work. Intelligence in its root means 'tying together'. Intelligence to me is the tying together of all the parts of the wisdom of the organism. It's necessary when we are talking to tape recorders or talking to books, just to use words. Primary living is sensing, feeling, intuiting, imagining, playing, doing; words are not a large part of all that.

PROCTOR: Do you see any demarcation between counselling and therapy within your framework? It's called Gestalt Therapy. You use it in what you would call counselling and in training counsellors. Do you see a distinction?

HOUSTON: I think I only see a quantitative distinction. When people are less experienced at being the Gestalt worker, they will limit themselves by that inexperience. They won't pick up too many of the signals and will limit themselves by a very proper anxiety about what will, at that time, be too far for them. There is no neat distinction for me between development, therapy, counselling and self-actualisation.

PROCTOR: What is amazing, to me, in Gestalt is the incredible speed with which people plummet through layers of blocking, to strong, true feelings. Are there dangers in that?

HOUSTON: A part of Gestalt that I've probably not stressed quite clearly enough here while I've been talking, but which I stress very heavily always when I'm working is 'What I do is what I've chosen to do' and 'What you do is what you have chosen to do'. The feelings I have are the feelings I've given myself and produced in myself. If somebody says to me 'I feel distraught and desolate', a response I am likely to make is 'How do you manage to make yourself feel that way'? – even if I suspect that their secret requirement is that I feel guilty or that I should try to comfort them. I'm very concerned that they see to what extent they are responsible for their own state and their own being. Having done that at the beginning, I'm not enormously concerned if they do give themselves quite bad feelings. It's very important to me that they should see that they have chosen to be in those feelings and that they have the power not to be in them. I trust their power to take themselves to where they need to be. I can point out, say, that they have not been in that infantile state of terror for a very long time: they have evidently developed the power not to be in that state unless they choose.

That returns to the question of 'conditioning'. I don't condition people who are working to feel that they ought to transcend barriers, or implode, explode, do anything. I try overtly to *condition them to set their own limits*. I know that I will value them as much if they choose not to work or choose to stop working, as if they take themselves through very risky areas.

PROCTOR: Does the client population with whom you mainly work influence you?

HOUSTON: The only answer that comes up is that Gestalt stresses that each of us owns ourselves and our actions and our responses and so that issue of owhership is very clear and very present in Gestalt; I have noticed more and more that unless I stay absolutely with that, I'm not working effectively.

PROCTOR: Have you ever used Gestalt with people who are very fragile?

HOUSTON: I've worked with one woman who was called a schizophrenic and that was beautiful. It was a good piece of work that she did and very integrative. I did a few weeks in a group of mixed advanced neurotics and schizophrenics and I didn't do any Gestalt with the schizophrenics – the 'gestalt' did not come into my mind of using Gestalt. I found myself doing something much more soft and reinforcing somehow, and I didn't know if that was in response to my fears, or to them.

PROCTOR: Have you any personal dilemmas in your counselling or training work?

HOUSTON: I think that there are parts of truth that I see in Gestalt and in training people for Gestalt that I don't live with and stay with in the rest of my life, for example, to do with property and women reducing themselves in many ways by self-imposed rules and self-imposed duties and tasks. My dilemma is not in the work but is in staying with the truth that's in the work.

PROCTOR: Looking at Gestalt in relation to counselling, do you consider that you are training people as Gestalt therapists or do you think that you are giving them skills or modes that supplement their other modes of working with people?

HOUSTON: I think I am training them as Gestalt therapists *and* I'm giving them a tool which works very well alongside other modes and is more appropriate at certain times than at others. Gestalt is especially neat at dealing at the level of resistance. It's particularly neat as a way of confronting people with their responsibility for themselves, of helping them to work polarities and conflicts within themselves and with projections. So where those things are up top in counselling, Gestalt may be appropriate for some people to use. I do not see a useful distinction between training them as a Gestalt therapist and training them to do those things.

I do see a jealous ownership of the word therapist by professionals who want to maintain an exclusivity. Probably a good confidante or confessor performed quite a lot of the therapeutic and counselling tasks which have become paid professional jobs now. Finally, you see, though I value Gestalt very highly, I suspect that relationship, not method, is the heart of any growth or therapy.

PROCTOR: Can you think of anything else that you have left out of the Gestalt picture?

HOUSTON: I find myself thinking of the word 'freedom'. I haven't used that word much. Freedom via high awareness isn't the freedom of irresponsibility, but of a vastly heightened response-ability. People are aware of themselves and the people around them and of the systems around them and the whole environment in which they make and realise their choices. I aim to help people experience freedom in that very particular sense.

Dave Wilmot

7   Reality Therapy

Dave Wilmot has worked for sixteen years in the field of mental health. He is a social worker, trained in psychiatric social work, group and family therapy. After working as mental health consultant for a London borough, he ran a therapeutic community with the Richmond Fellowship. For the past four years he has been Student Trainer and Consultant for Camden Family Service Unit.

Reality Therapy originated in the work of the American psychiatrist William Glasser, who worked for many years with 'hard-core delinquents' and wrote *Reality Therapy* in 1965. In England, Reality Therapy has been used with 'multi-problem' families and long-term mental patients where more verbal methods seemed to be inappropriate. Many Reality therapists are also indebted to the work of two other American psychotherapists, Virginia Satir and Paul Watzlawick.

SUGGESTED READING:
Glasser, William, *Reality Therapy: A New Approach to Psychiatry*, New York: Harper & Row, 1965.
Satir, Virginia, *Conjoint Family Therapy*, Palo Alto: Science and Behaviour Books, Inc., 1965.
Watzlawick, Paul, Weakland, J., and Fisch, C., *Change: Principles of Problem Formation and Problem Resolution*, New York: Norton, 1974.

PROCTOR: What pair of spectacles are you going to wear for the purpose of this interview?

WILMOT: Whether it's with a student, a staff member, or a family that I'm working with, what I'm trying to do is create the facility where people can begin to think about what they want for themselves and think about ways of getting it.

PROCTOR: And that formulation comes out of the Reality therapy school of thinking?

WILMOT: Yes, it is the idea of looking very concretely with another person at literally how to get what you want in your life. Reality Therapy – Glasser's work – would say that dealing with small, mutually-identified goals between you and another stands the best chance of being productive. The Brief Psychotherapy Centre in California would say 'Reality is what the person wants and let's work on that, rather than what *you* perceive would be a better state for that person to be in'.

PROCTOR: Looking through that pair of spectacles at human beings as a whole, what comes into relief as to the nature of human beings and the relationships between human beings, groups, social systems and ecological systems of which they are a part?

WILMOT: Whereas at one time I felt quite sure that what people were about was maximising human growth potential, I now think that is the payment you get for what I call the drive towards raising your self-esteem, the drive towards being seen and acknowledged as being a significant person – both to have that feeling internally for yourself and for it to be recognised amongst others. I think that self-esteem – individual, personal significance – is for me the clearly identified life motivating force and I look at it within systems (e.g., the family) as much as within individuals, as being that which creates the differences, etc. Where the self-esteem of an organism or each group of organisms is high, you can see where an individual, where a group, where a community, is going for itself. When self-esteem is low, you look at yourself in terms of what the other group, the other individual, the other community is getting for itself. It is a very simplistic idea, but it works. I can actually understand that and base a clear model of helping on such simple assumptions. It also seems to me that to look at individuals and groups in terms of the maximising of potential as being the outcome of how to do what you want, how to raise your self-esteem, allows me far more creativity to intervene as a therapist than if I acknowledged that life is at best a successful stalemate between dirty drives and sufficient controls. That doesn't allow me very much room to work. Nor does it allow me to have reasonably high ceilings for my views of other people or what I could ever achieve with them.

PROCTOR: Is there an infinite amount of self esteem available

for people to have? Of, do you see it as something fo
people are in competition?

WILMOT: I'm actually not sure about that. The Taoist training
I have had in acupuncture and boxing, in philosophy, says that
an organism is born with an amount of energy and that it's the
channelling of the energy that's so important. I can't conceive
of it being infinite just as I can't conceive of it being finite.
But I can conceive that we never actually get anywhere near
the upper reaches of what we can get for ourselves in terms of
raising our level of self-esteem. When self-esteem is sufficiently
low among a sufficient number of people, we can do a pretty
good job in making sure that no one gets very much. For
example, in my marriage, when my self-esteem is fairly high,
when I'm getting what I want for myself and I feel good, then
I can say to my wife, 'Yes, you go and do that – that's fine!',
and I give a great deal. When my self-esteem is very low,
then it can sometimes seem that anything my wife is getting
for herself must be taken from me – I am stolen from, I don't
actually give. That very simple idea helps me to have an
overview of the importance of quantifying self-esteem as a
totally non-magical thing, very much down-to-earth. You
can raise your self-esteem level, you can monitor it, you can
know where it's at reasonably simply.

PROCTOR: So, basically, self-esteem is the oil that makes the
human species machine go well if there is enough of it spread
around?

WILMOT: Yes. One way in which self-esteem is raised or
lowered is by feedback, the feedback you get from you as a
person in your role, the things you say, the things you do, the
way you look, etc. It seems to me it is a perfectly reasonable
state to wish for feedback about yourself. I know that my self-
esteem is often governed by my interaction with other people,
although I might have a core of it which over the years built
up to make it feel fairly good to be me regardless. Feedback
I get from another person has an immediate effect on my
self-esteem, so that is one way I can monitor my self-esteem.
But I don't see that as the only way of measuring it. For some
people it's more important to be with people and for some
people it's less important. I guess it could come to a point
where they could not survive without the feedback they got
from other people. Then it seems to me we're not looking at

self-esteem any more; we're looking at a much more desperate scrabble for feedback.

PROCTOR: What do you see as the purpose of human energy?

WILMOT: For me, the most palatable philosophy is looking at man, the world, etc., in terms of balance, in terms of harmony. That makes sense to me. I know I can be responsible in terms of my own harmony, my own levels of energy. That's my concern. In that sense, as is everyone, I am one model – I am what I say. Now if all these models add up to anything more than that, then I wouldn't be surprised. I wouldn't be surprised if my internal workings and the external world that I see are not part of some other system to do with the interplay of such forces. There seem so many similarities in the world of nature, in the world of science, in the world of man, that bring me back time and time again to the idea of the interplay of opposing, dynamic forces, basic energy levels, the rise and fall of energy levels. I don't begin to understand it but I have a tremendous sympathy with it. If someone proved it tomorrow I would just nod my head in a very self-satisfied way. Although I look at self-esteem as being the major motivating force I know that I am never satisfied by one state of mind forever and that as soon as I get too complacent in life I change it in some way.

PROCTOR: Yours is a model that's for you and of interest, but it isn't the definitive model for the whole of counselling and social work?

WILMOT: By no means! I can feel quite sure that somewhere other people are working on other things and that's all right by me. It enables me to stand still and do what I'm doing. And not feel regretful, guilty or whatever.

PROCTOR: What are the processes or structures within British society today that stand out to you as being helpful to the realisation of what you think are proper purposes, like the raising of self esteem?

WILMOT: It sounds a bit corny when I think of it but it looks as though we've got a sufficient level of development to be able to sit back and ask such questions and to ponder on such things. We can afford to look at how the quality of our lives could be better. It seems to me you've got to have a sufficient cultural development to be able to do that, when so much evidence from other countries lets us know quite clearly that in no way could that go on except in a hidden, covert secretive way. The fact that we have a reasonably developed democracy seems to me a fairly critical enabling factor. Going along with that is the fact that we have basic minimum conditions to survive, a guaranteed safety net, in this country. It is most unlikely that anyone actually starves, etc. Again, we can afford to look at these questions because we don't have to concern ourselves with hunting for our daily meals. Now that we've got the basic rules of survival established, we can afford to look in different directions.

PROCTOR: You don't consider that individual responsibility is diminished by the number of regulations there are?

WILMOT: I think no matter what the rules are, you can perceive them as working for you or against you, depending on your self-esteem level. For me, sometimes some rules stop me getting what I want, but it's the basic existence of some of the rules that enable me to go after what I want. I wouldn't say that we have too many rules. Since the drive is towards raising self esteem, you can get very mixed up in the process. You can be outrageously selfish in doing it. It seems to me that without sufficient rules, the society where people attempt to fulfil themselves could well become quite anarchic, unless we vested certain rule-making powers in a group of people, which is effectively what we've done.

PROCTOR: Do the rules provide a safe space for disadvantaged families to grow?

WILMOT: One part of it is clearly dealt with by being middle-class. You don't have to worry about so many things. It just is like that. As a therapist, I can intervene where people totally under-use their ability to get what they want for themselves and I know I can help them to get it. That's where I put my skills. It comes back to me trusting others will be working in a political way, where people are not getting what they want and cannot do that much about it. They can do some things. Since I work with them on getting what they want, my work is inevitably political and is rightly seen as being so. I like to work in that way of developing people's functions and systems for raising their self-esteem. I'm not so good when it comes to working on behalf of a community, or getting something for a group. So I get the best messages for myself out of the work that I do at the moment. Therefore, I am very good at it,

I think, and I put more into it and I become more skilled at it. When I've tried other things, I've seen that I don't do it so well. I don't get the payoff.

PROCTOR: Do you find any structures in British society which are unhelpful to the raising of self-esteem, if there are so many people needing such a lot of help in getting what they need?

WILMOT: The clearest one for me that prevents it is the very model of help that we offer to people. I know it's one small aspect of society, but I think that the generally applied model of helping as demonstrated in English social work is designed in an empty, mindless way to support, and take care of, instead of actually enabling any change to occur. It contains such an element of pathology in it that it, well, very crudely, does more harm than good. It's done well-meaningly and with skill and with care and is highly complex in its theoretical construction, but I think it maintains a pool of socially in-adequate individuals and families in our society. And that can be looked at in terms of justifying their being given more help. It's a pervasive thing in social work practice and training, and in all the helping professions. It is doing real harm to quite a sizeable section of the population. We now have it fairly fixed in our society that there are inadequate people and inadequate families that we must provide help for. A very crude model of identifying need and providing the service to do something about it without looking at what people do actually want. It's the same model that's used in medicine, in psychiatry, and in the penal system, too. There is a total confusion between wanting to be *punitive* and wanting to *put right*. We are not clear when we are doing which.

PROCTOR: Like the confusion in child care and education?

WILMOT: Yes, part of that model is that experts know what a better state should be for, say, a group or type of client. 'We have decided that the best thing for you, young man . . .'

PROCTOR: Can you trust people to know what's best for themselves?

WILMOT: To quite some degree – far more than we give people credit for at the moment.

PROCTOR: Where does the word 'reality' come in, in Reality Therapy?

WILMOT: For me, there are two things: it is what I and the person I am working with define as real between us. Real is *what that person actually feels*, whether it is real or not to others, and that's what we've got to work with. If that person feels paranoid, then that paranoia is real and that's to be worked with. Now at the same time, the other level of 'real', in reality, to me is the idea that there are *real consequences for behaviour and actions*. They undoubtedly exist since they are done to me and I do them each day. Anybody who chooses to put aside these matters in order to work on ideas and concepts that their body of therapy has come up with is, to me, unreal, and cannot work in the client's real world. It won't contain the actual real world parameters that the client is living within. Therefore, I would say to a therapist, it would be wise not to ignore your client's imminently losing his electricity supply. I would say to a client, in this real world you will lose your electricity supply unless we can find a successful way of dealing with your electricity payments. It's like a game of consequences – the client has to be aware that there are real consequences for choosing to do or choosing not to do. Just as therapists have to be aware there are real consequences in choosing what to do in this area or what not to do.

We bandy around the word 'self-responsibility' but I know I will not take responsibility for a client in any way because that would be unreal. That doesn't happen in the real world and I won't be able to maintain a long enough, close enough relationship with that person for it to become an alternative reality. That for me would be a different job to the one that I'm doing or would choose to do.

PROCTOR: Do you accept that responsibility for, say, your five-year-old son?

WILMOT: Yes, much more so. I have to acknowledge when I am working with a client that he may have the facility to take responsibility for himself. Now I haven't worked with young enough clients where I would have to cloud that by actually taking responsibility away from them as I would do with my five year old son. Working with children as a client group I think would be very, very difficult and I would have to re-learn the whole idea.

PROCTOR: You don't believe that there are some people who, although they may be of adult age, who wear adult clothes, maybe have an adult income, are nevertheless no more able to take responsibility for themselves than your five-year-old son?

WILMOT: No, I don't. Nothing in my clinical experience to date has shown me that. Given a model that takes into account what a person wants for themselves, it is always possible to do something to raise someone's self-esteem. It has never yet been impossible to do anything, if I have listened to the client, and if I've used my skills in designing reasonable, bite-sized chunks of work together that exhibit my skill in doing my part of the job properly. Models of help which look at people with quite severe determinance tend to start off with that sort of assumption and are, firstly, very highly problem-centered; secondly, probably are centered on a fairly rigid theoretical background. So the way you look at it would determine the outcome of it. For instance, looking at social work as a basic problem-centred profession, the case history is what I call a disaster catalogue. It is nearly always a history of all the tragedies, disasters, and messes that the individual or family have got themselves into. In the section marked strengths and weaknesses, I have yet to see lists of strengths in a family taken seriously. Weaknesses, yes, by the dozen. And the section on 'milestones for children' should read as 'stumbling blocks' because it's illnesses, failures, awkwardness at potty-training, etc. Not milestones, not places where achievements were noted but places where difficulties were encountered. This is the sort of thing that comes from a model which sets ceilings on (a) people and (b) what can be done between helpers and the people. And that's being done in my line of work with 'multi-problem families' very, very clearly. We are now reaping the result of twenty years of regarding families as just that, and of having designed work which fits in with our perception.

PROCTOR: Is what you're talking about still Reality Therapy?

WILMOT: It's what I consider as being realistic growth – growth tempered with reality.

PROCTOR: How did you come to Reality Therapy?

WILMOT: Having come into social work when I was sixteen as a trainee mental welfare officer, the first six or eight years were spent just absorbing a model which other people did. In 1960 the Mental Health Act had just come. For a practising social work agency such as I was in, there was no theory behind what was done. The job was what was done – which was putting people into hospital or not, mostly putting them into hospital.

When I did my social work training some eight or nine years later, what I got was space to look around – an opening up of my mind to look in different directions. During that time the whole existential movement was what was drawing me like a magnet. I was totally fascinated by not just looking at the mechanics of what you do to people described as ill, but actually looking at it in another way. That was the first step for me – taking a lateral look at people, rather than saying they were either ill, more ill, or less ill at any moment in time. Here was someone saying, 'We'll introduce the idea of mad, not ill'. I think I took a conceptual step sideways in doing that, which was great for me.

I went to encounter groups and marathons and whatever, which were in fact (a) only available to quite a small and fairly articulate, educated section of the population and (b) dangled rather priceless carrots in front of people like openness, honesty, growth without in any way describing any steps in order to achieve them. It was good in some way to be open, honest, clear-communicating, etc., regardless of consequences (for sure), particularly in an encounter group. But what it never ever dealt with was those poor buggers like me who did lie – on occasion – were not open at times, although at other times I was, who nevertheless was quite as well-meaning in my search as these other people were. It seemed to me what it pushed me towards was a very clear realistic way of looking at helping people. The books of Laing, Estherson, et al, are very beautiful books, high on theory, tremendously low on practicability. They don't actually tell you what to do and how to do it. It pushed me in the direction of wanting to know what are the ingredients and mechanics of growth – let's assemble them all and put them together. How do you do it? You can't ask those sorts of questions in the humanistic field because answers aren't the thing, it is the looking that is so important. I liked that but it didn't help. In my work on myself and in my work with people, I wanted something to get my hands around. It could well have been something to do with my being steeped in such a lot of community mental health. It's very down-to-earth social work.

Certainly, the thing that's given me the biggest push in the direction I'm now in is working with what are called 'multi-problem' families. We are trying to marry the idea of growth and self-esteem with people who have reached the bottom of the bin. We have discovered that the two are not mutually exclusive, and that growth is not a middle-class concept for a middle-class group. Certainly my own background from a working class culture has been a major force, as it has for Tony Manocchio, Mike Pegg, Bill Pettit, Pat Pegg and other theorists/practitioners who are pushing at the edges of knowledge of therapy.

PROCTOR: How did the work of Glasser and Satir influence you?

WILMOT: The put down the a,b,c, and the 1,2,3 of interacting with people in the real world. A book which had a great effect on me was a book called *Change* by three people in America at the Brief Psychotherapy Centre. It gave the ingredients of helping produce change in people who want to change something. It helped me think in terms of what is called *the '1, 2, 3' model* – '*what, how* and *when*' and sticking to it with people.

PROCTOR: What resources do you see yourself bringing to the counselling interaction?

WILMOT: One of them has to be objectivity for me. It's one which I was brought up with in social work training and then went so far away from it as I could, and now I'm coming back to it. I am not involved in what the client or family are experiencing. For me, I look at becoming involved in terms of getting taken up in other people's patterns which can be very seductive. I am sufficiently separate from the experience of the client or family to be able to look at it differently.

The other resource I bring is being a model, unashamedly so. If I talk about honesty, then it's important that I am honest. If I talk about being open, that I am open. Given those things, it doesn't matter that I don't do them all very well. What is important is how I handle my mistakes – that's where being a bit of a model comes in. If I can say 'Christ, I made a mess of that', it can be worth several hours of attempting to find out with someone what's happening, whilst not acknowledging anything I might be thinking or experiencing.

The other thing I bring into a helping relationship is being an ideas merchant for the family. I help design something that functions better, helps them more, relieves the pain, makes them happier. It's perfectly legitimate for me to teach what I've learned from other families and from my own experience.

Most of all, I bring being creative – to actually use my *brain* to think of alternatives for the family to design and try, much more than to use my *feelings* in any particular way. That's not to say I'm not sensitive or that I don't want a good relationship because I get a tremendous amount out of it. But social work spends far too long talking about 'building a good relationship' with no clear purpose in mind. A good relationship is something a therapist earns out of really creative work with a client. The relationship is one outcome of the work and must be terminated – and celebrated – if the therapy is to have been real.

PROCTOR: What do you see as being the responsibilities of the client and the counsellor in the counselling or therapy situation?

WILMOT: I am responsible for the quality of my intervention; I must do it fully, creatively, use myself to the best of my ability. I am responsible right up the very skin of the clients. Right to where I butt up against them but that's where it stops. I do them a disservice and myself a disservice if I take any more responsibility for the session than that. The responsibility the client has is for himself or the family for itself. I'm very fond of saying, 'Well, what are you going to do? It's your family. I'll help. What can we decide about what you are going to do?' And I maintain that, particularly with the families I've worked with who have been successfully de-skilled, maybe with fifteen or twenty years of social work. Now, the joint area, the mutual area, is what we're actually going to work on. And I will sit down for the whole first session finding out. I'll take what the family says and not think that they mean something else and try and guide them towards it. I'll take what they say as being real for them, and try and achieve it. I have learned from other families where they tend to get in a mess and I am quite prepared to give that to a family. 'Mothers quite often never look after themselves. Do you look after yourself, Mrs Smith?' I'll often give a suggestion, straightforward advice – I'm not afraid of giving advice. If it's advice, I always start it with, 'if I were you'. Once you're sure that you have constructed some sort of contract on things that they want, if that's the focus of your work, then it's ok to give advice. Sometimes I use it totally mischievously just to upset a family pattern. In one of Manocchi's books he turns to the anorexic girl next to him and says, 'Tell your mother she doesn't love you enough and that's why you're so thin' – a therapeutic instruction designed to 'rock the boat'. That's just the sort of thing I would use to disrupt a very tight, harmful, family system. Strategy is absolutely critical.

PROCTOR: You talk about teaching and social work and therapy and counselling. What are the differences between these roles and tasks and the therapist's task that you perform with a family?

WILMOT: In a way, the therapeutic relationship can be one of the most honest and delightful of relationships. For instance, I have a friend with whom I have an agreement that we don't talk about our work because we tend to disagree. I am prepared to forego saying a lot of things, challenging things, to him about the way he works in order to have our friendship. In the therapeutic relationship, it wouldn't work so well to do that – it's more upon me to be all the things that I treasure most and I'm more likely to be them in that situation with a family than perhaps any other situation.

PROCTOR: Do you have ways of trying to ensure that your clients and you have similar assumptions and objectives about the nature of the task and the interaction?

WILMOT: Yes, absolutely, because we do it all to begin with. I never start work with a family without finding out from every person what they want – what they like in the family – what they'd like to see different – if they had a magic wand and could wave it in their family, what would they change – what would make them happier – what would they like to see less of – what would they like to see more of – until I get the biggest, clearest picture of something that each family member would like for themselves to make the quality better. I put it all down on a very large sheet of paper with a very large coloured felt-tip pen and it's like a crude contract. It's like saying the problems often take care of themselves when the family begins to get what it wants for individuals and for each other. I know that works and so instead of working on the problems I start working on what the family can get for itself. It's a fairly structured first interview, but it's not rigid. I set out to have fun and look after myself.

PROCTOR: Do you actually say 'I set out to enjoy this and to take care of myself?'

WILMOT: Absolutely. It's a marvellous model for a family, and what I want in order to work well. I want each person to come out of that first interview thinking that it's worth their while to carry on. Therefore the loose contract of work has got to contain something for everyone in it. If there are conflicting goals, it stands to reason to me that one of them is going to be less satisfied than the other. It's the way that I go about it that's going to be crucial. If I can say to one person 'How much of that do you want for yourself in order to let him have something of what he wants? Let's try and design a way you can get what you want and you can get where you want'. And I'll use games, exercises or anything in order to get them to try it out, working with each other – 'let's try – you come here and you come here and let's sit down together and let's try that'. So there's a lot of the healing in the designing going on.

PROCTOR: Do you focus on any particular processes or engage some faculties more than others?

WILMOT: Certainly the family processes are fairly important for me in my work. But also with individuals, taking care of themselves in terms of working on their self-esteem, breaking self-esteem down first, 'what do you do well, how could you do more of it,' are all important processes. With families and students, I tend to work on self-esteem just like, if you went to a doctor for a broken leg, he'd give you a vitamin shot. I tend to concentrate on actually *doing* something with the family to achieve change, to promote change rather than on exploring in words their communication patterns or whatever. I like designing strategies to try instead of the one that's hurting. And then for them to practice it and see if they feel better. For instance, one family had £800 rent arrears and the social worker tried all sorts of finger-wagging social work questions – and got absolutely nowhere. So the questions we asked were, 'Whose job is it to pay the rent? Do you like it or don't you like it? If you don't like it, if someone else did it, what could you do instead as your contribution in this family? You could do some more cooking. Okay, if you're not going to do it, who else could have a go at paying the rent? Who'd like to try. Do you know where it is? Do you know how to get there? Could you make a day of it and go out?' So it was agreed that the wife made a day of it, took the baby in the pram, paid the rent, knew what bus to go on, went on to see her sister. She tried it for four weeks. The family paid their rent for the next six months non-stop, never considered it a problem.

PROCTOR: It sounds as if you do work on communicating but by helping them to communicate more clearly?

WILMOT: Yes, I suppose it's misleading for me to say I don't work on communication. The one thing I'm very careful about: I don't want to build up a great body of knowledge about the family unless it's immediately available to us all. In many therapies, work with an individual family results in the most immense amount of detailed knowledge about the client but it doesn't help change occur.

PROCTOR: How about feelings? Do you do any work on helping them explore how they are feeling so they can put that into a goal? Or are feelings actually not talked about or exploded at all?

WILMOT: Well, I usually say I never consider feelings but that's theoretical. In practice, it's different because I'm just as interested in feelings – in how people are feeling – as any therapist. But I know also that the whole idea of experts guessing what people feel and of saying 'I feel that . . .' instead of 'I think that . . .' and getting the two totally confused is a very unproductive area of work. I want to know what people in the main *think* about each other in the family and *think* about the work that is going on and I want to be absolutely sure that they separate out their thoughts from their feelings, because they're going to be lucky to find a social worker that can.

PROCTOR: What kind of climate do you seek to develop when you're setting up a therapeutic contract, and why?

WILMOT: One of the ingredients in setting up a contract is whilst taking everything that the family say seriously and sincerely, nevertheless, to keep the whole thing quite light and let it be absolutely clear between us that it is not a process that is going to go on forever. I want a climate that is highly productive, one that is not going to create dependency, will not get us stuck in impossible or deep areas that neither the family nor I can work on very productively. I've got to have all the ingredients that make for high productivity, because as soon as I assume that I've got plenty of time to work with this family – I'm already going off my model; and into another model that says 'well they're going to be like this forever so it doesn't really matter if we get going today or if I leave early or cancel next week's visit'.

PROCTOR: Does 'transference' have any meaning for you?

WILMOT: I know it's there. It would be very hard at this state of the field in therapy to ignore transference. But it is not a problem for me. I don't choose to look at it or include it in my model. It's not in my arena of work and I'll be using what's happening in a different way. Transference is, for me, part of a therapy which contains its own pathology. You've got to work on transference, counter-transference, the relationship, terminating the relationship, building the relationship: these are not the client's problems, these are problems you're bringing into it because of your model of help.

PROCTOR: Are you aware that you positively condition certain of their responses and ignore others?

WILMOT: Yes, I do it absolutely overtly. Part of it is helping a family to discover positive patterns and getting rid of negative patterns, painful patterns, unproductive patterns, dysfunctioning patterns. Helping a family to look at how messy and awful that is and getting rid of it and trying something new, practising it, role-playing it, almost a new conditioning process. I never actually look at it as conditioning, but as looking for and building on positive patterns for an individual or family.

PROCTOR: And they can contend with you if they don't agree with you?

WILMOT: Absolutely. They can fight me on a fair basis. It's a flat piece of ground – we're just a few yards apart. I'm not miles above them. That produces a very healthy thing, I think. To fight, to argue with your therapist, because I just could be wrong. I want the family to be able to say 'Stupid' or 'That was a wrong question'.

PROCTOR: Are there any other processes that I haven't mentioned but that you either very consciously, or somewhere slightly below the surface, notice as happening and expect and do pick out? Either within a family or between you and the family?

WILMOT: One of the things that occurs in the best work I've done with families is that I slowly work myself out of a job and away from the family. If therapy only works because I am there, it's a duff therapy. What comes out of it has got to be sufficient change, sufficient raising of the level of self-esteem, sufficient discovery and building on positive patterns so that the family life is still the family life. We came together for a period of time to change and to do good work together. Then I went and we celebrated saying goodbye and how nice it was. I've got tremendous friendships with lots of different families I've worked with who pop in from time to time, but I make sure that they are friendships. I like the idea of going to see your family therapist every now and again as you might go to your doctor for a checkup. After say six months, to have a session again and say 'Well, how's it going?'. Coming together, working hard, celebrating and going apart gives a good experience and with many of our families they've never been left well by anyone. Leaving's always been bad whether it's by the parents, or by their social workers. We know that you must leave the family whether you're a student here for nine months or a social worker here for two years, it doesn't matter. It's the quality of the leaving that I think is absolutely critical.

PROCTOR: Who decides when you leave? How does that get decided?

WILMOT: Hopefully it occurs between the therapist and the family. Coming to the end of the period of work, of the contract, you should have worked on things in the contract not so the family is cured – we don't cure what happens in families – but so that they find new processes to make that particular area function so the family can live with it happily – the best possible balance. When you come to the end of all that, it's like saying 'Well, there's the end of our work together. Let's assess it. How did you think I was as a therapist? How do you think you've worked? That's where you were at the beginning, how do you think it's gone?'

PROCTOR: So you've actually gone down ticking things off. You've had three sessions on how mum wanted her peace and you've had two sessions on what dad's going to do to enjoy himself a bit more and you've had some sessions for the kids . . .?

WILMOT: That's how I would do it. And I come to a stop and say 'If we work from now on, we construct a new contract.' You see it's very easy to say 'Well I think we ought to meet a few more times . . .' and then you can very easily slip into 'Well a few more times . . .' and if you don't know what you're doing at that moment, you start slipping into supportive casework. On the contract there's all those things and also I take something like arguments in the family and I use the same model 'What happens about arguments in your family? Who argues?' – you can think of the questions that arise. . . . 'Who argues most? What do you do when you argue? Do you hit? Who hits whom? Who gets the most bruises? How would you like to see arguments finish? Is there a better way for you? What don't you like about arguments?' till you really have explored what happens. 'How would you like to see it differently? And what could we try to do? When shall we do it?' So with each ingredient in the contract. The family get a big picture of it, how they'd like to see it differently and when we're going to try something different. I'd work on arguments until the family say that things are better enough for them to live with. If you set out to stop the arguments in the family, well . . . tell me if anyone can do it. It's only got to be so the family can live with itself and resolve it – so they're left feeling that they can deal with their usual behaviour. The reactive school of family therapy will set up the session and sit and watch the family and feed back to them what they see is happening. The family can produce their act in front of anyone day in and day out forever – what I'm interested in is what they want differently to that. I only want to watch that if it's to do with finding out or putting together something different for them. I might say 'Show me your last argument. Don't talk to me about it. Show me your last argument. What were you doing? You were doing this and you were doing that and then how did it happen? Show me – shut up'. But I wouldn't actually sit in on a family session and listen for half an hour or an hour – I'd be screaming at the end of it! It wouldn't be useful for me, in the way that I work and I don't like it anyway. what they see is happening. The family can produce their act in front of anyone day in and day out forever – what I'm interested in is what they want differently to that. I only want to watch that if it's to do with finding out or putting together something different for them. I might say 'Show me your last argument. Don't talk to me about it. Show me your last argument. What were you doing? You were doing this and you were doing that and then how did it happen? Show me – shut up'. But I wouldn't actually sit in on a family session and listen for half an hour or an hour – I'd be screaming at the end of it! It wouldn't be useful for me, in the way that I work and I don't like it anyway.

PROCTOR: Anything else you can think of in processes?

WILMOT: The major thing is the finding, discovering or re-discovering and building on positive patterns in that family. Not in 'family life' or 'family therapy' but literally in *that* family. I think that's the whole key and what everything else is about, raising the self-esteem or getting them to do joint family tasks. It's got to be geared towards that family. The major process of the work is towards that.

PROCTOR: Are there any other skills you haven't mentioned?

WILMOT: One of them is de Bono's idea of lateral thinking. Being able to develop your imagination to think of ideas, strategies or whatever. It's a totally different process to linear thinking, one which can really get you off the ground in working with a family. For instance if a student says to me, 'I went to see a family and they weren't in. I'll go next week.' That's the start of a linear model. I'll say then, 'You want to see the family. How could you see the family?' 'Well, they weren't in.' 'Yes, I know – how could you see them? Could you see the father at work and get him to come? Could you go later at night or first thing in the morning? If you want to do it, how can you do it?' That skill of stretching yourself broadly rather than going along a thin line is one of the most useful things I've learned. You can do the same thing in a family. 'Well why don't you all go away and think and here's a list. Do that – think about it. Then come together'. The family begins to learn that 'Christ, when we think about it, we can come up with the answers'.

I also use humour, the use of paradox can break patterns where all other things, even serious attentive listening or whatever, won't get you anywhere.

PROCTOR: Does the client population with which you work affect and influence the ideas and the model that you use?

WILMOT: Yes, it does. Anything that I do very much comes out as whether it works or not with multi-problem families and also comes out of getting feed-back from them – what helped and what didn't help and what was absolutely useless so the model of work is added to or subtracted from feed-back from families, students and colleagues in the unit. I would occasionally drop something which proves to be not effective.

Like for instance I used first to insist on every member of the family being there in a family referral meeting since I am a family therapist, therefore every member of the family must be there. I've learned that in fact I don't need to do that. I can in fact start with a few family members and make one of the first task's 'right, how are we going to get the rest of your family here? what's the best way?' So I've dropped the idea of insisting and cancelling a family meeting unless everyone is there, unless it is particularly appropriate that everyone must be there, and changed it to something that would work better because sometimes all the people are just too scared to come and you won't get them there, so you either say 'well, they won't suit the model' or you start playing with the model so that it works. Certainly in the unit, feedback from staff and from students on courses I run shows that that is the bit of the course they like. That really helps when they think what they are going to use when they get back to work on Monday.

PROCTOR: Do you have any dilemmas in your therapy or counselling work?

WILMOT: Well, it's hard. I can let things be a dilemma or a problem if I choose that they should be. I often say if I'm working with a family – a family has a difficulty and a social worker compounds it into a problem and a succession of social workers can make it into a multi-problem status. Now if I want to regard something as a problem, if I considered the transference as a dilemma, then I would have to take account of it. Now the easy way out for me which I often choose is not to make a problem and I in fact do the same thing with dilemmas. I can say. 'No, I don't have any dilemmas in my work.' In my actual practice, if I start thinking about wider implications – like I don't do that much making sure that families get all the benefits that are due to them – then I could regard that as a dilemma because I don't do it and many people have said to me 'but what do you do about poor families in society?'

PROCTOR: And finally, do you think that in the course of this interview you have given a fairly comprehensive account of your ideas and practice or, has giving it in the form of answers to this questionnaire slanted it in some way?

WILMOT: Yes. It hasn't pushed it in any other direction; in a way I represent Reality Therapy but, at the same time, it has not pushed my answers or responses in any way solely into what the Reality therapist would say. It's pushed it into the direction of making me look very clearly at what I'm saying and what I'm doing.

Eugene Heimler

8   Social Functioning

Eugene Heimler developed his self-help method of
Social Functioning in an attempt to find an alternative
method of casework that helped individuals who were not
often articulate to assess and make the changes they
wished for in their own lives. Central to the method is
the Scale of Social Functioning which allows individuals
to see and make priorities about the areas of their life they
wish to develop or change. It also allows the counsellor
to determine the amount of support and help likely to be
needed in the case of any individual. The method is
taught in this country by trainers, who are members of
the Association of Lecturers of Social Functioning.

Eugene Heimler developed the Scale of Social Functioning
when he was working as a psychatric social worker in
Middlesex in the 1950's. He has been consultant to the
World Health Organization and to the United States
government (1964–5) and adviser to the Supplementary
Benefits Commission until 1965. He was director of the
Hounslow Project from 1965–71. He is presently Chairman
of the Association of Lecturers of Social Functioning,
in England, and Professor of Social Functioning at the
University of Calgary, Alberta. He frequently lectures in
Britain, Europe, and the United States.

SUGGESTED READING:
Heimler, Eugene. *Survival in Society*, London:
    Weidenfeld & Nicolson, 1975.

PROCTOR: Since you are the only person I'll be interviewing
that has devised your own system of counselling, could you
start off by exploring for me how, when, where and why your
approach to counselling originated?

HEIMLER: It seems to me that things usually start before the
action takes place. My actual social work practice began in
1953, but the scene was set, I think, long before that – through

my own particular experiences of life under the National Socialist occupation of Hungary during the war, and subsequent deportation to various German concentration camps, including Auschwitz and Buchenwald. The motive for my own particular work was an enormous question, long before 1953, when I was qualified, about how can human beings do things like that to other human beings? The second one was not such a theoretical question, it was a very personal one: 'How can I endure all this? What happens to me as a man whose total action of freedom is taken away, and the only thing left is thought and feeling'? And even to share these thoughts and feelings with others was very dangerous sometimes – you had to be very selective.

It all started by a particular kind of conditioning, which not only I, but hundreds of thousands of people, millions of people, have gone through – Jews and nationalities of Nazi-occupied Europe. I wanted to answer this question: what will produce human freedom for myself, and for others? What is freedom? The loss of it I knew; but the other side I had never known. The only way I had some idea of it was when I was in a particular camp in Germany, and I saw the Allied planes high in the sky and then I said 'Well, they go back to freedom,' and unlike you and unlike, I hope, most of the people who will read this interview, I had not known what freedom was, except that I wanted to be free. So if you are asking for foundations, for motives, for why's, then I can give you the confused answers of a confused man who at that time was trying to find answers for himself, and consequently, after the war, for others. And the issue I formulated around this experience was how can a human being experience his freedom? How can a human being express his own potential that I was never able to express as a Jew or for that matter as a Hungarian? How is it possible that one can use what one has got and employ it out there in the world? How can one be free and creative?

PROCTOR: And how was it that you came up with your kind of answers or approach?

HEIMLER: I'd like to answer this in 'black and white', but I can't. I only know that unconsciously I was moving towards a particular direction. Britain had a great deal to do with it, as I experienced the country before I took my training. What struck me, and this is very, very difficult to convey to you – not because you don't understand, but because you were born in a country where you have never known, thank God, what it means to be pushed down and persecuted – to be able to experience step by step what political freedom was. I remember when I went to West Hampstead when I arrived in England in 1947, I was terrified of the police to whom I had to go every year, with a little Aliens card. I remember saying to myself as I walked down West Hampstead, 'It's going: this fear of authority is going.' Authority of a particular brand and kind is at the heart of the matter. England started it in a sense, because it convinced me that authority does not necessarily have to be dangerous; it doesn't have to be persecutory. So how can one help people in this country, as a social worker, as a psychiatric social worker, to find their own authority? This was the issue.

PROCTOR: What other insights come into relief about human nature? You said at the beginning something about wondering how human beings could do these things? What is the answer?

HEIMLER: How can human beings do that, I swear I don't know. But one observation of human nature is this: take away the civilisation from man, and he will regress, personally, according to any theory of regression, and, collectively, into an animal state. But not all men.

PROCTOR: Man is an anti-social animal by nature?

HEIMLER: I don't know whether he's anti-social by nature, but if he is cornered like animals are sometimes cornered, then he can be violent and angry and frightened. I said also: 'But not all'. Now again I would like to know what determines the other helpful, the non-animal, part in some that I have observed in the camps. I still don't know. I have some observations, some hypotheses. For example: people who have real faith. I am not just talking about religious faiths. The Zionists, for example, somehow did not regress to the extreme extent, because they had an aim. I don't like Communists, in no form, no shape, they remind me of the Nazis, but they also had this faith. I saw Catholic priests, Jewish rabbis, who had that faith. Not all, but many of these people are shining examples of what human beings can be. You have then a situation in which man regresses into an animal form, but some men remain outside that form, when they are motivated by something more than personal survival. I think that if you can 'plug in' somehow into the collectivity of an idea, or a collectivity of a group, really and truly, you seem to survive more than if you are alone. And an essential loneliness or even to put it better, aloneness, is what made those other people regress.

PROCTOR: What is human energy all about?

HEIMLER: I'm glad you ask this, because it is basic to the kind of formulations that I began with. Without trying to be too scientific, I want to divide human energy into two components which interact. One comes from the hormonal system and the whole bio-chemistry of the human body, and the other one is a psychic energy. The two have an interaction much closer than we had hitherto realised. A concern I have today is to see how they interact. Which is the chicken and which is the egg? When you are in a state of anxiety – that kind of horror and terror we all feel in the concentration camps – you feel the whole inside reacting, the heart, contractions, all that kind of thing going on. I observe this very often in people who are going through crises, anything which causes them pain. I notice that pain comes when there is beginning to be a ping-pong game between the body and the mind, and I think that you can't break in at just one end. You have to break it – you have to help undo the ties, the knots – at both ends.

PROCTOR: To come down to a nearer focus of how you see Man, you see him as partly reaching both his heights and his depths in groups, in collective ideas, and you see him having difficulty in co-ordinating his energy?

HEIMLER: In externalising his energy. If there is any problem, it is the problem of locked-up energy. Locked-up psychic and locked-up physical energy. I see that happening, unless this energy is *recognised*, not by *me* but by the *client* and unless this energy is *understood*. Recognition is not understanding. Unless this energy is then *used* by the client, in the world which gives him the opportunities to use them; to use hooks on which he can 'hang up' this internal energy, so the internal becomes externalised. If this flow of energy is not possible, his energy works against the individual rather than for him. So then this whole system, or approach, that I have developed across the years deals with the economic distribution of energy.

PROCTOR: It has to be in flow or it backfires?

HEIMLER: In a sense. It flows among a number of areas of

human endeavour. Where have we got the opportunities to experience this energy? And how do we experience the energy when it is blocked? We experience the energy as pain or frustration. If it is released, how is it then experienced? The experience is satisfaction. And if you look at this flow, it flows in the areas where the energies have the possibility to be externalised. Through work, through a concern in financial areas, within the human context – friendship, social relationships – in the family, whether it is primary or acquired, in the sexual and personal areas of human life. Unless there is some sort of balanced distribution of this flow, in these areas, you have a measurable, and I say a measurable, blockage. This can be unblocked, undone.

PROCTOR: And so it's helping people to find channels of energy, to take care of their energy efficiently and satisfactorily?

HEIMLER: That's right. To recognise that pain is potential, that the energy is there as a massive thing which can work for you, not against you. Therefore, to call a man in a state of 'anxiety' or 'depression' is irrelevant for me. What has relevance for me is that the energy is used or blocked, and my task is to stand by, be a catalyst, in the process of expressing it.

PROCTOR: What do you see as the resources that you bring to the counselling task?

HEIMLER: I think that the counsellor or the social worker or the therapist – I group them into one, because it's time now to say: 'this is what we are, we are what we are and to hell with apologies'. Who is guaranteeing that a particular person with another qualification is doing it better? I think that the person who is doing 'counselling' should be a person who respects his own satisfactions, frustrations, his own human conflict – not in the abstract, not saying 'Oh I respect human life'. Because human life, according to what I said to you earlier, is really something which *wants* to grow and which *wants* to express itself. Now you, as a counsellor, can stand by and say: 'I'll bring this flower out of the earth, never mind how long it takes it to grow, I'll pull it higher', and in the end you pull it and the roots are coming out as well. Or you can stand by and say: 'My job is to stand by and water this flower', to give your own personality; I don't want to withhold the word 'love'. Love means that you have forgiven yourself in a sense, forgiven that you aren't perfect to start with. Then,

I think, you are able to create an atmosphere in which it can grow, despite you. You have got to work, all the time, not to interfere with this growth, and my God, how difficult it is to do it.

PROCTOR: You talk about having personal qualities, and acceptance as being *the* most important resource a counsellor brings to the task. What about training?

HEIMLER: It starts with personal qualities such as a true recognition of yourself being as much, in reality or potentially, a suffering human being as another one is. So this wall between normal and abnormal is done away with because there is not such a thing.

Out of suffering comes a solution. Suffering has a purpose; it is not in vain, I am sure of that. The question is not 'Why does this happen to me, suffering?', it is 'What am I going to do with it'? This is really the counsellor's second task. In order to be able to deal with that, he has got to have training: proper, appropriate, good training. And this training is not only a training of what you know of things, or what Freud, Jung, Adler, Maslow, Rogers, Laing, or Sergeant have done. The counsellor has also got to have a training about recognition of his own particular life, the changing pattern of his mechanism, of his own particular satisfaction, and frustrations. And this is the most important part of his training. This should be coupled with the 'hooking on' of this personal thing to what others have said. What happens at present is that students are given lots of books to read which have no relationship to where *they* are. I would like, when *they* are reaching a particular point, to give them a particular book to read in order to understand what *they* feel. People are not alone, other people have been thinking about the same thing. It is the way that children learn. They don't stand up because anyone tells them to stand up. And they learn because they want to learn, and I regret to tell you, that as a University teacher I see that we are overburdening students with a particular kind of approach so that learning is the last thing they want to do. My function as a therapist, counsellor, trainer, whatever you like, is *to help you*, one way or another, to *have access to your own experience*. Let us presume that you tell me something. If I then use either a tape recorder or myself, or both, and play this thing back to you, then you are listening to what you have heard either from me or from that machine, or both, with a different ear – with what I call the 'third ear'. Then you are going to be able to be free from the pressures of the present and relate to your experience of the past.

PROCTOR: What do you see as being the responsibilities of the client and the counsellor in the interaction?

HEIMLER: The client's responsibility is very clear because the ultimate responsibility for his life, and by that I mean for his recovery as well as for his so-called 'illness', is with him. Therefore I can only take responsibility for creating the structure; creating the atmosphere; offering myself as another human being. But the responsibility lies entirely with the client. The notion that any psychotherapist can himself help with the process of another person growing is an illusion. So I feel that the contract is known and implicit, although not spelt out.

PROCTOR: And the implicit contract is that the client is responsible for himself?

HEIMLER: Yes, and that he learns almost immediately in the first interview, or if not in the first, certainly in the second. He will find the ultimate responsibility is his and cannot be anybody else's.

PROCTOR: How do you ensure that he carries the same contract as you do? How does it become explicit or understood in the first or second interview?

HEIMLER: Through the process of interviewing. You see, in the beginning of the first interview, when a client comes and talks about himself, I listen for a while and then at a certain point of time, I will say to the client, when he comes to the end of a flow: 'All right now, correct me if I am wrong, but did I understand you saying so and so?' And I play back. It is true it is selective, but a summary has been given back to the client. And to this he has got two or three reactions. The first reaction at the very beginning is usually 'Yes, this is what I said'. He still accepts my authority whether I like it or not. At the second or third time he is more and more involved with what he's been recording and talking about, and he is going to say 'Yes, I *said* that, but now that I think of it, I really meant so and so ...' or he will say 'No, I didn't quite say what you said'. Then you say, 'Well, what did you say?'. So very soon there are two adults who are exchanging theories; this is where the contract becomes implicit. Without my having to tell him 'Now look, this is what you do, this is what I do'. I don't believe in that. Things have to become natural. And by the very way that I treat him, and the way that he learns things about himself, this contract begins to take shape. I think I've left out from this process one thing, and it's an important one. Hearing, insight, understanding is not enough. When he begins to formulate his plan, then I need to put him into that plan. What I mean by this is: perhaps somebody says, 'I'm going to go for an interview, and I'm scared about it'. Well, than I wouldn't ask 'What are you scared of?' and then interpret him the unconscious reasons why he's scared of that particular thing. The issue which I would raise with him is 'Imagine yourself in that situation and now please tell me what is happening in that situation as you perceive it'. So he will give me a description of the situation that he will experience in advance. Imagination is what artists use. And since the client experiences it as an artistic thing, he hears himself back either from the tape or from me or from both. Then he'll be able to make the appropriate adjustment to manage in that particular situation. So he is well prepared for the task ahead. When somebody says to me 'I've had a quarrel with my wife', I say 'When was this?' and they say 'Last night'. 'ok. Now can you put yourself back to last night? What time is it? What's happening?' – 'I'm sitting in the big red chair and Kate, my wife, is screaming with the kids' – 'ok, carry on' – so the client re-experiences something. Another thing I have learnt since my concentration camp days, through hard and really terrifying struggles of my own life, is that no change comes about without experiencing it. In other words, however much interpretation you get from someone, unless you experience the original situation which you are talking about, and I mean *experience* – it if it was terrifying, you feel the terror in your stomach – no change will ever take place. In order to free yourself from the bondage, you have got to experience the bondage once more, to say goodbye to it. And the goodbye is not by experiencing it alone. The experience has got to be transformed and translated into the appropriate action in life. Then it's out there and it's manageable.

PROCTOR: So it sounds as if at least some of the time you focus on re-experiencing or the fore-experiencing of an emotionally charged situation that has been or may be unsatisfactory?

HEIMLER: It may not be emotionally charged because not all situations when they are experienced are felt to be emotionally charged. He may just tell me casually 'Something happened last night', and I say 'Tell me about it', and it turns out that an experience which seems to be not emotionally charged was a very relevant experience. So it is the re-experiencing of something, feeling of something, and the appropriate plan of what it means and what he can do with it in reality. What I call 'Human Social Functioning' is a particular kind of approach where I said, now twice, recognition and then planning. Planning and then we can discuss the plan and by discussion he re-lives it or fore-lives it and tests it out in reality. In his own reality first.

PROCTOR: And in any one particular interview, with one particular client, how do you arrive at where you focus? Do you have ways of arriving at the important point?

HEIMLER: In the end I invariably ask my client 'What is the most important thing you have said here today?' So in actual fact, I try to focus on that which is of relevance to him. There is another way in which this relevance comes out. This is not much practised as far as I know by social workers, or therapists, and I think it is very important. After some time, when you as a client talk about something, I would say to you 'Well, what does it really mean? What does it all really add up to? Will you jot it down on paper? It doesn't have to be a long piece, just a few words so that you know at the end what we've covered' – these are the areas of focus. So it is not *I* who define what the focus should be, although this may also happen in some cases. But it is *he* who decides.

PROCTOR: When do you use your Scale of Social Functioning and what is it designed for?

HEIMLER: This is a tool which looks at the human situation in various areas, from the point of work, money, friendship, family, sexuality, faith, hope, meaning, things like that. It is something which we can score, and so far it looks like a simple psychometric test. But there is an enormous difference in it. I think it may very well be the only instrument used today, which is handed back to the client. All the other instruments are scored by the experts working it out and making their diagnoses and the patient never knows what it is about.

In this instance it is handed back. They are very simple questions. Experts of social work or professional psychotherapy look at the questions and say 'Oh, this is so simple'. But the questions are devised for the client, who knows what they are all about. When he says 'Perhaps I like my work' and I say 'What does that mean?', he has got a magnet with which he can focus and say what it means to *him*. He can spell out his own experiences. Now when this happens through fifty-five questions, he has pretty well mapped out his whole situation for himself. He feels an integrating process taking place, rather than bitty pieces here and there.

PROCTOR: So it is a formal way of doing that externalisation you're talking about? Of having it on paper?

HEIMLER: Of having on paper and writing down the client's comments so that at the end of it, out of this list, he can take out what is most relevant. Also, we can use this for diagnostic purposes. We have an accurate method of scoring that can be discussed with the client. Up to a certain level of figures, the correspondence with a random sample means that this person really struggles terribly hard to remain in society. Above a certain point he needs help and above another point again he can function without help. Now what constitutes help? It's not just professional help, it's all kinds of help, it's support of some kind. This is the Scale of Social Functioning. And this had been greatly misunderstood and misrepresented, because it's very simple. What is being reported by clients time after time is that they are surprised at how quickly they can see a map of their lives, which would have taken a long, long time.

PROCTOR: You see your kind of skill and insight as being things that are for dissemination rather than for ownership or guardianship by a particular set of professional people?

HEIMLER: You have to have some professional training. A teacher can learn it, a clergyman can learn it and I think a number of them are using it. It isn't something which belongs to a particular selected group like the chosen people who have the ten commandments. People come to us for a number of reasons but they come because they are blocked, and they want to be unblocked. But you can use this particular approach in education. You can use it in a classroom. I would say that psychotherapy, in the sense that I understand it, and education are not far removed. Learning and therapy are just two lines which sometimes move into each other. So naturally I have been much more preoccupied with the therapeutic side because it happens to be the area in which I function. But lately, as I function in an educational field, I use this approach more and more in an educational setting.

PROCTOR: In the way you work, do you recognise that transference happens and if it does, what do you do about it?

HEIMLER: There's a lot of confusion about transference. First of all, what does it mean? It means the likes, dislikes, conscious and unconscious, that take place; transference in that sense exists between you and I – I happen to like you so it's a positive transference, you may not like me, and it may be a negative one! The point I'm trying to make is, transference exists in every human situation. Naturally it will exist between therapists and client. But it's another story whether I use that transference. I do not use the transference by allowing myself to be used as a screen – a symbol – and saying 'The way you act towards me is the way you acted to others'. This I would not do. The question is then, where does the transference go, what happens to it? And I suggest to you that if a person is given the opportunity and the structure to be truly occupied with those people, persons, and things out in life which produce pleasure and pain, he would not be that concerned about a therapist. So if he's continuously given a structure in which he talks about his wife, his mother, his boss, his girlfriend, likes, dislikes in the work situation, or hobby – if this is the focus, then I became a kind of friendly bystander. I have certain definite skills, but is not hooked on to me and if something is hooked on to me, I can very soon recognise it. If I recognise, for example, there is warmth, I say: 'Well tell me about the people you like in your life'. Doctor Michael Balint developed a very similar kind of approach, so I don't claim any originality for this.

PROCTOR: It sounds like a ricochet – as if you take the bounce and send it back in the direction you feel the energy ought to be.

HEIMLER: Yes. And then the energy lies there. So transference exists but it is not used, certainly not in an interpretive form.

PROCTOR: How about modelling? Do you think you act as a model for your client, and if you do, what is it you hope you are modelling?

HEIMLER: There may be some clients, not the majority, who might ask me: 'How did you arrive at this particular point in your life, what did you do?'. And I would answer their question. Modelling in the sense taking me as a model, no. I am sure it does not happen. They are going to find their own particular models outside me, the same as with transference. You see, I think they have got to model themselves to their own shape not mine. No, I think modelling is not part of this particular approach.

PROCTOR: You don't think they try your way of functioning out for size, like a child tries his parents' way of functioning?

HEIMLER: Yes, but how could they know anything about my own functioning when, intensively from the moment of go, the structures and the patterns are such that they are intensively involved with their own lives? In one case, a particular client got so involved with what he was doing that he said to me, when he was working and listening to the tape recorder, and writing down his thoughts, as they occurred to him – he looked up and looked at me and said: 'Why are you still here?'. And I thought that was possibly an exaggerated way of putting it but if I leave the room in the middle of the interview, as I have done once or twice, the process still goes on. And one of the advantages of this particular approach is, and this has been reported from around the world, that it is much easier for another therapist to take over, because of this transference situation, or rather, lack of it.

PROCTOR: And the process that will be going on when you leave the room is listening to his own tapes?

HEIMLER: Listening to the tape on which for fifteen or thirty minutes he spoke about something. As he listens, he finds something that catches his mind or feeling, stops the tape recorder and writes it down. So there is no chance for me to become that relevant in his life. My relevance is to provide the structure, framework, the observation in which he can function. And that brings me back to the very beginning, that I would feel, in my limited way, I can offer a man freedom to be his own guide.

PROCTOR: Are you aware that you do in fact sanction, or

approve or encourage some forms of interaction?

HEIMLER: No. As far as the interaction is concerned, between the client and myself, I don't think I would select preferences. Until the end when he is beginning to make steps. If he were to tell me in the end, as the result of his conclusions, that he is going to kill his wife or he is going to kill himself, then I would say 'Very well, you won't'. But outside these limits, I give him enough scope and freedom. The only stop I would put on is one another human being would do almost spontaneously – I've seen an SS guard killing people right, left and centre with a machine gun, but when one American prisoner fell into the river, this SS guard jumped into the river to save him. Now this, you see, would be my natural reaction, to save someone from killing himself or hurting someone else. But outside these extreme limits, I would not interfere with the processes.

PROCTOR: Presumably when you send them back to the tape you are actually encouraging them to operate at a kind of coordinated thought/feeling level?

HEIMLER: Yes.

PROCTOR: And those are the faculties you would encourage them to use on their own problems?

HEIMLER: Yes. Here I think I come to a difficulty. I think one of the most difficult problems is why this particular approach will work sixty to seventy per cent of the time but it will not work in something like thirty per cent or more of cases. In the question of conditioning I wouldn't point out to the person: 'Well, this is head stuff'. I would hope he would notice eventually what he is doing, and they usually do. There is a certain percentage of people who have just no reaction of that kind. And even after repeated attempts, they don't. This is a real problem that I have been unable to solve and it is unlikely that I ever will. I either have to return to other methods that I learned or refer to somebody else or whatever. This system will not work one hundred per cent, but when it works, it works well.

PROCTOR: Does your client population that you've worked with mostly influence the way you work?

HEIMLER: Yes. You see, originally I worked with unemployed people and the intelligence range varied. I found that people who are used to work with their hands needed to have some kind of precision, some kind of neatness to understand themselves. The language of the Viennese couch wasn't appropriate to those people in the 1950's in London. So very gradually, a particular kind of approach began in which there was a continuous recap of my understanding, and this recap did two things. One was that it confirmed that I was intensively involved with them and when I put it back to them, they were grateful that somebody at last listened. The second one was that people who have got severe problems have the fear that they are going mad. And the fact that I could sometimes formulate for them in a, hopefully, intelligent fashion what they were saying, meant to them that it was understandable, and hearing it back they did not seem that mad then. So this was the beginning of a psycho-feedback system which in some way is similar to the Rogerian one, only at the time I evolved it, or it evolved itself, I had never heard about Carl Rogers. Since then I have learned that there are similarities but there are differences too. So the client population did affect it very much because they had taught me to make their statement to me understandable before they should go further.

PROCTOR: Perhaps if you could spell out a bit the differences with Rogerian therapy, you'd give a clue to people who don't know about your system as to what it looks like from the outside.

HEIMLER: I'll illustrate it. In the beginning you would see two people engaged in a conversation which could be any kind of therapeutic interview you care to think of, except that I would hold myself back less in the partnership. I would show much more affect, particularly in the beginning, and concern about them – human concern – but that I suppose others do too. When the real work starts, at the beginning if possible, there is a verbatim repetition, not a repetition of content but a verbatim repetition, having trained myself (and this is part of the training) to use words the client has used. Because those words are symbolic to him and through those words he can open up communication channels. If you listen to the Rogerian interview as he describes it in his own work, then it is a repetition, re-worded sometimes, of what has taken place, of what the client has said. I might use *selective explanation*. Selective explanations means that you take out from a mass of information what the client feels, what he said in the interview, what he finds significant and connect it. So, you have said this and you have said that now, tell me what it means to you. The third and I think most important difference – a crucial difference – between Rogers and myself, is that I seek always the roads of externalising the energy, while Rogers remains, and I'm not criticising him for that, with feeding back information in order that the client should feel it, that it should be liberating. I do not think any form of human liberation from internal problems can come about until changes have taken place in the external world. In other words, not manipulating his environment, but getting him to *act* differently. The fourth one is that when it comes to action, the method changes somewhat. It isn't any more a repetition, but it is a testing out of various possibilities. So if he says, 'Well, I want to do this', he will test out, how does it feel? I may put another alternative, so that by combined effort we test out what would be the most appropriate actions to take. These are basic differences.

PROCTOR: So exploring avenues of action is the next step?

HEIMLER: Yes. Also in my method, I interplay with time. Now I have learnt from my own personal experience that time is very relative. I put you back to yesterday or the day the problem existed. Can you describe it. We talk about that, you really experience it, ok? Then I will ask you to give me the first memory that comes to your mind in connection with this problem, and ask how you solved it then. So unconsciously you get some feeling of that problem. Now I say to the client, 'All right, now you are five years older, how did you solve that problem?' So this interplay with time, where imagination plays a major part, is a creative process. Therefore at the beginning of the process you see something like the Rogerian system, but as it moves on, you see basic – not differences – but additions.

PROCTOR: In the first interview you talk, and they fill out the Scale?

HEIMLER: No. There I can't give a set rule. It depends very much on the situation. Sometimes they do, sometimes they don't. More often than not I don't give it to them then because the scale will only be accepted by the client when he discovers that he can stand on his own feet. Once this is discovered he will do the work as he likes it. He's free and he will accept the notion of the questions, because he knows I am not testing him for my sake, but for his. Another difference is that if you were to ask Rogers a direct question, 'What shall I do? What do you think?', Rogers would, as far as I understand it, put it back again to the client. I wouldn't. If he is asking me something, I do two things. First I answer it, whatever that moment I feel about it. Secondly, I will then go and explore with him what he feels. But if a human being is putting to you a question, then another human being has to answer that question. Because at the very moment you don't do that, you've lost all the free communication that exists between two human beings. And therefore, on this very basic issue, you can lose a client's confidence completely and he feels again in a regressed state, examined, or whatever. You ask me, 'Is your sexual life fine?' and I would either say to you 'Yes, no or perhaps' or whatever. But give a direct answer. And I would not say to him, 'Excuse me, but why do you want to know?'

PROCTOR: Is there a learning process that is, if not predictable, recognisable across the board for most people?

HEIMLER: Yes. I know two opposing factors that emerge and I can recognise more often than not at the very beginning if this approach is going to be successful. I still carry on if they are negative – in order to test myself out to see whether I am right or not. When the client comes in, a part of him wants you to solve the problem for him, so that part is regressed. Another part of him resents this and essentially this constitutes an uphill ride, even before you open your mouth, that conflict in the client. Now in order to break this pattern, I give him back the summary the first time and the second time and if the third time he says 'Yes, that's what I said' – if that is what he hears only, I would predict failure. I may be wrong, but I have carried on with people of this kind and I was not successful. In the beginning I will always accept that he will say, 'Yes, that's what I said ...'. Once the process of self-observation begins, then I am very comfortable and would predict that the possible outcome of the whole process – although I can't be one hundred per cent sure – will be ok. This process fits this individual.

Now prediction is another thing. I've got to agree with the client what we are aiming at. This is part of the implicit contract, but it doesn't come about by setting it down on paper in the first place. As we go on we explore what it is he would really like from this particular contact, relationship, therapy and when we have achieved that particular aim, I'll apply the scale again. There are certain parts on the scale which really show basic changes, for example, the perception of the past. In a particular mood you see the past in certain ways, in another mood, you see the past in another way. So the past is not something which is actually a rigid reality but depends on the perception of the moment. Now change can occur, and when it occurs, we can see the change there on the scale. So there are certain predictions possible.

PROCTOR: And the end comes when . . . ?

HEIMLER: When the task we have set is achieved. Now may I say this, and I say this with greater conviction this year than I said last year. If this system works, it's going to work very, contract, but it doesn't come about by setting it down on very fast. I would therefore say that I would consider Human Social Functioning a possible, fairly effective short-term method. But short-term is in no way defining a long-term result. This autumn and this winter I have followed up a number of people whom I have seen many years ago, and the effect is still there. It is not there because of insight but because of continued action.

PROCTOR: Is there a distinction, in the way that you work, between therapy and counselling?

HEIMLER: I can't see any. I have seen excellent counsellors and I have seen lousy therapists. These things have been created by a social system which is based on hierarchy and not on true understanding of knowledge. This is my own personal feeling. I am no less the good therapist, or worse for that matter, because I have or have not a medical qualification. Or, somebody can be better than I am who has. I don't consider, for example, that counsellors do inferior work, provided they know what they should *not* do. To learn what they should do – that's not the difficulty – but to know what not to do, that is the problem. And that, they have to learn. And that is the reason why thorough and good training is necessary, with personal supervision of a kind which the counsellor is willing to give himself over to. Then I think he will become aware of the dangers. This Social Functioning method is a help in supervision.

PROCTOR: What in society, within Britain today, helps people to find their energy flow and what are the things in the social system that make it difficult or give bad training?

HEIMLER: I'd like to start with that last one, because I feel very strongly about it. Our whole educational system is outdated in terms of philosophy. It is geared towards people working, even if that work is totally meaningless. For ten years of my life I have been working with unemployed people. I always felt that people should be prepared for life tasks. It was clearly seen with automation. Automation means people are out of jobs and the unskilled will be the first ones. But the system of education is still primarily based on work, and this protestant ethic that you have got to work still lingers on. Something is very wrong with you if you don't work. We have got to recognise and realise that a large percentage of the population increasingly will not work. Therefore the educational system has to find alternatives to work and this is life tasks.

PROCTOR: And are there any good things in our society that can help people?

HEIMLER: Yes, potentially the opportunities are here. Society can change and is not rigid. The voice of the underdog at last is being heard.

John Heron

9 Co-counselling

John Heron founded the Human Potential Research Project at the University of Surrey in 1970, and is currently the Honorary Project Director. He is Assistant Director of the British Postgraduate Medical Federation in the University of London and is Educational Consultant to the Federation; in 1974 he co-founded Co-counselling International. He conducts courses and workshops on Co-counselling and on varied aspects of personal development, professional development, and educational development throughout Europe.

Co-counselling was developed by Harvey Jackins in Seattle, USA, in the 1950's and 1960's. Under his auspices, it spread throughout the USA and to Europe in the late 1960's and early 1970's, and networks of Co-counsellors were organised under the title Re-evaluation Counselling Communities. Several Co-counsellors found that this organisation became too theoretically rigid and internally authoritarian and founded Co-counselling International as an alternative network that federates entirely independent communities of Co-counsellors in several countries. Co-counselling as a practice primarily occurs in people's own homes on the basis of one-to-one informal arrangements.

SUGGESTED READING:

Heron, John. *Reciprocal Counselling Manual*, University of Surrey, May 1974.

Heron, John. *Catharsis in Human Development*, University of London, August 1977.

Jackins, Harvey. *The Human Side of Human Beings*, Seattle: Rational Island Publishers, 1965.

PROCTOR: Looking through a Co-counselling pair of spectacles, what comes into relief about the nature of human beings, and the relationship between individuals and the groups, social systems and ecological systems of which they are part?

HERON: What comes into relief about the nature of human beings is that I see them as persons who happen to be very intimately associated with bodies. Persons intimately associated with bodies are highly vulnerable beings. For me the challenge of human existence is for human beings to be able to accept their vulnerability without taking out the consequences of it on each other, and to create social systems within which persons are able and free to accept their own and each other's vulnerability in such a way that all are fulfilled.

PROCTOR: What is the purpose of human energy?

HERON: For me, the purpose of human energy is really the celebration of three distinct human capacities which I would distinguish in theory only to unite in practice. The three basic forms of personal energy are the capacity to love and be loved (incidentally each of these has a passive and active form), secondly, the capacity to understand the world and the capacity to be understood, and, thirdly, the capacity to take charge of life, to be self-directing, to be an agent of free choice and in the passive form, the capacity to be part of a larger whole, whether it is social, ideological or even cosmological. So the purpose of personal energy is to celebrate these capacities and their inter-relations in a way that enhances the ability of other humans to celebrate them.

PROCTOR: Can you tell me briefly how and where and when your approach to counselling originated? Out of what social soil did these sets of insights emerge?

HERON: Briefly, I was, prior to 1970, for many years involved in meditation methods. I discovered that these methods were in many ways remarkable in what they did to the nature of human consciousness, but for me – and I noticed for others – they left unresolved infantile traumas and tensions. In 1970 when the radical therapies moved to this country, from California largely, I became interested in the whole range of them, and eventually was most impressed by Re-evaluation Counselling which was developed by Harvey Jackins in the States in the early 1950's. In the 1960's it began to spread around the world. Of all the radical approaches to personal development which were available in 1970-1, the most relevant was Co-counselling, at that time in the form of Re-evaluation Counselling as developed by Jackins and his colleagues. It appealed to me because it was a peer, self-directed, cathartic, growth method that resolved all kinds of tensions and distresses in a human being, where these tensions and distresses for me personally had not been dealt with - not even been identified - by the kinds of meditation methods in which I had been nursed previously.

PROCTOR: So its revolutionary aspects were that it was a peer-system rather than an expert-system, and that it was cathartic?

HERON: Yes, it was the insistence in Co-counselling that these cathartic methods - the use of abreaction, the discharge of painful emotion, distressful emotion, from early and later traumas - is something that each human being can take charge of herself, and it is not necessary for this to be managed, directed by an expert, a psychotherapist, a psychiatrist, a counsellor in the more traditional sense of the term. This is something that a person can basically manage herself after a relatively brief period of initial training. Well, certainly this is true of the average citizen in the community.

PROCTOR: What processes or structures within British society today stand out as being helpful to people celebrating those capacities you mentioned?

HERON: It seems to me in the last five years there has been a significant change of climate in continuing education for professional people in the helping professions. There is a much greater interest in the development of interpersonal skills, in the development of some minimal kind of emotional compe-tence, a greater willingness to accept that people in the helping professions really do not have any adequate training in how to handle their own tensions and difficulties. I have found in working with many different groups in the helping professions, a great willingness to explore, initially in a modest way, some of the new approaches which stress working with feelings, which stress cultivating an awareness of what is going on with people. Many of the techniques developed in Co-counselling are techniques which can be extrapolated to professional helpers of various kinds.

PROCTOR: What processes and structures appear to impede?

HERON: Well, although there has been a change of climate, I

would still see the whole society in which we live as a non-cathartic society. In the home, in the schools, in the hospitals and in all our major organisations there is a widely accepted and adopted norm of emotional repression, by which I mean that the tensions and distresses, negative feelings which human beings have, are on no account to be dealt with in any other way than being contained, controlled, repressed and denied. This, I think, affects the whole climate of life in our society. In every home, and in some instance in the schoolroom and the office and the hospital, there is an air of alienation because human beings in normal situations are given no emotional space; no acknowledgement is made of their need to deal with the effects of their vulnerability in appropriate ways. The culture is devoid of concepts of how to enable people to deal with their tensions and distresses.

PROCTOR: What do you see as the objectives of the counselling task?

HERON: The objectives of Co-counselling I see quite clearly – to train Co-counsellors – and this is primarily to train the *client*, the person who is taking her turn, with the counsellor in support – to train the client to take charge of her own feelings, and to provide her with skills for releasing distress feelings – anger, fear, grief – originating in the more recent and the more remote past, so that these distress feelings are not driving compulsive, distorted, disorientated behaviour in small ways and in greater ways. As it were, to restore to the human being the capacity for managing her own disturbing emotions which if they are not managed, I believe, significantly distort behaviour. Anger discharges through loud sounds and vigorous storming movements (harmlessly directed), fear through trembling, grief through sobbing, embarrassment through laughter.

The full cycle of catharsis involves a release of emotional tension followed by spontaneous insight if the discharge is sustained sufficiently. You will then have an uprush of re-evaluation of past traumas, and this is a very important phase – the phase of insight into how those incidents in the past have affected and condition present behaviour. The third stage, I think, is also very important, the stage of cele-bration. The post-cathartic client, having gone through the phase of spontaneous insight, emerges from the session as someone whose humanity is for that period very available for celebration. It is as if the client delights in the fullness of her emergent humanity, and this may then be taken further into a goal-setting and action-planning phase. The effect of catharsis in the longer term is the break up of rigidities, compulsive and maladaptive forms of behaviour, the release of the capacity for celebrating basic human energies and capacities, and for fulfilling those capacities in relation to the real world, in a rewarding and satisfying way.

PROCTOR: What resources do you see yourself bringing to the counselling task?

HERON: Basically, the resources brought from the practice of Co-counselling in the original training workshops, where I acquired the basic skills of the 'client' which I think are the primary skills. The skills of the counsellor are important but in a sense, secondary. So my prime resources are those skills brought from the practice of Co-counselling, exercising the techniques of the client on myself in working with my own tensions and past distresses and traumas, and finding ways of starting to celebrate my own being.

PROCTOR: What do you see as the responsibilities of the client and the counsellor in the counselling interaction?

HERON: This question is quite fundamental in clarifying what Co-counselling is about, because in a Co-counselling relationship the primary responsibility of the session rests with the client. The client is the person who is taking her turn, working on herself, using the techniques on herself, and she is primarily self-directed. That is to say that she is managing the session in a way that seems meaningful to her. The function of the counsellor is to give sustained, very aware, very supportive, attention with the gaze, posture and facial expression, and so on. The counsellor, above all, does not criticise, advise, interpret, analyse, categorise. The contract between the client and the counsellor is that when it seems to the counsellor that the client is lost – has got stuck in her own defences, is blocking, has lost her way, is confused, is no longer able to work effec- tively with herself, is unable to reach the state of discharge – the counsellor will then intervene with a practical suggestion about what the client may say or do, a simple suggestion of technique for the client to get the process started again. It is the client's privilege, either to accept this suggestion, or if it really feels to the client inappropriate, to reject it. Now, in making the suggestion, the counsellor, of course, has some kind of metal hypothesis, has some mental interpretation, of what is going on in the client, but this mental hypothesis is not verbalised. The only thing that is verbalised is the cashing out of the hypothesis in a very practical suggestion such as 'May I suggest that you now try saying so-and-so . . .', or, 'May I suggest that you now try doing so-and-so . . .'. Again, I would like to stress that it is always the client's privilege to reject the suggestion, as the fundamental principle is that the client is basically self-directing in her session.

PROCTOR: Obviously the counselling encounter is different from other roles?

HERON: In one sense it is different because the counsellor is giving sustained, supportive attention to the client without wavering, so far as is possible, for the whole hour of the client's session and the client is, in a very particular kind of way, working on herself. What is similar to other roles in life is simply the concept of human support reaching out to another human being.

What is practiced in Co-counselling, in terms of the counsellor's role of giving attention, is enormously potent in humanising encounters everywhere. What is different, of course, is that the client is doing something very countercultural – explicitly seeking to release in herself the discharge of old painful emotion. This is very untypical of encounters in other roles, which tend to be non-cathartic or anti-cathartic.

PROCTOR: If the client and counsellor train in similar workshops, there isn't any difficulty in knowing that your client and you have similar assumptions and objectives about the nature of the task?

HERON: No. Co-counsellors usually enter Co-counselling through a training workshop which may be five days or two weekends or an on-going workshop once a week, three hours an evening for fourteen weeks. In the training workshops that I run, one of the very first things that I do is expound my view of the theory of Co-counselling, and then after a good deal of discussion about the theory, I like people to say whether they find the theory sufficiently plausible for cashing out in practical training. I try to ensure that there is a rough agreement about some of the basic theoretical assumptions, sufficient agreement for both client and counsellor to feel that they are concerned with similar objectives.

PROCTOR: Going back to the previous question about where you focus, you've already said that you focus on the release of distress, and that you engage emotionality. Is there anything else that you want to say about that?

HERON: It works out that what the client tends to spend a great deal of time working on are early relationships within the client's family, that is to say, relationships with their mother, father, brothers, sisters, all people close in their early life. In terms of the particular processes within the counselling session, then, it is important that which is just as important as the emotional release, and give herself space to express a positive celebration of herself, to do some quite specific action planning and goal setting about the management of her daily life, from the personal side and the professional side, indeed on any other front, political, economic or whatever.

PROCTOR: Is the kind of climate that you seek to develop covered by your *free attention*?

HERON: In the training workshop, and in any Co-counselling session, where trained Co-counsellors are working, the key note is support, safety, security. This is extremely important because I find that human beings, for good reasons, will not open up early areas of deep hurt, deep scars, unless they feel very safe, very secure, and are assured deep within that when they open up these areas they will not receive further hurt. This is the child's fear, that if he opens up once again, yet more hurt will come in. So safety, security and support, and deep unqualified affirmation of the worth of a human being, are the two elements of the climate.

PROCTOR: Does the idea that people tend to recreate old patterns of relating in the counselling relationship, i.e. transference, have much significance for you and if so, what do you do about it?

HERON: Yes, I see this as very important, but would not work with it the way the classical Psychoanalyst works with transference. Where any two people who are already trained are Co-counselling together for the first time, we would suggest that they do what we call a check for identification, to discover whether the client who is taking her turn has any hidden projections directed at the counsellor, is unawarely projecting emotions and feelings that relate originally to some past person and past distresses and past events. So we run through a simple identification check to break this hidden projection or unaware transference, to make it explicit so that it is brought into consciousness and worked with. Thus, the process goes: 'Whom do I remind you of?', the counsellor says, and repeats this question until the client starts to peel off layers of association. When a basic association or identification comes up – say, the counsellor reminds the client of Mr. Green, a childhood art teacher – then the counsellor says 'Well, in what ways do I remind you of Mr. Green?' or 'In what ways am I like Mr. Green?'. The client shares this. The counsellor then says, 'What is left unsaid, what are the deeply felt feelings that are unexpressed, and which still need to be expressed, to Mr Green?'. This may take the client into a role play situation where she discharges some underlying tension about Mr. Green, gets an insight into connections between Mr. Green and the present situation. Finally, the counsellor says, 'In what ways am I not like Mr. Green?' so that the client can see the counsellor as herself, not covered over with all kinds of associations with Mr. Green. Now we find that this works remarkably well and clears the channel. The client may not deal with all the feelings associated with Mr. Green, but the client has insight that the counsellor is indeed herself, a distinctive human being and is not to be confused with Mr. Green, or anybody else. So in other words we are trying to make any transference, any hidden projections, quite explicit, and working with it through emotional discharge, gain some insight into the function of the projection and make a clear distinction between the counsellor as a person, a distinct human person at the present time, and projections from the past.

PROCTOR: Do you feel that people are always capable of being aware of those projections?

HERON: You have got to remember that a Co-counsellor may co-counsel with many different people, and, in a sense, each counsellor that the client works with will evoke a slightly different sort of projection which may be positive or negative. As a function of working successfully with different counsellors in the community, as time goes by the counsellor is going to dig down to progressively deeper layers of projection that may be fouling up all sorts of present relationships. In a sense, the identifying of hidden projections, of becoming aware of the process and how these hidden projections affect current relationships, is a continuous process with different counsellors. So that the hidden projections that the client is unable to reach in the early stages of counselling start to come up and be available for working in later stages. But the whole dynamic of transference is radically affected in the Co-counselling situation since this is a two-way reciprocal process. The counsellor is *not* any kind of impassive peg, constantly there week after week in a counselling role, on whom the client can throw an array of projections. It is a two-way process. So in many ways it is a whole different climate for two human beings who are seeking to help each other, to become aware of their hidden projections. This is a very different climate, for example, to classical Psychoanalysis.

PROCTOR: Do you regard yourself as a model? At least, do Co-counsellors regard themselves as a model for each other?

HERON: I think this is it. Since the process is reciprocal, and each person takes the role of counsellor and client, and since the primary role is the role of client, in a sense each client is a model, an example, for the other. If I, in a Co-counselling session, am a counsellor first and my partner is a client first, then if my client has a very good session and has worked creatively and really reaches deep levels of work, then this is an inspiration to me when it is my turn, in the second half, as the client. In this sense I think undoubtedly clients are models for each other and if you are an experienced client in a beginners training course, working as client is an inspiration and help to the beginners in the group.

The client models for the counsellor not as counsellor, but the client models for the counsellor when the counsellor then takes her turn as client.

PROCTOR: What kind of behaviour do you expect or sanction or encourage in clients and counsellors? Are you aware of positively conditioning certain communications and negatively conditioning others?

HERON: Yes. There is quite an explicit method here that what the counsellor would encourage, and what the client above all would encourage in herself, is self-appreciative, self-affirming, self-validating behaviour in words and posture: celebration of self. In her session, the client will do and say things that contradict, go against the grain of her deeply ingrained distress, recording that she is no good, has no value. She works against the grain of that recording by engaging quite intentionally in self-appreciation, self-validation, celebration of self. Also, we work with these for their own sake, enhancing and building up the centre of human strength within us. This method has a powerful effect at the time or later, of promoting discharge of the distress that is congealed in the 'I'm no good' recording. Conversely, the behaviour that the client would seek to overcome in herself, and the counsellor would encourage the client to overcome is all that verbal behaviour where the client both identifies the negative recording and gets trapped in complaining about how dreadful she is, and 'how life is troublesome', 'how all is against her' and 'I'm no good and you're no good and we are all in a mess'. The counsellor encourages the client to find opposite ways of talking and thinking and being.

PROCTOR: And are there any other patterns of interaction or patterns of learning which you would identify as a process, which you have recognised and made use of?

HERON: There are quite a wide range of simple techniques which the client is encouraged and trained to use with herself during the session. These include a literal description of a traumatic incident, not taking an analytical standpoint but evoking the event, rather like a novelist. The feelings lie in the interstices of the literal details, the smells, the sounds, the colours, what people actually said and did. We use repetition, inviting the client to repeat words and phrases – maybe repeating them somewhat louder and several times – if they carry a hint of emotional tension, a slight charge as evidenced by all kinds of non-verbal cues. We encourage the client to accept sudden – apparently random – thoughts, images, associations, connections and ideas that appear to enter the mind from nowhere. We find that these are an invaluable part of the process and we like the client to be sensitive to these, to verbalise them and accept them and work with their implications. A fundamental process I've already mentioned is finding words and phrases that contradict the depressive recording 'I'm no good', and we work with this principle of contradiction in many ways. To go verbally or nonverbally *away* from distress loosens the system up and provides a leverage outside the distress to discharge the distress feelings that are within. There's one basic method which we call role play. The client recreates an old traumatic situation but seeks to express the previously unexpressed, the feelings that were cut off at the time, whether they're positive feelings of love, or whether they're negative feelings of anger and fear and grief. She directly expresses the feelings by speaking in the session to the other person in the original traumatic scene; and the counsellor stands in for this other person, the mother, the father or whoever it is. The client uses these techniques on herself, prompted by the counsellor when she overlooks an opportunity or gets stuck. There are, of course, many other techniques which it would take too long to go into now.

PROCTOR: Given that there are a fairly limited number of ways that we can respond to a request for personal help, or seek to intervene in another's personal exploration, are there any responses that you have worked on being able to use effectively?

HERON: One thing I haven't mentioned is the importance we give to affirming the worth of the client, indeed of other members of the Co-counselling community. I can, at the end of the session as counsellor, affirm the worth of my client. Any time they meet, people in the Co-counselling community can reach out to each other to affirm their humanity in an unqualified way. This is a central intervention in Co-counselling, because if I appreciate in an unqualified manner, sincerely and genuinely, another human being, then that human being is lovingly confronted with her own tendencies to think of herself as no good, and invited to accept my celebration, invited to agree with it, and take it further.

PROCTOR: What if there are people who you find it hard to affirm in their humanity or it would be insincere for you to do so?

HERON: If you really can't do it in a sincere and genuine way, then avoid it. Next time there's a Co-counselling session available, try to find out what's going on in your relationship with that person that you can only see the negative side of their make-up, and are unable to see what's either very evident or lurking within the negative side. There may be some unidentified projection that makes you unable to appreciate the other which can be dealt with effectively by Co-counselling.

PROCTOR: And any other interventions?

HERON: Stepping outside the particular domain of Co-counselling, I use another training method which I call the Six Category Intervention Method, which is for any practitioner in a professional relation with a client, from bank manager to psychiatrist. I suggest that there are six fundamental types of valid and legitimate intervention which I call: (1) *prescriptive*, giving advice; (2) *informative*, giving new knowledge and information; (3) *confronting*, challenging the restricted beliefs, the rigid attitudes of others; (4) *cathartic*, eliciting a release of tension; (5) *catalytic*, facilitating self-directed problem-solving in a client, seeking to provide opportunities for the client to engage in self-discovery; and (6) *supportive*, affirming the value or worth of the client.

In any practitioner/client situation, if the interventions are productive, then they fall in either one or other of these six categories. I would not regard any one of the six types of intervention as superior to any other. Each is equally appropriate to a particular type of practitioner/client situation, or to a particular phase in a practitioner/client interaction. Let's remember here that we are now thinking in a very general way across the board, for all types of professional relationships with clients and not in the very special type of relationship between co-counsellors where the client is largely self-directed and where the counsellor's interventions, when they do occur, are primarily cathartic and supportive.

PROCTOR: Are there some interventions that are less appropriate for a counselling situation or a Co-counselling situation than for a bank manager situation?

HERON: What I have found in using the Six Category Method with a wide range of professional groups, is that there are two categories in which people regard themselves as being unskilled, weak, inadequate, or relatively incompetent. They are the cathartic and the confronting categories. In all the workshops so far, without exception, people have demanded that I spend time in suggesting techniques, exercises, methods for building up skills in cathartic and confronting interventions. In human growth counselling, I would soft pedal prescriptive intervention. Giving advice is more appropriate, the more the client is coming to a professional with special technical expertise such as a solicitor, a bank manager, an architect or a doctor. But where the client is going to a counsellor primarily for the purposes of human growth and development, then advice, in the sense of the counsellor suggesting how the client should live, is less and less appropriate. Catalytic intervention, encouraging the client to find ways of setting her own goals and finding ways to meet those goals is more appropriate.

PROCTOR: Do you see any demarcation between counselling and therapy?

HERON: The concept of therapy is for me largely outdated and my own preference would be to have the notion of therapy restricted exclusively to physical disorders – to take it right back into the realms of physical medicine. I would like to eliminate the term 'therapy' from the whole field of working with people on their emotional growth, their possible development, their problems and difficulties as human beings on this strange planet. I would sooner see the counselling that addresses these kinds of issues as part of education, as part of an educational process that includes training people to build up skills in working with their feelings, skills in working with other human beings, skills in decision-making. One of the troubles with the present social system, as I see it, is that since emotional competence and interpersonal competence have been largely relegated to the domain of therapy, they are nowhere adequately represented in the educational system. Therefore the vast majority of people in the helping professions of all kinds have – as a result of their education and training – remarkably little skill in working with their own distress feelings and to this phenomenon the suicide figures bear eloquent testimony.

PROCTOR: Does that mean that you feel anybody could Co-counsel?

HERON: No, I don't believe that anyone can Co-counsel. I think for people to enter a Co-counselling basic training workshop pre-supposes that they have manageable amounts of distress, so that they have enough attention outside their anxieties that they can hold together a coherent lifestyle; above all, they have enough attention outside their anxieties to give attention to another person, who is the client. And there are clearly a significant number of people who are too deeply distressed, to be able to Co-counsel. They need sustained and intensive one-way counselling, until sufficient distress has been discharged so that they have enough free attention to move over to co-counselling. This sequence needs to be acknowledged more in the whole field of what people still insist on calling 'therapy'. In psychotherapy there are clients who undoubtedly need sustained one-way counselling but then, particularly if cathartic methods are being used, there comes a changeover point when they have enough attention free from their distress to engage in Co-counselling.

PROCTOR: Do you select for Co-counselling?

HERON: If you do Co-counselling through so-called growth centres, then the people who attend are a highly selected group – in my experience the kind of people who are 'together enough to Co-counsel effectively. If I am running a Co-counselling workshop through an adult education department at the university where I am using the ordinary publicity resources of the adult education department and reaching out generally among adults in the surrounding community, then I would use some kind of screening process. I give an introductory lecture and then say to people, 'Well, if these ideas seem to be plausible and you would like to practice, come back next week, but before you come back, please give me a ring. I would like to have a talk with you about what's involved in this kind of course and whether this is a course that is appropriate for you, that it's something you really wish to get involved in'. Then, in the telephone conversation, or maybe indeed a personal interview, I would apply some light screening procedures. I would check out the conventional psychiatric history of the client and if the person, for example, was on very heavy doses of psychotropic drugs, then I would suggest that a basic Co-counselling workshop might not be the best place. Because as the discharge process starts, the client wants to come off the drugs, and if the client does this too quickly, there is an uprush of distress and then he needs instant counselling to handle the panic. This isn't the kind of situation that other beginners can cope with. Another criterion is chronic patterns of invalidation. It's very easy to tell in a short discussion if a person is carrying around an enormous weight of invalidations that she is endlessly, repetitively and compulsively putting herself or other people, or the world at large, down. The weight of invalidation that a person is carrying around, directed at herself is a partial index of the degree of distress. You can ask a person to tell you what she likes about herself and how a person will respond to that question is some initial indication of her level of distress. Screening or selection is always problematic, but certainly what very heavily distressed people need is a special setting where counselling on a one-way basis can be given when the intense distresses suddenly rush up.

PROCTOR: You talk as if the trainers in Co-counselling really have to develop over time a good deal of almost professional experience.

HERON: I am very wary of the concept of professionalism because my own view is that it is largely a defensive one. It can be used in all helping professions to sustain norms of emotional repression. It is tied in with labelling and categorising people and seems to me to be a vast conspiracy to sustain emotional repression in all kinds of practitioner/client situations. So rather than say that the teacher of Co-counselling needs to become a professional person, I'd say that she needs to develop very aware human skills of judgement.

PROCTOR: Does your client group influence your way of working? Does the fact of having worked largely with what I imagine is a middle class, or at least, articulate, group of people, influence the way you view counselling?

HERON: There is no doubt that the vast majority of people who come to Co-counselling training workshops are middle class people in middle class professions: teachers and tutors and social workers and psychiatrists and psychologists. This means they have well-developed verbal skills, are familiar with some of the theoretical concepts that are used in introducing Co-counselling. Co-counselling is seriously under-represented in working class culture and probably needs to be significantly restyled in its presentation to become effective, relevant and meaningful there.

PROCTOR: Do you have any personal dilemmas in your counselling work?

HERON: I am interested in the relationship between catharsis as a necessary condition for human growth and the whole range of so-called transpersonal methods: meditation, yoga, contemplation, concentration, prayer, praise, worship. Because of my earlier experience, I regard these methods also as a necessary condition of full human development.

Now there's no doubt in my view that both approaches can be used for the negation or repression of the other. That is to say that people can be immersed in the cathartic way and remain quite blind to transpersonal methods, and one of the symptoms of this is rigid, dogmatic theorising about cathartic methods. On the other hand, many people can be caught up in meditation processes and the whole mind-expanding edifice can be built upon planks of repression of unresolved distress. The symptoms of this are attitudes and behaviour like undiscriminating guru worship, spiritual authoritarianism, and so on. One of my interests is in ways of combining meditation and related methods with the cathartic methods that are central to Co-counselling and indeed in advanced Co-counselling workshops we do explore this. Another interesting thing is that in Co-counselling discharge precedes insight. There is a possible partial reversal of this, where you have a whole set of concepts that enables you to tag and identify compulsions, programmes, scripts and recordings deep down in the psyche. As a function of tagging them, some discharge may be elicited subsequently. Transactional Analysis workshops work a little bit in this way.

PROCTOR: How do Co-counsellors arrange to work with each other?

HERON: Part of the notion of Co-counselling is that of community, meaning an association of people who Co-counsel regularly. It will have a programme of follow-up groups meeting once a week or once a month. There are also one-day week-end and longer workshops which regular, practicing Co-counsellors attend to improve their skills and work intensively with each other. There will also be people who take responsibility for providing address lists of those who have done basic Co-counselling training and ensure they are available to anyone who inquires. Minimal organisation is necessary to sustain communication between people. The original American organisation is still active under the title of 'Re-evaluation Counselling Communities', and I was instrumental in establishing it in Europe. I resigned in 1974 and became involved with a group of Co-counsellors in the United States, in this country, and throughout Europe, in establishing Co-Counselling International, so that the peer principle which is central to the Co-counselling relationship can be fully represented in community procedures and organisations. It's my belief that in the original Re-evaluation Counselling Communities, the peer principle is not adequately represented in the way the whole organisation is structured. Also the original American organisation, in my view, began to suffer from theoretical rigidity and theoretical closure. So in Co-counselling International we provide international workshops, where completely independent counselling communities can meet and discuss developments of theory, method and practice and ways of organising peer communities. I also wish to extend the notion of community to mean not just minimal association with those who Co-counsel and go to workshops to share their common methods but an association of Co-counsellors who are interested in finding new ways of relating with each other as well as Co-counselling.

PROCTOR: I've noticed that you haven't much talked about any other kind of repression but emotional repression.

HERON: My view of Co-counselling theory would be that individual emotional repression and the subsequent distortion of behaviour becomes, as it were, collectively congealed in rigid and repressive social systems and norms. These acquire a dynamic life of their own and become an independent source of human distress. One of the issues about recovering full humanity and planning for a richer, more meaningful life involves deciding what to do about restructuring social systems.

It does seem to me that in the human development field it is possible for people to become deeply engrossed in personal growth as a defence against and as an evasion of the whole question of social change, political action and re-structuring our organisations. Conversely, it's equally possible for people to get deeply involved in a revolutionary commitment or involved in political or social action, and this can be seen in some people as a defence against working through feelings, against dealing with repressed emotion. I have a good deal of concern about the committed revolutionary who has not dealt with repressed anger.

PROCTOR: Is there a danger that people start to lead the more significant parts of their life within the community where they can be sure of validation and a safe area in which to discharge their distress, and escape from the more difficult way of living with their own vulnerability in their own social situations?

HERON: I present Co-counselling as a tool for living, a tool for taking charge of every area of life, injecting meaning, significance and value into it. The discharge process, the insight that follows it, celebration, goal setting: these cash themselves out every day in trying to find new ways of handling existing relationships – personal relationships, family relationships, professional relationships. The whole point about the process is to step out of old, compulsive ways of being in the world and to find new liberated ways of expressing every situation, taking a new look at it, taking risks and exploring new ways of being.

There is one final point which I would like to add and it's about the balance of attention in the client working on herself. A client needs to have a certain amount of her attention outside the distress on which she's working, so that her system is free to discharge the distress. There is also the corollary principle that the client works with what's on top. We don't use methods which precipitate the client prematurely, steeply and sharply into very heavy layers of distress. If the client works with the associations that are available, that come up spontaneously, then she can be assured that she's always dealing with what she's ready to handle. The discharge process then becomes relatively undisruptive.

PROCTOR: Do you feel you've given a clear picture of Co-counselling?

HERON: Yes. I think as an initial sketch it covers most of the main points which you would include in such a sketch. There is one important further point: persons happen to be very intimately associated with bodies. So that for a person to alleviate the tensions, the distresses, at the level of personal feeling also involves a release of somatic tension through sobbing, or crying, or laughing or trembling. The initial methods that I teach in Co-counselling take a gentle route with use of words, associations, light non-verbal techniques. There is also a way in through the body, through mobilisation of breathing, of body energies through vigorous movement, through pressure points, through massage. These are, I think, important and central cathartic techniques, very effective and powerful. They can lead people deeply to early distress quite quickly and in my strategy of Co-counselling training, these are techniques which I introduce at a later stage. But they can effectively be integrated with Co-counselling procedures without in any way detracting from the basic principle that the client is fundamentally self-directed and is in charge of the way she runs her session.

Tom Osborn

A Radical Perspective

Tom Osborn is a consultant in group work and is one of the staff of the Counselling Courses at South West London College. A doctor and psychiatrist by training, he has worked in the theatre as a director and writer. He spent some years as a lecturer at the Polytechnic of North London, where he helped to set up the Diploma Course in Applied Behavioural Science. He runs groups in a wide variety of situations and he practices, and sometimes teaches, massage and bio-energetic therapy.

A radical approach to counselling is based on a position in psychology and a position in politics. The position in psychology is a reaction to Behaviourism, which is seen as turning people into objects and controlling them; and to Psychoanalysis, which is seen as authoritarian and, again, controlling. This *psychological* position is known as humanistic psychology, a phenomenological approach which accepts as valid the experience of people as they themselves describe it. The position in *politics* is linked to a socialist analysis of society. The work of R. D. Laing and Herbert Marcuse are of basic importance to radical counsellors, who believe that no therapeutic theory or practice which does not place people in their social context is adequate.

SUGGESTED READING:

Cooper, David, *The Grammar of Living*, Harmondsworth: Penguin, 1976.

Heather, Nick, *Radical Perspectives in Psychology*, London: Methuen, 1976.

Laing, R. D., *The Divided Self*, Harmondsworth: Penguin, 1970.

Laing, R. D. *The Politics of Experience*, Harmondsworth: Penguin, 1970.

Laing, R. D., *The Politics of the Family*, Harmondsworth: Penguin, 1976.

Marcuse, Herbert, *One-Dimensional Man*, London: Abacus, 1972.

Radical Therapy Collective/Rough Times Collective, *The Radical Therapist*, Harmondsworth: Penguin, 1974.

Reich, W., *Character Analysis*, London: Vision Press, 1976.

Rowan, John, 'A dialectical paradigm for research' (abstract), p. 28, Vol. 31, *Bulletin of British Psychological Society*, 1978.

Rush, Anne Kent, *Getting Clear: Body Work for Women*, London: Wildwood House, 1974.

Schatzman, Morton, *Soul Murder*, Harmondsworth: Penguin, 1976.

PROCTOR: What is your relationship to counselling and what kind of spectacles are you wearing?

OSBORN: The relationship I have to counselling is primarily through groups. In fact, when I first looked at the questions I wondered whether I ought to talk about the little actual 'counselling' that I do with individuals. But it seems to me that what I do in groups is based on an attitude towards the people that I work with which is closely related to counselling. It is based on the idea that people have their own potential and what I am concerned with is how they get in touch with that and use it. And I believe that whether people can do this or not depends very much on their social context, on how they relate to each other as political beings – which must be what lies behind my choice to work mainly with groups.

PROCTOR: What is your background in counselling?

OSBORN: I haven't grown up in one particular school of counselling or group work, or adhere to one now. I started as a doctor and psychiatrist, although I haven't practised orthodox medicine for over fifteen years. I gave it up for reasons that I didn't understand very much at the time but I knew it felt wrong. I then worked in the theatre and it was in improvisation workshops that I first worked with groups. My real life started when I stopped being a doctor. It was the first time I think I became autonomous. I started using my *own* potential.

PROCTOR: So your medical background affects your viewpoint by your reacting against it?

OSBORN: The medical model has been useless to me. I never use it, or if I do it is a hindrance. I think that a medical training does not serve, at all well, anyone who wants to do healing work, and I include physical healing work as well as counselling. In the medical model, the person who is labelled sick or neurotic is the problem, and the medical expert is someone who represents the authoritative view of what is normal and what you ought to be like. Society defines its own sanity in terms of people who are mad and its own healthiness in terms of disease. It actually contains its sickness by loading it on to certain people who are then patients. I would like to abandon that completely.

The model I use now is that of phenomenology. Laing and his colleagues have written a great deal about this in the context of schizophrenia. It means attempting to accept people's experience in the terms in which they themselves describe it. That is different from the group approach which is used in management training. The prime purpose of management training is to get people to work effectively in an organization which is owned by someone else. That begins to use the language of politics. Group work in management training *uses* the phenomenological approach for its own ends, but puts strict boundaries on it wherever the actual experience of people conflicts with those ends. In a truly phenomenological approach you don't apply those boundaries, or at least not consciously, though they may still be acting through you to some extent. In counselling I would say that is closest to Rogers, and to Perls in therapy. You accept people where they really are, and you help them to accept themselves where they really are.

PROCTOR: How did working in the theatre affect you?

OSBORN: I can remember a particular moment when something started to happen for me. There is a technique of working with half-masks. You put the mask on and you look in the mirror, and you can see a new creature which is partly you and partly the mask. The forehead, the brow, the cheek bones and nose are the mask's, the mouth, and chin and jaw are yours. The mask evokes something from deep down, something which is not deliberate. For me, it first came with a sound. That was when my work on myself at gut level started, and my approach to counselling is very much concerned with helping people to get in touch with that.

PROCTOR: That seems to connect with Reich, and you do Reichian body-work. What about Reich?

OSBORN: Reich is marvellous in opening up access to a whole range of new experiences. One of the things I don't like about

Reich is that he seems to put a new set of criteria on people. The most obvious example is that you should have a particular kind of orgasm and that to me seems anti-phenomenological, anti-experience. You should have the orgasms that you do have, and grow from there.

PROCTOR: What do you take from Reich?

OSBORN: What Reich shows very powerfully is the structural relationship between bodies and personalities. His first innovation was to insist that you must work with the resistance as shown by present, physical reality in the psychoanalytic session, before doing any deep work. He tackled this directly when people evaded or laughed or were charming or seductive as ways of diverting attention. This is all described in his book *Character Structure*. Then he went on to work directly on the body structures by touching and manipulating them, as in massage. And this, together with his work on the orgasm, led to the field of bioenergy, orgone and cosmic energy. A lot of people dismiss his later work about orgones and so on. I take it very seriously. Reich covered a tremendous range. He foreshadowed almost everything we do in the growth movement today.

PROCTOR: And does Reich provide a link between the individual and political viewpoints?

OSBORN: No. I wish he did. He certainly was important politically himself, with setting up the Polyclinic, where he counselled working class people on sexual problems. He also anticipated later concepts in psychology on the nature of fascism and the authoritarian personality. But, ultimately, the way I understand him, he fell back on the idea that individuals have to change first, that social change *depends* on individual change and that gives his followers a let out from developing the sort of political consciousness that he himself applied early on. Whereas I believe that both have to happen together.

PROCTOR: Can you then say what the basis of your political spectacles is?

OSBORN: In groups, I was influenced by working with John Southgate. We both wanted to run large groups and give participants more power. A large group inevitably becomes political because it is an analogue of an organization, and it has to relate as an entity to its environment and its resources. In a small group you can stay with face to face relationships.

In a large group you can't. Of course, in a large group it doesn't need to be radical politics that are expressed, it could be reactionary. The Bion/Tavistock groups teach about leadership in hierarchical systems. We ran large groups where people learned possibilities of changing the existing structures.

And in my life, my experience of communal living and some collective political struggles such as in the Poly (The Polytechnic of North London) and a squatted street were all a basis for a political outlook which affects the way I look at counselling.

PROCTOR: So for you several perceptions overlap. What comes into relief as to the nature of human beings and the relationships between individuals and groups and social systems and ecological systems?

OSBORN: I see our whole society as going through a fundamental transition from living in the competitive, exploitative mode, to attempting to live in some sort of balance. You can see that on many levels from ecology to politics. It is to do with not regarding people just as objects to be used, or animals for that matter or anything in nature. In politics it means extending our awareness to understand how a lot of the time our lives are based on using people as objects to exploit, in factories or in under-developed nations and so on. A great deal of what goes for normal in our lives actually depends on that exploitation and objectification.

That transition is reflected at the person-to-person level in counselling and therapy. The counsellor doesn't maintain an authoritarian position. The client is no longer an object to be healed.

I see our work as one focus of the general process of social change which is related to the transition from exploitation toward balance. Of course we must attempt not to be exploited ourselves either. The strongest political urge is to throw off your own exploitation. Many counsellors are in situations where they are easily just used to further the *re*productive processes of our society, to provide well-behaved, manipulative people who will fit into the existing *productive* machine.

PROCTOR: Most counsellors start with the individual, but your world view starts with wider systems. How do individuals develop and grow within groups and systems to find or not find balance?

OSBORN: It is to do with people fulfilling themselves. There is a core of energy inside each person which tries to express itself. People grow by finding their way to that energy, and finding out how that energy is stopped. If you are in the growth movement you say people stop their own energy. If you are a political activist you say it is stopped by the system. I don't want to be doctrinaire about that. What is important is what way of looking at it at any particular time is going to help the unfolding process.

The process of therapeutic change can be thought of in three stages. Accept yourself – because not accepting yourself blocks your path to the core of your energy. Get in touch with your own vital energy. And change your world in accordance with your own vital energy. Sometimes, parts of that process are very individual. They concern one person and that person's self-exploration. At other times, they are very universal. You may need to withdraw to do that, but at some point you need your social connectedness. We all depend on the world around us and are part of it. You have to understand in what ways the world around you and the way you are part of it prevents you from moving along this path and prevents others too. At some point that structural effect may be so crippling that it has to be changed. Your world becomes *the* world.

Counselling is primarily practised with an individual focus and is usually thought of in that way, which is why I give a lot of emphasis to the wide, social, universal view. I read an article by Edward Bond, the playwright, just the other day and I wrote this down in my notebook – it struck me as being very well expressed. He says: 'It is a hard lesson, but we need to learn that moral behaviour depends more on social practice than on individual action. In a society structurally unjust – as is ours – good deeds may in the end only support injustice'.

PROCTOR: That sounds as if you feel quite impatient with counsellors and counselling.

OSBORN: It is a constant tension. I am responsible for myself and I can choose my destiny. And also, my world, including my ability to choose and the nature of my choices and my power to be responsible, is made for me by the time and place I was conceived and born and brought up. For me it is essential that we remain in the middle of that tension. Any counsellor or therapist who is not aware of both its ends is limiting their own view and their own part in the large change process and the possibilities of change in their clients. Yes, I get frustrated that a lot of therapists and counsellors who are marvellous with individuals are just naive politically.

But this wider view for me is not only political. We are not just individual energy systems. That energy which is in us relates to other people's energy and also to some sort of cosmic energy. It has helped me to understand what religion and people's relation to God are about. It is built into oriental philosophy. You breathe in *prana* and you distribute it around your body and you get vitality from it. In the eastern martial arts, this universal energy is called *chi* or *ki*. It is related to prayer and gaining strength and finding centredness.

That not only has therapeutic implications but it is connected with the whole transition from exploitation to balance. If I want to relate to someone at a psychic level, like in giving a massage, I need to be in a state of centredness which is quite different from the competitive exploitative state that I am often in the rest of the time. When I worked in bio-energy and massage I began to make contact with the energy aura around people as a commonplace, physical experience. I mean physical as distinct from metaphysical. The trouble is none of these phenomena can be related to orthodox Western science. At the moment there are no concepts to make sense of them.

PROCTOR: How do you value your scientific training, then? Have you thrown it all out?

OSBORN: I'm very critical of it. Science and technology and control and exploitation are all linked. The conventional scientific training is entirely a part of that system. This kind of science turns people into objects and invalidates subjective experience. This is reflected in much of what goes on in psychology and psychiatry. Also, it separates the intellectual from the practical. Some people study physics and design machines. Other people follow designs at a factory bench and oil machines when they're running. That takes away the intellectual power from the doers and the practical facility from the studiers. The doers become stupider and more irresponsible and the studiers actually can't do the simple jobs which are needed to look after themselve. This is to do with class. The conventional scientific training simply reinforces the division.

Science is tainted for me at the moment. Obviously, we

need to make an integration. I recently read a paper about non-alienating research by John Rowan who is constantly trying to relate and link up those two aspects and I really value that.

PROCTOR: What do you see as the purpose of human energy?

OSBORN: Something like to fulfill itself. I don't have an answer which says that the purpose of human energy is X, and X is something. If you are religious you call it God's purpose. The trouble is that it is too often invoked to legitimate what happens to be a particular interest. But I don't like the feel of saying there isn't a purpose. I think purpose is a word we give to the direction of an unfolding. I prefer to value the unfolding itself. So the purpose of human energy is for me to pursue and allow that unfolding.

PROCTOR: What processes in society today stand out as being helpful to the proper exercise of human energy?

OSBORN: We need to relate to what is called the counter culture or alternative society. The extreme alternative for organisation is what often happens in a children's playground. There, the organisational pattern is a clustering around activities. An event is not structured in terms of roles and time boundaries but in terms of the dynamic of the event itself. It draws people into it while it lasts and they go away again when it is over. It looks very chaotic and it can be quite threatening. I am not saying it is a permanent organisational form, but on an organisational level it is how the alternative society works. Or to qualify that, it is at least how the *transition* to an alternative society works. Unless we can experience and learn to tolerate that sort of situation where we can suspend our role boundaries, our time boundaries, and our possession boundaries: unless we can get accustomed to that, we are not going to be able to make that move which is actually happening around us. As individuals and as institutions we are going to get stuck and increasingly defensive.

At the same time as moves *towards* that kind of alternative, there are all sorts of *reactions* to it, attempts to maintain the system as it is. The conflict goes on in society and it goes on within individuals. It is expressed *by* society *through* the neuroses of individual people. I think a lot of people who are counsellors see clients who are involved in that process, and who are made unhappy or mad by it. As counsellors we have to realise that is what is going on and we actually have to take part in that experience ourselves.

PROCTOR: You see the alternative society as being strong and good not because it's a permanent way of dropping out but as a way of finding out about how useful structures can be devised that are more responsive to the needs of people? Or do you see it as drawing people out of society?

OSBORN: The alternative society is trying to move from exploitation to balance. At the moment there is a great polarisation. The two different modes are so incompatible. I think that the psychological structures of interdependence and the organisational structures of collective decision-making are really very different from the traditional structures of dependence and of hierarchical decision-making. So are the economic structures of joint ownership. They conflict and it is very difficult for people who are used to one to function in the other.

PROCTOR: From your answers it is clear that you have a position on the right use of human and physical resources. How does that sit with your phenomenological attitude of accepting people where they are, even though their perceptions of the world may be very different from yours?

OSBORN: Not very comfortably – but that is one of the discomforts that I think it is useful to live with. The acquisitive and co-operative impulses exist side by side in people, and societies. The pressures of our relationship to resources and technology bring out one or the other. For example the oil crisis shows us that we can't go on being profligate with physical energy, so whatever I do or anyone else does, the transition will happen anyway. I see my task as validating the expression of the cooperative impulse in people. A lot of the time the alternative society has a great deal of trouble because of its own growing up within the exploitative mode. The process of getting at resources controlled by existing society often involves using the exploitative mode. I think that the most educative experience anyone can have today is to be involved in a factory occupation or a communal squat or a college occupation or any collective venture where resources are shared and decisions are made jointly.

When people actually live in a communal situation, they go through a process of becoming politicised. That means understanding the nature of the sort of oppression that is going on, and secondly, it means experiencing the positive side of the excitement of what collective things are about. What I would foster are situations where that positive process happens. Living or working collectively is not a moral duty or a deprivation. It is a rich experience. At the moment it is often blocked, both within individuals and in society. It is a question of releasing positive energy.

Perhaps that is what the Rogerian approach does in counselling; it sets up a dyad which is a bit of a collective living experience. It is not an experience where the counsellor is either somebody who knows the answers and will not tell you, or who tells you the answers. It is one where the client experiences something of what it is like to relate collectively. But it is much easier in a group. That is why I choose to work with groups. People need opportunities to discover that they do not have to be isolated individuals, competing with each other and so on. Or isolated groupings doing the same. One of the things group work does too rarely is to aim at collective interdependence – for example, so that people learn how to join together to push for what they want. Whenever I work on a course I try to put that into the conscious goals, to help people to actually link with each other in order to get what they want together, because that won't happen if they try for it as individuals. Maybe that consciousness could be brought more into our actual counselling work.

PROCTOR: You have talked a lot about the experiences you bring into the counselling task. Are there any other important resources that you offer as a counsellor or as a trainer to somebody else?

OSBORN: I think the work I have done on myself is important. We can only relate to other people in a helping way when we are not too loaded with our own needs or fears. Many things depend on that: the ability to be with someone and listen to where they are; maintaining a distance. There has got to be a tension between involvement and distance.

PROCTOR: What do you see as your responsibility when you are counselling?

OSBORN: I think I have a responsibility of not laying my trip on a client. Or at least of not doing it covertly because it may be impossible not to do that.

PROCTOR: How do you know you're not?

OSBORN: I try to be aware of what is happening to me as much as possible. That is another responsibility I have, to be aware of what is going on, not necessarily to speak about it. To decide what to say and what not to say about what is going on for me as counsellor, in terms of where the client is at that particular moment.

PROCTOR: What about the client's responsibilities?

OSBORN: Any kind of institutionalised counselling starts off with the counsellor, in relation to the client, as someone who has more training, more skills and probably special knowledge of a particular area, and is being paid or is being employed by someone to do this job. It is not an equal relationship. A client has no responsibility for making decisions about what should or should not be said, whereas a counsellor always has. Even in a deliberately set-up peer-counselling situation the counsellor has to say 'well, I mustn't say this now because it's his session'. The client's responsibility is to use the situation for learning. But it may be up to the counsellor to show how that can be done.

PROCTOR: Is the counselling relationship different from the other roles you are involved in?

OSBORN: I think it is very different. It is a one-sided, helping relationship. In friendships I try to be as open as possible, and I try to bring into that relationship whatever is happening. I'm not all that good at it but that is my ideal – it should be possible and if it isn't happening, then it's not as perfect a relationship as it could be. Other work relationships I also regard as two-sided, though they are not usually as open. In the relationship with my children I feel much more like I do in a relationship with a client. For instance, there are times when they go through bad patches, or developmental phases, when I really would like to be rid of them – but then I realize that they need my love, my understanding, my validation, my help, and I override my irritation. And it is possible to do this – that is where the unconditional positive regard comes in.

PROCTOR: How does co-counselling differ from the traditional counselling interaction?

OSBORN: There is a sense of equality and of exposure. Why I think peer counselling is valuable in training counsellors is that you actually are the client half the time. For a lot of social workers, particularly, the idea of being a client in social work is absolutely out. In peer-counselling, half the time you are in a position of weakness, of exposing yourself, regressing and so on.

PROCTOR: Do you have ways of trying to ensure that you and your client have similar assumptions and objectives about the nature of the counselling task?

OSBORN: I don't find it easy to do that at the outset. If it is a joint enterprise, then not only do the conditions of a contract have to be arrived at jointly but even the process of making a contract at all is one which I don't want to just lay down. But the client has to learn the nature of this relationship and how to use it.

I try to say certain things. For instance, that the client takes responsibility for coming again or not. I actually think that the sooner that person feels able to discontinue the relationship, the better. One of my most successful individual therapeutic relationships was one in which I gave somebody the name of a book, called *Getting Clear: Body Work For Women*. I also talked to her about women's workshops. I only saw her three times and she wrote to me and said that she had bought this book and was getting a tremendous amount from it, and I saw that as getting her in touch with her development in another way.

I try as far as possible to make my decisions and my views visible. I attach great importance to that.

PROCTOR: Do you focus on any particular processes or engage some faculties more than others?

OSBORN: I move around quite a lot. I tend to use things that are actually happening at the moment – and that might be physical or symbolic. If it is symbolic, it is in terms of how people relate to their chairs or how far away from me they are sitting or the way they are holding their hands or something like that. I don't like deep symbolic interpretation very much, because I think a lot of people resist it. If you try to push a symbolic interpretation what you get into is not the area of interpretation but the area of resistance. On the whole I tend to work with building up people's strengths and skills. The sort of processes that I engage with are 'What is it that you can do – what is it that you want to do', helping that person to get in touch with their own abilities, their own powers, their own directions, their own skills. Also to do with their own feeling that they are inadequate, so that they are invalidating themselves.

PROCTOR: That doesn't sound very Rogerian!

OSBORN: What I like about the Rogerian approach and why I attach importance to it is that it is not judgmental. I think if I were to characterise my technique with a word, I would say that it is action-orientated. What I am concerned with is helping people to take actions. And I do believe people are themselves the best knowers of what they need to do, what action to take; this is a Rogerian approach to action. I also may focus on a person recognising how the inadequacy was part of one's past and who in one's life it is connected with and the feelings that evokes. But, ultimately, I am not looking for a person to work with their feelings. I am hoping that the person will come out with their own actions. It's true an action-oriented approach is close to making suggestions or offering solutions. But that woman whom I gave *Body Work for Women* to didn't just take the book and do the exercises as a way of pleasing me. She actually went off on her own with it. An action approach is easier in a group, because you can see how each person affects what happens next.

PROCTOR: What kind of climate do you seek to develop and how do you see it being important for your joint task?

OSBORN: When I recognise that a good climate is there, it is usually rather sparky and spontaneous and I and the client and all the participants, if it is a group, are actually feeling free to suddenly make a joke or get up and do something or go out for a piss if they want to instead of wondering if they should. One of the signs of a good climate is that when one person is talking and somebody else suddenly has a marvellous idea, the person who is talking actually stops. In counselling, if a person is able to interrupt their train of thought with something that has cropped up suddenly and they are eager to say that and that doesn't irritate them or me then I know the thing is going well.

PROCTOR: How do you set that up? Is that something that just happens?

OSBORN: I try to partly be like that myself. I may draw attention to the ways in which that has been blocked, or say that I am feeling a bit constrained when it isn't like that.

PROCTOR: Do support and confrontation come in here? An analytical climate is basically a confronting climate but a Rogerian climate is predominantly a very supportive climate. Do you see yourself switching between the two?

OSBORN: I see myself switching, but I see myself as being basically supportive. In the beginning of any relationship I set out to support whatever that person wants to do. But that would have to be combined with attempting to make my own position clear and my own aims clear. The ideal climate I like is one where everybody is able to come out with what they are after and, at the same time, tolerate what other people are after, however different it may be. Obviously, that often means one has to work out consequences and come to accommodations but at least that openness is possible.

PROCTOR: Do you find it difficult to decide between support and confrontation?

OSBORN: If somebody is regressing into the state of being a child, there are times when that really needs to happen and you need to take the role of the parent. And there are other times when you need to say 'Look here, I don't want to be your parent at this moment', and to confront that and not collude with it.

One rule that I always make for myself in a group is that I never confront individuals until the group is working as a group. If you are basically supporting then you can be confronting in the framework of support. It is possible to confront people with their strengths and I think that is often the most valuable form of confrontation.

PROCTOR: Does transference have much significance for you and, if so, what do you do about it?

OSBORN: It certainly has a lot of significance for me. Anyone who works non-directively or has a goal that people should become self-directing is bound to become involved in transference. People want your approval, your love, or support, and they seek it in all sorts of ways. When I am in the role of counsellor or group leader, people relate to me in that sort of parental way, and I attempt not to be related to like that. However, I don't work primarily through transference like a psychoanalyst. I don't focus predominantly on the dependent or counter-dependent way people relate to me – or to each other for that matter, because that happens too. I notice it a great deal but I tend to side-step. My aim is to establish a new kind of relationship, an interdependent one, more directly. I don't think it is only that people are stuck with unresolved or unfinished relationships or early developmental relationships, like in an oral or anal stage, that they are not able to be independent or interdependent. Often they simply don't know *how* to relate in other ways. They have not had the experiences, they have not developed the skills. My feeling is that to focus too exclusively on the transference actually in some way perpetuates the non-mature way of relating.

PROCTOR: If you don't induce it and don't ignore it, how do you relate to it?

OSBORN: If I refuse to respond to demands for love or approval or refuse to rise to aggression then that refusal is obvious, and I may also mention it. And I recognise my own counter-transference as well – my anger at what people are demanding of me or my love for them. The thing about the transference approach that I don't like is that it is a hierarchical approach. It keeps me in a position of superiority if *I* label some actual experience as transference and it becomes material for analysis – analysis by *me* – instead of a live part of a relationship which has to be dealt with in equality. I do work with transference, in the sense that the way people are relating to each other or to me is due to things they are bringing in with them rather than what is present. I may respond temporarily to needs of that kind, but I don't analyse it at a deep symbolic level. You can work deep without transference. Gerda Boyesen, for instance, does not work with transference, but she works at a very deep level.

PROCTOR: Do you regard yourself as a model for your clients?

OSBORN: Anybody who does not regard themselves as a model for their clients is kidding themselves. If we don't want to model anything, then we are modelling somebody who does not want to model anything. What this question does is to bring me up against the areas where I feel I am weak. There are lots of parts of me which I would like to work on. I give a very honest lip service to the usual things like honesty, openness, bringing myself into the relationship and so on. Quite often there are situations where I am not very good at that and that often comes into it too.

PROCTOR: You mean you are trying to model a human being?

OSBORN: Quite right – thank you! One thing I try to model is an ability to make one's own provisional working theories about oneself all the time. Using one's intelligence, using one's nut about what is going on in oneself and around one, and trusting one's view about that. Another thing I try to model is the idea that I am actually working on myself and that the self-regulation of an ongoing process is something that everybody actually has the power to do once they discover it.

I may make different choices in my own life from the ones I make in the role of counsellor or group leader, and that is partly to do with modelling. In the beginning of a relationship it seems to me part of being a human being that one is reserved about some parts of oneself. It could be very threatening for a client if we reveal all of ourselves as a counsellor straight away.

PROCTOR: What sort of behaviours do you expect, sanction, encourage in the client, and are you aware of positively conditioning certain communications and negatively conditioning others?

OSBORN: I don't like to think that I do that, but I know I do give the odd flicker of a smile or look of attention or glazed look. I feel much better about doing that in groups than I do in individual situations. In a group, a communication will get different responses from different people. If you don't support somebody at the time when they need it then somebody else is going to. In fact, if you support people all the time, you take away the responsibility from the other people for doing it. In an individual situation I feel a bit different.

PROCTOR: It's almost a closed system, isn't it?

OSBORN: Yes, there are times to actually inhibit my judgemental parts. I see negative conditioning as essentially a judgemental process, a punishing process, and in that sense it is basically against what I feel is the most fruitful approach to counselling which is an accepting one. I think the main quarrel I have is with the whole idea of 'conditioning' someone through isolating a single stimulus and response. I just don't believe that makes any sense in terms of human behaviour, which operates at a very complex level where every message has many meanings. Its main meaning is determined by the context and its symbolic nature. Most of that is excluded when you isolate a stimulus and a response. In conceptual terms, Behaviourist theory just does not work for me. It is mechanistic, and alienating in the sense that it separates the person from the conditioning expert. It ignores the self-developing, self-regulating capacities of people. I suppose it could be used differently. But then can you still call that conditioning? I can't forget the theory was developed on experimental rats. Noam Chomsky's review of B. F. Skinner's *Human Behaviour* in the journal *Language* is forty pages long and devastating.

PROCTOR: Are there any other patterns of interaction which you would identify as a process which you habitually recognise or make use of?

OSBORN: One thing which comes to my mind is the dynamic of an event. Each session and the total span of a counselling relationship has a kind of dynamic of its own. It has high spots and low spots – crescendos – it has some music of its own and a shape of its own. It is helpful for the client to be in touch with that and I draw attention to it. It is connected with the self-regulating process and it is helpful in terms of being in touch with one's rhythm, so at certain times it is not a good idea to take action, at other times it is the right moment. And learning to trust that. Also as a counsellor, accepting where the person is and trusting that even if you don't understand it – *particularly* if you don't understand it.

Another thing is the way that individuals are different in different situations and how they become part of a social organism. In one situation somebody may be effective and powerful and in another situation, weak and ridiculous. In one situation, somebody may be confronting and in another, accepting. They may take the role of father or at another time or place, the role of mother. Often people are pushed into that role by the situation. I want people to develop a consciousness of that going on.

The basis of the Laing school is to do with that – what people project onto you. In that way, I think it actually conflicts with what are becoming traditional 'new therapy' ideas – that you are totally responsible for yourself and self-determining, and so on. I support the Laing side. I do think that what other people project onto one is terribly important, particularly when one is a child or an infant, or maybe in the womb. I think it happens in groups, here and now, with adults, because certain people have more power given by the social structures of that situation. An example is the kind of evolution that women have gone through in the last few years. They have stopped thinking of themselves as being neurotic or hysterical and they have thought of themselves as being oppressed and they have started throwing off that oppression and gaining more power.

PROCTOR: Is 'consciousness raising' one of the interventions you make?

OSBORN: Certainly. I think joining a women's group, or it might be a Gay group, can sometimes be much more valuable than having private therapy.

PROCTOR: Are there responses that you have worked on being able to use effectively?

OSBORN: Yes, I have. I can remember one specific one, which is speaking in image language, in metaphors. I was impressed by it as a method used by Gunnar Hjelholt in a short two-hour demonstration T-group. I deliberately used to set myself times in groups when I talked only in image terms. I just said to myself 'for the next half hour I am not going to think of anything else except the images and the central image that are coming to me'. And I'd say them to the group every now and then. I think that the important thing about deciding to develop a particular way of working is simply allowing yourself not to use the things you think you are strong on.

PROCTOR: Are there any responses you have deliberately soft-pedalled?

OSBORN: I have deliberately soft-pedalled my explosiveness because with some people it really has a paralysing effect. Not as an overall part of me because I also think it is quite productive at times, but it has had some really bad effects.

PROCTOR: Do you see any demarcation between counselling and therapy within your framework? If so, what are the dangers of the uninitiated going beyond it? Let me add to that an illustrative question. Would you regard bodywork and work based on Reichian assumptions as appropriate when you are counselling or training?

OSBORN: I regard it as doing therapy. Bio-energetic massage, for instance, is a very special skill and quite additional to any natural healing hands one may have. I think that therapy does depend on special knowledge whereas in a sense I don't think counselling does. I don't mean to denigrate counselling when

I say that. To be a counsellor needs a lot of experience and skill. But the kind of language and the basis of the interaction that is used in counselling is actually something that is common. It is not one that is always *used*, and many people are so out of touch with it that it feels like special knowledge. But we are all expert human beings. We are not all expert therapists. What we have to learn, to be counsellors, is to actualise what we know as expert human beings. What we have to learn to become therapists is special knowledge in addition to that.

PROCTOR: What about the dangers of the uninitiated?

OSBORN: I don't like the whole business of initiating and certification and so on. So much has happened by people exploring things that they weren't initiated in and did not have any kind of certification in. But I recognise a therapist is obviously in a powerful position with some very powerful tools. Leboyer was asked about how he decided what to do when he put a baby in warm water. He refused to talk in terms of any specific skill. He always returned to his attitude – to regard that new born baby as a person and so long as you are in touch with that person and accepting that person the way they are, you are not going to do something that violates them. The only kind of initiation I want to see is in the ability to have that attitude. I don't know how we get that. Our habitual responses in ordinary life tend to be judgemental, solving, interpretative and so on, and they are a part of the system we live in. How many therapists have that attitude? And if they do, is it because they are isolating themselves from that system? I think there is just as much danger in therapy conducted by initiated people as there is by uninitiated people.

PROCTOR: It's interesting that counselling is going to set up as a profession at this point in time when quite a lot of people in the counselling world, but not by any means all, recognise the unsatisfactoriness of previous professional organisations, initiations, and professional mystifications, but also recognise that society has a responsibility for doing something to protect vulnerable people.

OSBORN: Yes. I don't complain about people trying to do that. I have no energy for doing it myself. I just want to press my view to make it as openly creative as possible. The world demands a standard and there is nothing one can do to deny that demand. We demand it ourselves. If somebody wants to come and work with me I try to find out how competent they are.

PROCTOR: Does the client group with which you work, or have worked, influence the way you view counselling?

OSBORN: I have done hardly any formal individual work for money in the last couple of years but I have a number of times worked very briefly with people whom I have met in the course of my ordinary life. Most of them would not be able to afford an ordinary therapist's fee. And I doubt whether they would want to get involved with something like the Health Service either. Well, that changed the way I worked to some extent. If you are a normal human being who is part of a personal circle, you are not setting yourself up as the expert knowledgeable Therapist who sits in a consulting room and so on. And the way I view things at present is that there is much more that we can all do for each other than we do at the moment.

PROCTOR: Do you have personal dilemmas or tensions in your counselling work?

OSBORN: I have a personal dilemma to do with being a highly educated, skilled person, in a certain set of areas, with a fair amount of intellectual power, and earning power; and, at the same time, feeling that the wielding of expertise, the being an expert as a role and the using of that earning power is actually something I don't much want to do because it conflicts with the social culture that I want to live in, or move towards. The culture that I want to move towards is one where there is great role flexibility, where people are able to change their jobs, where the divisions between the intellectual/academic and the practical/manual disappear. At the same time, even within the social direction that I believe in, I do believe in skill and I do believe in the need for competence, I believe in doing things well. That dilemma expresses itself a great deal, at every level, in the way I earn money or don't earn money, in the kind of job I do or don't do, in the way I have clients or don't have them and the kind of clients and colleagues I work with. You can see that I am myself moving through the kind of transition I've been talking about. I don't believe I am just projecting my own development on to the outside world. I think if you look around with open eyes you will see plenty of signs of the unfolding I've been describing, or something very like it. I have by no means resolved all this.

Part III

Exploring the Interviews

I   Relating to New Theory

RECENTLY in the Course I run, some students and I set up and participated in a series of workshops in which we looked at, and learned to practice, Behavioural Counselling and Reality Therapy. These two models have their differences in emphasis and outlook, but they combined together very usefully. The students had all had a good deal of practice in Rogerian counselling as well as in Gestalt therapy. After the first week, they were enthusiastic about the new workshops, but rather dazed. It seemed a sensible, effective and interesting way to work – but so had Rogerian and Gestalt, in the eyes of all but a few of them. I, as a trainer, was apparently equally involved in all of them. And yet, as one student said, it seemed like a completely different and even contradictory game – the rules were different, the assumptions different, the practice dramatically different.

This book of interviews may have the same effect on many readers. The contributors are all articulate, experienced and wise-seeming practitioners. On its own, any one of the interviews could be, if not definitive, at least an introduction to a sufficient account of the helping process. Each interview brings into sharp focus some simple basic axioms. Yet they are ten more or less distinct systems. Gestalt psychology (the theoretical base of Gestalt therapy) offers a useful framework for making sense of that kind of confusion. For example, a film is a very complex piece of work. As a whole, it is in itself a 'slice of life', abstracted and communicated through simulation and through the medium of moving film. It makes a sort of 'whole' (or gestalt) in itself. In order to edit it, or write a criticism of it, it would be possible to pick out smaller 'wholes' for consideration. These could be in various dimensions. They might be themes, incidents, single characters, the beginning, the ending. They might even be single frames viewed as separate entities.

In viewing each separate 'whole', it would be necessary to keep in awareness as much of the 'total whole' as possible, in order to edit in a way that retained consistency within the smaller, say, theme, but was also consistent within the larger context.

Showing all the separate 'wholes' alongside each other, separately, would not be showing the film. The film is more than the sum of its component 'wholes'. Equally, the film, although comprehensible within itself, is viewed within the context of awareness of the 'real world.' And of course the actors, while playing their parts, hold in awareness their 'own' lives, which in turn affect their performance.

If a film is that complex, the total world of human living and experiencing is infinitely more complex. Scholars long ago divided the study of man into separate compartments, to try to simplify and make possible such a massive undertaking. This dividing up into biology, psychology, sociology, history, the Arts, etc, does damage to the 'total whole', wherever that may be set. On the other hand, the vast increase in knowledge demands ever greater specialisation. Without specialisation we would not have the amount of knowledge about different processes and structures that we have. But the meanings we give them may be less full than they need be, if we are insufficiently aware of the smaller systems which are part of them and larger systems of which they are a part. Social work teaching and practice is an interesting example. Twenty years ago, trained social caseworkers mainly relied on insights derived from that partial field of study of the total human experience called psychology. In the last decade, they have increasingly made use of sociological insights. The meanings attached to their work, by social workers trained in that time, are often quite different from those of their older colleagues.

Continuing with the image of the film, counselling, in my imagination, is an undeveloped theme which weaves through and contacts many of the constituent 'wholes' of human experience in various dimensions. It relates to individuals, to groups, to institutions. It draws on many fields of study, and is a part theme of many professions. The contributors to this book all acknowledge that they are strands in that theme. By consenting to speak alongside each other, they tacitly affirm each other's right to some part in that theme. Each has specialised in a particular approach. Several of them have already made useful contacts with other approaches. Others share common origins.

The core interviews seem, to me, to be those which explore the Psychoanalytic, Rogerian, and Behavioural insights and practice. The three contributors who are responsible for those interviews have spent all of their considerable counselling experience developing, questioning and exploring the implications of that particular approach. They each carry a sub-theme, which may have the potential for developing the theme 'counselling' more fully. To carry their part strongly, they need to have specialised. The elegance of each of their formulations is very appealing. The impression they convey, of each being, in itself, a sufficient account, reminds us of the satisfactions we take in seeing a whole theme clearly. It can be almost painful to hold in mind that it represents only one perspective, one focus, one set of basic assumptions. Yet, taken separately, each could be deceptive and misleading as an insight about human social experience and the art of helping people.

In deciding how to provide a useful setting for the interviews, I experienced that tension. My need for my own closure – to tie everything up as neatly as possible into a single theme – was strong. To quote Ellen Noonan, I wanted an Access card to take the waiting out of wanting. To go for closure would have resulted in over-simplifying, and doing damage to, the variety of insights and dimensions presented. As yet, in my opinion, there is no single satisfying framework which could serve as even an interim statement. What does seem useful is to start by exploring whether the models relate laterally to each other, and if so, how.

I have done this in two ways. First I have looked at certain *dimensions* along which the various *theories* differ. Secondly, I have identified six of the very many possible *themes* which emerge out of the discussions of *counselling practice*, and looked at them in the light of the different frameworks. I hope in this way to open up those 'wholes' to each other, and to help readers begin to move about among the various models.

In addition, I have looked at the barriers which can interfere with being open to any new ideas. The most difficult part of training, for many students, is the initial questioning of their basic assumptions about people and social experience. In her interview, Pat Milner mentions the difficulties that this stage of training presented for her, while Dave Wilmott speaks of the release that the permission to 'think wider' afforded him, as a mature student. Since this book is an invitation to just such an exercise, I want to explore what is involved in that process.

Each of us can make our own theories and draw different conclusions from our own experience about what kind of species we are. But the language we use to make the theories, and the frames of reference we offer to our observations, to give them meaning, are the products of our social experience and our cultural heritage. If we were someone who forged new language and created a new frame of reference – 'if the world were *round*, how would those facts look?' – we would almost certainly suffer extreme pressure to relinquish such a hypothesis. Only if we were someone who could present our insight powerfully, back it well, and who lived at the right moment of history, when some new explanations were imperative, would we stand a chance of social validation for our vision.

Meanwhile, for the most part, we take for granted the rag bag of common sense assumptions in which we were brought up, relinquishing some of them as they prove ridiculous or inconvenient, and taking on board new ones that we are offered, that make fuller sense of our experience. If we accept the responsibility of intervening in other people's lives, it is important to know the assumptions on which our interactions with them are based. Otherwise, our actions may appear arbitrary to them and theirs to us and the uncertainty of the situation can lead to confusion rather than to helping and being helped.

What we are able to see and what sense we make of the world and human behaviour will be determined by the frame of reference we forge. It allows us to see and it prevents us from seeing. This dilemma can make people anxious. In the folk-song, an old woman, coming from market, went to sleep on the King's Highway. A beggarman cut her skirts up to her knees as she lay sleeping on the roadside. Partially 'unframed', when she awoke she began to weep and wail 'Dearie me, this is none of I'. In order to re-establish her identity, she relied on her dog Stout wagging his tail in welcome. When he began to bark, she began to cry 'Dearie me, this truly is not I.' In the same way, we depend to a greater extent than we usually realise on our mental clothes – the way we see the world – remaining stable. To feel that what we see out there is 'only perception' is alarming. What so clearly 'is' in one framework is not necessarily so looked at another way – maybe that woman was not possessed of a devil, as the Bible suggests, but sick; maybe not sick as the psychiatrists say, but driven crazy by unreliable and contradictory messages, as Laing says.

Nevertheless it is often possible to try out different frameworks for size, if some experience is puzzling. But there are certain very basic assumptions about the nature of man that we become socially invested in. Basic life styles, methods of working, the bringing up of children, attitudes to education, politics, and indeed every sphere of human interaction, are built on those assumptions. If those assumptions, which are more akin to belief, since so much becomes invested in them, prove faulty in practise, it takes a good deal of courage and discomfort to try out other sets of assumptions.

Basic Assumptions

There are five such sets of basic assumptions which figure, to a greater or lesser extent, within the models chosen for this book.

There are *Behavioural assumptions*. These are, firstly, that human beings are determined by their conditioning. If we were to achieve a high viewpoint and look down on the patterns below, we would see that each movement of any living organism, including a person, was determined by its prior conditioning responding to present stimuli. Choice is illusory. Secondly, they are that only what is observable and measurable is reliable evidence. It may well be that the stimuli to which the human organism responds are *subjective*. So phantasies, ideas, etc and the person's *perceptions* of outside stimuli may be the effective stimuli, but until those are measurable and observable, behavioural theory does not take account of them. By staying with the measurable and observable it is assumed that we can monitor our 'changing behaviour' behaviour and adjust it reliably.

Skinner, the main proponent of this philosophy, has been attacked and refuted many times. However, there are very many Behavioural psychologists. These basic assumptions offer them a sufficient enough explanation about the nature of human beings on which to base a consistent and apparently effective model of counselling and therapy.

I think these assumptions are acknowledged, by many holding them, to be partial. They attend to the simple and avoid the paradoxical. In his interview Dougal Mackay appeared to act as if he and others were *responsbile* for making *choices*, two words which are meaningless in Behavioural theory. But he set aside that paradox and attended to the concrete. In the same way he 'knew' that respect for his client and enthusiasm for his method were important elements in therapy, although these are not easily measurable or monitorable variables. It is this decision, to disregard such paradox because it is not amenable to measurement, which frustrates and angers many practitioners who work on different assumptions.

The traditional Freudian assumptions are that man is inherently anti-social. The individual is a product of the biological drives of sex and aggression. These must always be at war with the social needs for control and co-operation which the child internalises. A man is the product thrown up by these conflicting drives. Since he is also at the mercy of his perceptions – how he sees the world is a reflection of his inner conflicts and defensive mechanisms – he is ultimately determined by his history.

In its determinism, this is similar to the Behavioural view. As Dougal Mackay pointed out, transference, in Behavioural terms, is the triggering of acquired child-like behaviour by stimuli which are akin to those provided by parental figures. However, in the Freudian view, outside, objective stimuli do not exist. What we perceive is personal to us, and is determined by our inner fantasies.

Ellen Noonan does not entirely share this set of assumptions. While seeing the world in many ways as Freud did, she sees sex and aggression, when destructive of self and others, as drives perverted by harsh and unsympathetic environmental forces. Her basic assumptions, like Winnicott's, seem to come more into the category of the basic assumptions which I explore under the label 'existential'. If man can be freed to view the world more nearly as it is, rather than he fears it to be or would have it be, he can lead a life more satisfying to himself and others.

The third set of assumptions are the assumptions of *humanistic psychology*. The majority of the models in this project are based on those. Carl Rogers is a major contributor to the body of theory which has grown out of humanistic premises and Developmental Counselling develops and extends his ideas.

Eric Berne, in developing Transactional Analysis, took Psychoanalytic insights, but altered them by presupposing a humanistic model of man. Harvey Jackin's model of Co-counselling is humanistic, as is the Reality Therapy approach of Glasser and Satir.

Humanistic psychology suggests that human beings are inherently social and, as a species, need and care about each other.

If they are nurtured and brought up in such a way that th
spect themselves and are free to trust and respect the humanity
of others, they will use their aggression and sexuality in the
service of 'loving and being loved, taking charge of their lives
and being part of larger systems, and understanding their
experience and being understood' (to paraphrase John Heron).

This set of assumptions does not emphasize the reality (or
common human perception) that good resources for physical
and psychological survival are scarce and have to be competed
for. Nor does it concentrate on the way in which social systems
are mostly built out of, and maintained by, quite different
assumptions. That perception is in no way denied. Pat Milner
points out that Rogers, for instance, has worked hard to alter the
education system so that it offers the experiences which allow
people to realise their human potential. Glasser also has turned
his energy to recreating educational systems, and Satir to education for families. For the most part, however, the assumption is
that if individuals are realising themselves fully, they will
automatically create fitting environments for themselves and
others.

The fourth set of assumptions represented in these interviews
are those of *existentialism*. They are quite similar to those of
humanistic psychology, but are more present-centred and action-
oriented. They do not posit humanity as a species which necessarily has a potential programme for successful social evolution.

There are two branches of the existential river. The *European*
one rose out of the bitter experience of aggrandisement, suffering
and death – of space and resources diminishing, and of man's
inhumanity. In this view, man by his awareness of death is
anxious and guilt-ridden, and by his need to be part of a larger
more substantial whole, is open to commit all sorts of savagery in
the maintenance of the group, or the herd. Caught between this
fear of personal freedom and fear of death, he is in a condition of
alienation. Only by faith in himself, or paradoxically, in some
wider purpose, can he create himself every moment, and live in
contact with himself and others by virtue of recognising and
owning his choices.

The *American existential* branch was nurtured in the still
abundant and hopeful soil of California, not yet in the sixties
overtaken by our modern puritans, the ecologists. Romantic
and almost hedonist, it still centres on the present moment and

man's capacity for making his life by his choices. But in this model, anything capable of being imagined is capable of being realised. What man does by his choices can be to fulfill human potential, not merely to survive in a less alienated manner.

What both these existential variations imply is the need to take action to change systems which increase man's alienation from himself and others. Both stress an individual's responsibility for, and dependency on, not only himself but also any system with which he feels identified. The English tributary of European existentialism, represented by R. D. Laing, has especially stressed the way in which confusing messages, offered by families and wider systems – for instance schools – effectively maintain people in confusion and submission.

Eugene Heimler represents the European existential view, although by his action-oriented therapy he transcends the expectation that all we can do is to learn to live more creatively with our pain.

Gestalt therapy represents the American existential view, coming as it does out of Esalen, the centre of the encounter movement.

The Radical perspective of Tom Osborn indicates the extent to which the existential viewpoint is consistent with radical political assumptions. The existentialist is centred in the insecure security of the here-and-now. This perhaps allows for the possibility of 'mental and social clothing' being disrupted without a consequent fear of lack of identity. Ideas, assumptions, and even social systems can be allowed to change if the individual is living in the present. It is also of interest that the existential view is consistent with, and often goes along with, an appreciation of Eastern philosophy. Both rely on following and becoming part of process, rather than on structures of any sort. Neither predict 'an outcome' and both emphasize the art of living in the present, rather than planning for or worrying about the future.

The fifth set of assumptions are *Marxist assumptions*. These are that the real, or engineered, scarcity of resources in the world is the basic determinant of human, social and thus personal life. The struggle to maintain power over economic resources is a continuing struggle. This power is maintained by control of communications and social 'myths' as well as in more direct ways. These myths, and the social structures built on them, are built into people's personalities, and serve to blinker them and frighten

them when they consider other ways of living. Thus someone
with a personal problem – marital, economic, study or whatever
it may be – cannot be viewed as purely 'a case for personal
counselling,' but as someone who is prevented from ending his
frustration or suffering by being blinkered to some of the
possibilities, and confused as to the realities. To the non-Marxist
cry of horror at counselling or therapy being used as a political
forum, the Marxist response is that that happens all the time.
Counsellors, like social workers, are by their nature involved as
agents of covert social control. If there were no safety valves for
the escape of human suffering in steam, the revolution would
have come and created less alienating structures. Counsellors,
social workers and psychiatrists are today's opiate of the
people.

Tom Osborn shares some of these Marxist assumptions. At
the same time, he points out that very few people are both high
on sensitivity and understanding of themselves and other individuals and small groups, and also skilled at understanding
and using the political processes. Because of that separation,
it has seemed possible for radicals to delude themselves and
believe that, come the Revolution, politics will change people.
However, the very nature of internal personality structures,
which mirror outer structures, means that the revolutionary
finds it hard to create something different from that which he
experienced and from which he has not been internally freed.

So the wheel of assumptions comes back full circle, to the
power of conditioning, and the way in which external structures,
in their turn mirror, and are maintained by, individuals intent
on keeping their own internal worlds intact.

Despite the range of assumptions touched on in these interviews, all the counsellors appear to share a respect for individuals
and a persistent mild optimism and they make clear that they
believe individuals can, if they choose, find ways of taking charge
of their own lives, or changing their behaviour in desired
directions.

The theories discussed in the interviews differ in other dimensions as well as in basic assumptions. These differences are not so
integral with 'life-style'. It is possible, for instance, to change
viewpoint, historical perspective, time orientation, and focus
quite easily. They are 'mental clothing' to which we become
attached, but we are not usually socially invested in them.

Different Perspectives

Theoretical models are based on differing perspectives. There are three basic stances from which the contributors view the world. Traditional Psychoanalytical and Transactional Analysis models are derived from a view of the world that allows patterns within and between people to appear.

The Behavioural model derives from the scientific/objective stance. Observations are those of an outside observer, looking at what presents itself, either from the front, or from the side.

The rest of the models are all based on a phenomenological vewpoint. That is the world is viewed as if the observer were an essential part of the scene he is viewing. Everything that presents, out there, is at the same time in interaction with, and has personal and cultural meanings for, the observer. There is no true objectivity.

Reality therapists and Behaviourists share a number of *assumptions* in common about the changing of behaviour. The difference between the two is the phenomenological *stance* of the Reality therapist, and the scientific/objective *stance* of the Behaviourist.

The T.A. model holds basically humanistic *assumptions* about the nature of man, but shares the analytical *stance* with the traditional Psychoanalyst. In the Object Relations model of Ellen Noonan, Psychoanalytical insights are retained, but seem to be enhanced by perspectives from an increasingly phenomeno-logical stance.

The philosophical stance of viewing the *world* may not be the only way counsellors using a particular model 'look' at their *client*, in practice. Although phenomenologists may predomin-antly see the world through their clients eyes, they are some-times wholly in their own experiencing, and share, with their client, views out of their own 'windows'.

Both Pat Milner and Gaie Houston talk about this. Reality therapists, Developmental counsellors and Behaviourists, in practice, seem to move between looking at their clients world through their eyes and with the eyes of an objective observer, or consultant. The Psychoanalytical practitioner may often look from the underneath, up, at what is happening between her and her clients. But she will also spend time seeing the world as her client sees it. So *practitioners* interact with clients from a variety of stances. The *philosophical* stance is the stance for gathering data and drawing conclusions. The *theory* is made out of the view from that stance.

Different Focuses

Since the theoretical models discussed here are considered in relation to counselling, the 'range of convenience' of the models does not need to be extensive. On the whole they use telescopic or close-up lens rather than fish-eye, although I have deliberately, in the questionnaire, asked people to try out their fish-eye lens. It is apparent that some are more accustomed to doing so than others. For instance, Dougal Mackay firmly believes a lens which focuses on sets, or even items, of human behaviour to be the only appropriate lens for a therapist.

Rogerian Counselling focuses almost exclusively on how individuals bring the intrapersonal into the interpersonal arena.

From the analytical stance, the range of convenience of Psychoanalysis and T.A. is wider. Both can be used to analyse wider social systems, but for the purpose of use in individual or group counselling, the range of convenience covers intrapersonal and interpersonal processes.

Developmental Counselling, with its high awareness of the cultural frameworks and systems within which individuals develop, has a range of width, from the telescopic lens on individual behaviour, to the wider range which encompasses individuals within social systems. Social Functioning is similar, starting with a view that holds in focus the whole individual within the social roles that he occupies, although within that range, smaller areas can be picked out for focus.

Co-Counselling is somewhat wider. It focuses on the details of processes of discharging distress but it also widens out to see the individual within his social setting. Reality Therapy has a range which starts where the individual is in the world, and includes the social systems of which he is an integral part.

Gestalt, by its emphasis on the fullest possible awareness has a highly flexible lens, widening and narrowing according to what process or systems become figure and ground. The Radical perspective is also wide set, since the study of social systems is seen as essential for the understanding of the social experience of individuals.

Time focus is another way in which theories can differ. Which aspect of time is seen as most significant follows from the various basic assumptions. The psychoanalytical assumptions necessarily concentrate on the significance of the past for the present experience of an individual. The humanist and existential assumptions, concentrating as they do on the individuals acceptance and affirmation of himself as he is now, focus on the present. The past and the future are seen as aspects of present awareness. Behavioural assumptions, which stress the possibility of adjusting the environment to create desired altered behaviour, focus on the future as the end product, and the present as a means to that end. Marxist assumptions, too, concentrate on analysis and action in the present as the means to a desired future.

These differing time focuses do seem to have direct significance for practice. While a counsellor is working within a single set of assumptions, it is inconsistent to alter the time focus of the work. That is not to say that a wider framework may not allow practitioners to use different 'pairs of spectacles' with different clients, or with the same client at different times. For instance, working within the framework of Developmental Counselling it is consistent to start with what manifests in the present, move to dynamic understanding which includes focusing on the past and then change to the Behavioural focus of working in a structured way towards future objectives.

Relating to Differing Historical Perspectives

One of the ways in which I am reminded of my age is in looking at the fashions in social work. When I trained on the first generic social work course in this country, we were quite preoccupied that, on completing our training, we should be recognised as professionals. We were unthinkingly scornful of 'do-gooders' – voluntary lady bountifuls who we considered were only in it for the fulfillment of their personal needs. Since then I have seen the wheel turn full circle, with social workers being scorned for their alienating superiority and volunteers being found more effective in helping people, because of the therapeutic value of simple goodwill and respect for others. At the same time, I have seen psychiatrists turning from being considered 'the experts' to being considered arch-confusers and the enemy of all men of goodwill (except when required to help with someone whose bizarre or dangerous behaviour is beyond the time and patience limit of anyone who cannot offer a permanently manned place of asylum.)

Such changes in social perceptions have much more to do with our human ability to notice what is lacking or inadequate over and above what is present and adequate, than in changing social role performance. As we swill from polarity to polarity like water in a bowl, some of what is real advance gets laid down and integrated. In these interviews, contributors acknowledge the extent to which the net of the Welfare State frees many people from the necessity of using all their energy, just to stay alive and fed. At the same time, its presence allows us to see its short-comings and even its pathology.

Most of the models discussed here show evidence of reactivity. The Freudian model itself was a reaction to the moralistic approach to mental illness. However, it was conceived in a medical, clinical setting where 'illness' was the verbal package appropriate for bizarre or confused behaviour, and diagnosis, prognosis and treatment were the ways of relating to illness. This convention was not questioned by Freud – it did not need to be. His loosened and altered perceptions allowed fresh knowledge and understanding to come out of practice.

Based on this new information, new hypotheses emerged and other aspects of psychoanalytic theory were questioned. The humanists and existentialists came to feel less threatened by, the more trusting of, the inner space opened up to exploration by Freud. They began to trust people to make sense of their own experience in their own imagery, rather than making the territory safe by having it parcelled up in an imagery derived from Freud, or Klein. Moreover, they were at a place where they could afford to pursue the avenue of the difference between knowing 'about' what is happening 'to' a person and fully experiencing what is happening 'in' a person. In this exploration they were all beholden to Moreno, the developer of Psychodrama, for every psychodramatic technique mentioned by any contributor here – two chair work, five chair work, role-play – was first thought of by Moreno. It was his pioneer work that found the means to bring the past into the present, and the internal into the external, in ways that allowed people to re-experience their past, or own their present, rather than merely 'getting insight'.

Behavioural therapists, impatient with the introspection and subjectivity of academic psychology and clinical psychoanalysis, reacted by stressing external observation and objectivity. Reality therapy and Social Functioning, unsatisfied by the pace of change in traditional therapies and the unsatisfactoriness of being unable to measure, demonstrate and take satisfaction in that change, turned to working on action, rather than with symbols – words, fantasies etc. Also, impatient with the 'ivory tower' attitude to real life consequences, Glasser reacted in Reality Therapy by always checking on possible consequences of change, ahead of time.

Co-Counselling and Radical Therapists became aware of the dependency inherent in the medical model. So long as any frightening and bizarre feelings and experiences are considered the domain of experts, individuals are not helped to learn to relate to their own experiencing, and feel safe with it. These practitioners therefore put a lot of energy into demystifying the 'how' of the therapeutic process, and the role of the 'therapist'. Developmental Counselling is the model which is not reactive, but rather integrative. It takes the models which are around and which work – the reflective model of Rogers and the action based Behavioural model – and mixing with those the post-Freudian understandings of life tasks at ages and stages, it offers a sensitive, practical counselling model of wide applicability. Again, however, it is a model that could only be created at a certain moment in the history of counselling.

It was interesting to me how many of my contributors responded to the question about history in a personal way. I had originally intended it to be cultural/historical – how, and in relation to what other trends, did this model get developed?

It seems to me that their accounts of how they, personally, came to adopt a model does represent the history of its cultural development. Each new generation and culture works over old, perhaps eternal, dilemmas and polarities in its own language, symbols and action choices. Each individual, caught up personally in those dilemmas and polarities, addresses them personally in his own personal language, symbols and action choices. Free-will versus determinism; morality versus utility; classicism versus romanticism; structure versus process; the individual versus the collective; conservation versus change; the intuitive versus the rational. These are not only polarities which are represented in the various theoretical approaches, they also represent personal choices for each contributor.

Summary

In summary, relating to *new theories* may produce anxiety. We may be required, temporarily, to suspend our basic assumptions, in which we are socially invested, to explore quite different assumptions. Less drastically, we may be required to alter our viewpoint on the world, to expand or narrow our habitual lens, or alter our comfortable focus. Last year's accepted truths may be being questioned in the light of this years fresh insights. The reward is the possibility of altered, enlarged and more flexible perceptions.

The anxious stage of relating to new theories and wider awarenesses seems usually to be temporary, provided the encounter is one of choice, and not enforced.

If, for a while, an attractive new insight is tried out for size – used, tested, explored – the parts that genuinely enhance experience and practice become integrated, and the parts that confuse, or do not sit naturally amongst existing mental and practical furniture, wither away.

Thereafter, that pair of spectacles becomes another pair among a range to choose from. Occasionally this choice may be conscious – 'let's try Reality Therapy' or 'if I looked at this through T.A. spectacles, would it make more sense?' More frequently, the choice happens at the intuitive level, below the threshold of conscious awareness. Just as we have learned when to wear our 'wife' spectacles, when our 'teacher' spectacles, and when our 'consumer' spectacles intuitively, so we have learnt to know intuitively when to wear our Rogerian spectacles and when our Behavioural ones.

2 Using Theory to Inform Practice

THE central purpose behind conducting the interviews in this book is the encouragement of more creative and better informed counselling practice. It seems to me important that counsellors should be able to share, both with their clients and their colleagues and peers, what they do and how they do it. However, it is even more important that they are actually counselling as effectively and as satisfyingly as they can, both for their clients and for themselves. The first section of the questionnaire, and the first section of this part of the book, is designed to allow readers to clarify their theoretical understanding, and to help them communicate it in an orderly fashion. The following sections of the questionnaire, and this particular section of the book, are designed to help readers develop the 'hows' of their practice by looking at some of the 'whys' about which individual approaches are particularly clear. From the preceding section, it is clear that most of the different approaches are fairly restricted in their range of perspectives, in their focus and even in their basic assumptions. Yet, if their ideas are useful within that range, it seems unlikely that they are not also applicable in other areas.

In this section, therefore, I have selected various themes which run through all the interviews, and by looking at them in the light of the different models, I have tried to suggest how they are amenable to being opened up, laterally, to each other. At the same time, I have tried to stay clear about when I think there are real, and possibly unresolvable, differences of view and approach. As I said in the Introduction, useful communication between counsellors, as between people, depends on seeking for consensus where dissension is more apparent and also on openly confronting those differences which on the surface may look unimportant, but which are actually of basic significance.

The themes I have selected are in three different dimensions. The first two – *safety* and *power* – are elements in what is usually talked about as 'the counselling relationship'. I did not use that expression in the questionnaire, because I thought it was such a diffuse and much-worked concept, that it was likely to obscure rather than further communication at this stage. In the interviews, these two 'sub-themes' are explored through the questions in the second section of the questionnaire – The Game Rules of Counselling – and in the question on climate in the third section of the questionnaire – The Game Tactics of Counselling.

The next three themes – *feeling*, *thinking* and *doing* – are significant areas of focus in the various models. Each approach facilitates change through working directly on one or more of these processes. These themes are explored in the third section of the questionnaire, largely through the questions on focus and processes.

The last two themes are in the area of definition and accountability – *monitoring*, and *counselling and therapy*. Definitions of counselling are explored in section two of the questionnaire – through the questions on how the counselling role differs from other roles, and what the mutual responsibilities are. It is also the subject of section four – The Limits of Counselling. The theme of monitoring was not explored in the questionnaire at all, although several contributors talk about it indirectly. In retrospect this has seemed a significant omission, and I want to make that omission good by looking at the issues which the interviews have raised for me, when thinking about actual, rather than token, accountability.

These themes are only six out of the very many that it would be possible to label and isolate. I think, however, that had I selected say, structuring; counselling interventions; conditions for change; significant change processes; etc, very much of the discussion would have covered the same common ground. I suggest that readers select their own themes which are of particular interest to them, and work them in a similar way. It is probable that even similar themes, explored by someone wearing different 'spectacles' to mine, would look very different.

Safety

Whatever is seen as the particular focus of the counselling task, all the practitioners in this book require, of their clients, a willingness to reflect on themselves in their situation and a preparedness for change. This process – of taking a look at themselves, and of resolving to change in the way they are in relation to themselves, or in the way they interact in their social situation – is in itself potentially anxiety creating. Change always involves the relinquishing of the known however unsatisfactory, for the less known or the unknown. This much is agreed by all the contributors, and in response to this anxiety, each wish to offer a situation which is experienced as safe for their clients, in order to facilitate this process. What each approach perceives as the particular purpose of the safety can differ, however, and arising out of those different perceptions, different degrees of safety are considered useful, and different ways of communicating safety are utilised:

For the Behaviourally based approaches, the client is required to talk about the dissatisfactions he has with his own behaviour, and to share in setting up a programme of graduated change. The safety required is such that will result in the client feeling 'totally relaxed with me, and able to speak freely.' (Mackay)

Most of the humanist or existential models are focused on the area of feeling and sensation. Their practitioners are highly aware of the extent to which the handling and communication of strong or ambivalent feelings and sensations is discouraged in most sub-cultures in which formal counselling is likely to be practiced. They are also very conscious that when a person first comes for counselling he is likely to be experiencing strong, confusing and ambivalent feelings. They therefore consider that there is a need for a policy of 'positive discrimination' in the direction of accepting and validating the experience of a client, in the form in which it is shared. 'The objective is to provide a situation in which a person feels safe enough to lower the defences which he's made to protect him against thoughts, feelings, events that threaten him, by creating an atmosphere in which he feels accepted, understood and valued . . . to give freedom to look at real feelings and thoughts which are often fairly negative and have often had to be denied or distorted'. (Milner)

The Psychoanalytical approach recognizes the need for safety for the same reasons. However, being more aware of 'what has gone wrong', and of the recalcitrance of defensive structures which people erect, it is less optimistic that just an experience of safety will allow a client to discard defences which have worked well for him at some stage, and which still protect him from discomfort and pain. For this to happen, a certain level of anxiety is required, produced by the counsellor's ability to maintain a confronting relationship which is '. . . not necessarily aggressive . . . a kind of doggedness, a persistence, a refusal to let them avoid an issue'. (Noonan)

Associated with these perceptions of the need for safety, there seem to be three discernible styles of communicating to the client that he can feel safe. Clearly these three are points on a spectrum, rather than distinct entities. It is interesting to consider whether they are necessarily associated with particular approaches, or whether particular approaches attract counsellors with personality characteristics which 'show' in distinctive styles.

At one end is an optimistic, almost salesmanlike approach to the client (except that it includes an element of respect for the client which is often lacking in the sales interaction). It employs a light-hearted, humorous discounting of trepidation and pessimism. It stresses the possibility of quick and visible results, and of the satisfaction that this offers to the client. 'I am here to have fun and to take care of myself, and I expect you to do the same'. (Dave Wilmott)

At the other end of the spectrum is the serious reflective approach which allows ample space for exploration and discovery. The safety offered is that of *not* having present anxiety, fear of, and reluctance for change discounted, but rather hearing it treated very seriously. It stresses the satisfaction of recognizing and grappling with the apparently irrational parts of the personality which resist efforts at change. For some seriously disturbed clients, the climate offered is one of simple acceptance and containment, but for the most part '. . . there has to be a certain amount of anxiety. . . . You have to mobilise a lot of energy. It's not a secure, comfortable relationship at all'. (Noonan)

Somewhere along the spectrum fall the other approaches, most of them characterized by warmth and trust. They do not discount ambivalence towards change, and all offer space for exploration and discovery. However, unlike the psychoanalytic approach, they all offer, at least at the outset, a complete absence of anything which could be received as structuring or evaluating the client's experience in terms other than those of the client's own imagery and language, 'safety, security and support, and deep unqualified affirmation of the worth of a human being.' (Heron) Particularly the Rogerian, Gestalt, and Radical models stress the satisfaction to the client of learning to trust his own processes, no matter how convoluted or irrational they may appear, for only processes which are 'owned' are able to be the occasions of choice and change. 'Until someone has got a feel of what they are doing to themselves, they are not in a position to move on'. (Houston)

Apart from differences in style and intent with regard to safety, the differing approaches employ different structures and methods. One of the most commonly used safety structures is the 'contract'.

The word 'contract' is used by most of the contributors, but I think it has two different meanings. For the *action* based models, a contract can consist of an overt, and more or less formally entered into, agreement, specifying particular learning objectives. These objectives arise out of the clients own wishes, and the exercise of defining them is clearly reassuring to both client and practitioner. It provides the safety of defined limits and clear objectives, lowering present anxiety and making the concept 'change' something concrete and tangible.

In the Reality Therapy and Behavioural models, an initial contract is drawn up in the opening session. However, in the models which have changing behaviour as only one component of the counselling task, such contract-making may be considered premature. Michael Reddy speaks of the possibility of buying into an 'ought' contract, Tom Osborn speaks of the contract needing to be built up gradually, as the possibilities and the responsibilities become clearer, and Eugene Heimler does not administer his Scale of Social Functioning, on which agreements about what to work on are based, until he is sure that the client will see the Scale as for his own information, rather than for 'experts' to evaluate him by. (Heimler does not like or use the word 'contract' because he dislikes its overtones of formality.)

For the *process* based models – those which, like Rogerian, Gestalt and psychoanalytic, focus on learning to become acquainted with the process of full experiencing – such a contract approach is more difficult, if not impossible. An objective which states 'to become more in touch with my own experiencing' is not useful, and in that it can be a recipe for reinforcing 'I am never quite good enough', it can be positively harmful.

So in this context, the 'contract' describes an informal establishing of the mutual expectations, ground rules and general area of work.

During the first or second session, the counsellor displays the way of working she has 'on offer' – 'sets up the stall' – both verbally and by modelling and conditioning. This conditioning is not covert. By her responses, the counsellor focuses the client on the areas that she has told the client she thinks are useful to focus on. Every contributor talks of finding ways to explain his or her wares, and of encouraging the client to choose to 'buy in' or to 'buy out'. This is clearly important, since one to one counselling is potentially a 'closed system'. Michael Reddy and Tom Osborn work almost entirely in groups mostly to prevent 'offering help' becoming coercive. Dave Wilmot suggests that by not taking clients wishes into account, social workers often covertly condition clients to dependency. In other settings, Behavioural techniques are used to reinforce 'acceptable behaviour' as Dougal Mackay is uncomfortably aware. So each contributor explains to the client their particular method (or, in the case of T.A., language) and they spell out, progressively, their understanding of the counsellor and client role.

It comes out clearly in the interview with Tom Osborn that the client role is not one with which many people are familiar. The idea, even, of *talking to explore* rather than to please, inform, etc is not understood. Most counsellors have had training or experience in developing their counsellor role so that it is comfortable and familiar to them. In so doing, they may have come to make covert assumptions about the 'good' client and the 'bad' client. When clients do not know what behaviour is expected of them, they are likely to feel at a loss. At such a time, they will exhibit, beautifully, their customary wary and defensive postures. They are especially likely to exhibit lack of trust and unpreparedness to engage themselves fully in changing the way they are and act. Gaie Houston spells out the dilemma of the non-interpretive therapist who delights in creating this exhibition of defensiveness and is then thrown back, in desperation, on interpretation to lever the client out of his safety position. The corollary to the Rogerian emphasis on providing a safe climate is that clients will take care of their own safety in their own way, if we do not help establish a safe environment.

The concept of *systematic desensitisation* on which so much Behaviour Therapy was based can be extended usefully to make better sense of how different counsellors establish a climate of safety. Behaviourists are interested in stimuli 'out there' to which a client is phobic. Psychoanalytically oriented counsellors are interested in the *phantasies* associated with external and internal stimuli to which a client is phobic, and which trigger apparently 'irrational' behaviour. It seems to me that when a client comes for counselling there may be here and now stimuli to which he is phobic. Through generalisation (another concept from Behavioural theory) the counsellor may be reminiscent of all authority figures. Or by emitting 'stimuli' close to those of a particular parent etc, she may be experienced as the immediate bringer of fear, or, what is sometimes just as frightening, a bringer of hope. So however much the counsellor may try to divest herself of similarities to possibly feared stimuli, she may miss the mark for a particular client (although I think a sensitive counsellor has an intuitive 'feel' for what approach is least threatening to an individual client). The Rogerian approach seems to me to be an intuitive way of allowing a client to set up his own internal 'anxiety hierarchy' in the face of such fear. If a client is allowed to present himself in his own way, he may sit by the door in the first interview, side-ways on the second, face-to-face but eyes down the third, and full-face the fourth. A Behaviorist might point out that process later on, so that the client learns to understand and trust his own processes and feels self-rewarding. Conversely, it would be very consistent for a Behaviorist to work initially on helping the client systematically approach the therapist.

The same principles apply in the Rogerian and Gestalt approach to learning to experience, more fully and clearly, feeling and sensation. For very many people in the Anglo-Saxon cultures, the sensing and feeling mode has been, systematically, negatively conditioned or extinguished. Rogerian and Gestalt methods give clear 'permissions' (in T.A. language) for clients to feel and to sense.

The danger area is demarked and mapped verbally, and the counsellor has the client's permission to focus him within the mild, bearable danger area. The counsellor then allows a client to move in and out of the high danger area of his feelings and sensing as he is able. High danger areas are approached, recognised, and 'owned' (Gestalt) when and as the client elects. Meanwhile the ways in which he interrupts himself are also experienced and valued for the safety they have offered. In the same way, Transactional Analysis, by spelling out, at the start, that Games and racket feelings are the result of decisions that were made in the past, when the information that the small child had was inadequate, seeks to offer clients clear choices about whether or not they wish to relinquish a particular 'safety device'. Having recognized his 'pay-off' in the present, a client may decide not to relinquish some of his Games.

So these interviews suggest that there are many ways of approaching, and being with, a frightened person. In practice, I believe that the most effective way of allowing a fearful person to start on his way towards exploration and change will depend on the two people in the situation, rather than on theory. What theory can do is to ready the counsellor, through her increased awareness, to respond more flexibly. For anyone, when he risks approaching some little known or unknown 'expert' for help knows at some level what safety he requires and what structuring feels safe for him, and he will communicate that in many subtle ways. If the counsellor has sensitivity and self-awareness, she will respond appropriately to that communication. What the ideas talked about here can do is to increase 'the range of behaviour' which she has at her disposal to express that response.

Power

The word power is not popular with counsellors. Many of them say that they do not like the idea of having power, so they choose to work in a 'non-directive' style. However, none of the contributors in this book feel that it is possible to deny that the counsellor is experienced as having power, by the client, at the start of most counselling encounters.

The counsellor occupies a social role similar to that of other professionals who frequently 'reward' either overtly, or covertly, deferential behaviour (the doctors and social workers of whom Dougal Mackay and Dave Wilmot speak). The client brings with him into the relationship both the needs and hopes which have been unfulfilled by other powerful people in his life, and the consequent 'holes' in his own perception of himself – the central Psychoanalytic insight. He brings his 'generalized conditioned responses' to such powerful hope or fear carriers – the parallel Behavioural concept. Even if he does not wish to act dependently, he may never have learned a way to be interdependent, as opposed to dependent or independent. (Tom Osborn) The counsellor in imagination, and hopefully in reality, has some powerful resources, to give (or perhaps withhold.) She is almost certainly seen as having some answers. The client comes for help when he is feeling confused, distressed or unskillful and the counsellor at that time is unlikely to be experiencing, or at any rate expressing, low self-esteem, 'Let's face it, I seem to be coping better than him'. (Mackay)

So the issue does not appear to be whether the counsellor has, or is perceived to have, power, but how she can most usefully relate to it, use it and share it. Presumably people deny power because that word so often implies coercion and manipulation. It can be used in both these ways in the secret and potentially closed system of the counselling relationship. However, reading through these interviews, it seems that it can also be used to assist people in the direction they want to go, to prevent people going where they do not want to go, to support people while they are discovering where they want to go, and to share with people so that they can get there themselves.

Counsellors are usually invested with some *authority* – that is they have appointed positions in schools, colleges, counselling centres, Health Centres, hospitals etc. In many other cases they wear another hat, or hats, as well as their counselling one – doctor, nurse, teacher, social worker, priest etc. Not infrequently, with that other hat on, they have power to give and withhold tangible rewards and punishments, or else they are clearly identified with those who do. Francesca Inskipp points out how hard it is for a school counsellor to detach herself from the more familiar teacher role, and Pat Milner states that she will never perform a dual role, though others do. In school, children are systematically conditioned to obey for most of their life, and considerable sanctions are employed to discourage initiative, as many contributors point out when they talk about our education system. Initially, when he enters the counsellor's room, the child is unlikely to know that this situation will 'reward' quite different behaviours. Even when he realises that, he may still feel relatively powerless, since the only other behaviour he knows is probably independence. The ability to use and respond to resources and information offered by 'experts' in a straight forward, non-deferential way, and to appraise and evaluate it for its appropriateness, is one that very few people are ever taught informally, and even fewer formally. Until this particular skill, or trick, has been acquired, the counsellor cannot share her power, however much she may wish to do so. 'The first time he will say "yes", that is what I said" ... Later he will say 'Yes, but come to think of it ...' Once this process of self-observation begins, then I would predict that the possible outcome will be O.K.... Over a number of sessions if it doesn't work, then I would predict failure.' (Heimler.) While this learning is taking place, the counsellor seems to use her power to provide safety, and to act as a kind of battery, until by using new ways of working, the client creates a more efficient dynamo for himself.

For *resources*, the counsellor has some skill and knowledge which she cannot easily share fully with her client. The kind of things mentioned by most contributors are specialised experience, through life and training, of people in difficulty or distress, and self-awareness when working as a counsellor; and also an ability developed with time and training, to listen and to be sensitive to her client's communications.

This itself may provide a powerful atmosphere, and can give rise to hopes which the counsellor does not want, or is not able to fulfill. 'It may be the first time in their lives they've experienced this sort of friendly relationship and they expect much more than the counsellor is able or willing to give'. (Inskipp) Her experience in other counselling situations, the concepts she has met and her own comparative ease with feelings, embarrassment etc, in the client, are likely to give rise to the hope that here is someone with *answers* to offer. The lowering of these expectations and the withdrawal from a position of perceived power of this sort is done in different ways by different contributors. Pat Milner, for instance, says that it is not appropriate in the first interview to say 'I do not have any answers'. That is what the client has come for, and he will only be confused if he is disabused of that idea before he can begin to glimpse other possibilities. The 'setting up stall' phase of counselling, during which the counsellor shares with the client the way that she works, and possibly makes a contract, is not just about providing safety. It is also a 'modelling' of the way that this kind of opportunity could be used by the client – an open demonstration of real skills and knowledge which are offered for sharing, as and when the client is able to join in. In Transactional Analysis language, the counsellor refuses to be 'hooked' by the client's Adapted Child, but deliberately sets out to 'hook' her client's Adult. No one suggests that 'knowing the ropes' may assist a client to skilfully *avoid* changing – a concept that I have heard at other times. All the contributors here seem to agree that once the partnership is one of consenting Adults, the client can cooperate actively in his own change process. The experience of the Co-counselling community suggests that from then on expert skills can be learned through simple training, for use in the client or counsellor rôle. 'In a co-counselling relationship the primary responsibility of the session rests with the client . . . when it seems to the counsellor the client is lost . . . she will intervene with a practical suggestion . . . to get the process going again. . . . It is the client's privelege either to accept . . . or reject it'. (Heron)

There is a crucial and obvious difference between practitioners of Co-counselling and the majority of people who come for counselling. They all share a set of norms about 'healthy' behaviour which is quite different from the norms which are usually followed in the dominant culture. From the outset, in training workshops, and in co-counselling sessions, they are working towards shared and common aims, whether they are 'client' or 'counsellor'. However, counsellors in the general community are commonly holding *norms which may be very different from those of their clients*. They have very obvious axioms, which they can easily share, but which may go against all the axioms on which their clients' behaviour is based. Going through the interviews, I picked out one such axiom from each model, and to underline their simplicity, I expressed them colloquially. These ideas and this information is not such that it needs an 'expert' to deliver or take credit for it.

- Listen to your feelings as well as your thoughts, to help you know where you are
- Sometimes what you do, and the way you see things, makes more sense in terms of what is happening inside you, than what is happening outside you
- If the way you act isn't satisfying for you, you can deliberately learn new ways of doing things.
- If you have a difficult or painful experience which you can't 'get off your chest' (dis-stress yourself of) at the time, let nature do its work as soon as possible. Afterwards, you will be able to make better sense of things, and act more sensibly.
- If you make a map of all the important things in your life, you can find out what makes you feel good, and what makes

you feel bad, and decide what to do about that.
- If you allow yourself to be the marvellously sensitive 'receiving set' you were meant to be, you will be able to get your bearings better and 'transmit' more accurately.
- You have a lot more personal power than you usually imagine
- You go better when you are well-oiled with self esteem, and you can find ways of helping yourself realise you are O.K.
- It is alright to want things for yourself
- You may have to assert yourself to guard your territory and get what you want, even if it is something which harms no one else. There are acceptable ways of doing that.
- If you change the way you are it will have consequences which you can imagine, make choices about and, if you want, prepare yourself for
- If you begin to see yourself in the light of all that, you will begin to learn that you can trust yourself and other people more than you might imagine, and you will be able to judge more accurately when you can and cannot trust.

These axioms do not sound very revolutionary; indeed, they sound almost corny. Most teachers and parents would probably not disagree with them in theory. However, if most of them (including, I suspect, many of us who give strong credence to such ideas when counselling) were watched while carrying out teaching and parental duties, I think the following list would be shown to be more like a set of working axioms.

- Pull yourself together. Don't speak until you can talk sensibly
- Why did you do that? there's no reason to be like that
- You'll never learn – you can't teach an old dog new tricks
- Don't carry on so, make a fuss, be afraid
- Don't think about things too much – Life is not a bed of roses, you have to take things as they come.
- Listen to me. Do what you are told. You don't want to know about things like that.
- You are powerless, and if you're not, you're being naughty
- Some days you feel good, sometimes you don't. I don't know what gets into you
- Don't be selfish, or greedy, or pushy
- Go on, take a risk, but don't be surprised if you get your fingers burnt
- People really aren't to be trusted.

These 'norms of repression' (Heron) are the covert norms

which people hold to for much of the time. It is not because everyone who does so is wicked, or stupid, but because these axioms are familiar, and therefore safe. All axioms in the second list have familiar phrases to express them, those in the first list do not. Most of our institutions rely on those within them adhering to such norms. People who try to live by other norms are actually disturbing institutional balance. 'So schools in which children feel too threatened to be themselves, to acknowledge their own experience, are likely to produce maladaptive consequences for the children, though not for the schools'. (Milner) '. . . there are all sorts of attempts to maintain the system as it is. That goes on in society, and it goes on within individuals. It is expressed *by* society, *through* the neuroses of individual people . . . a lot of clients are involved in that process, at some level, and are made unhappy or mad by it. . . .' (Osborn)

So when someone comes for counselling, it is likely that the kind of ideas which they will be introduced to, and the ways of working that they will be offered, will cut across the ingrained 'messages' which they have previously received from their parental figures at home or at school. Using the T.A. framework to look at the counselling transaction again, the counsellor is bound to be *involving herself in some part of the client's internal dialogue*. At the outset. she is identifying with his Nurturing Parent, saying in effect 'You're ok, its safe to be yourself here, to try out new behaviour, if you want to you can change and I can help you, its alright to want things, what you say doesn't seem silly to me etc.'

These are powerful interventions, and they need to be if they are to have effect. As Michael Reddy points out, for people to 'hear' new 'permissions' they need to be delivered as powerfully as were the original 'stopper' messages, which withheld permission. (I, personally, have yet to meet a counsellor in training, let alone a 'client', whose ability to give themselves 'nurturing' messages is not almost totally eclipsed, initially, by their tendency to criticise themselves.)

I think there is no model which does not acknowledge, in some form, this conflict. It is in the response to the *fact of conflict* that a real difference between approaches shows up, and it seems to unite strange bed-fellows. The Rogerian based approaches and the Behaviourally based approaches (including Social Functioning) all respond to the fact of conflict by *not* (in Behavioural terms) reinforcing it with attention. Rather, the Behavioural approaches deliberately seek out, stress and reinforce what is going 'right' – 'build on positive patterns' (Wilmot). The Rogerian approach by reflecting and accepting whatever is uppermost, pays equal attention to whichever side of the struggle appears uppermost at any one time. All those models reproduce a nurturing climate, as we saw in the section on safety.

The remaining models all respond to the fact of conflict by *confronting* it is some way, at least from time to time. As we have seen, the Co-counselling model is based on shared norms. The person who takes her turn as counsellor is contracted to assist the client to *counteract* his conditioned tendency to avoid discharging distress. The Psychoanalytical model, being clinically based, as Ellen Noonan points out, is focused on 'what has gone wrong.' The Freudian view of conflict – based on unconscious drives which are by their nature not readily available for working with – predisposes a Psychoanalytical counsellor to prepare to enter powerfully into her clients internal dialogue in a way which she does not anticipate will necessarily make her popular. Reluctance for change is not seen in terms of conditioning or modelling which is no longer adaptive, but in terms of 'defences' which may manifest themselves in the content of the interview or in the relationship. They are focused on, at least from time to time. In this case, the nurturing climate is still considered appropriate, but as we saw in 'safety' the counsellor is at pains not to communicate it as indulgent.

T.A., being psychoanalytically based, also confronts from time to time. But the typical style is 'confronting with the T.A. language' (Reddy). Eric Berne devoted a whole chapter of his book *Games People Play* to 'Games therapists play'. By taking the confrontation out of the arena of the relationship, the danger of that particular kind of power game is minimised. Fritz Perls, too, found a way to stay with the awareness of conflict, without interpreting it as it manifested in the relationship. Like Rogers, he was at pains not to encourage one side of the conflict over the other, but rather to point up to the clients' awareness the physical and verbal signals of conflict, and the manifest 'interruptions'. 'The Gestalt method is to dramatize the conflict. . . . I invite them to set up a dialogue between those running legs and that steadfast heart. . . . I don't interpret, I use their words, very purely returning them to the speaker . . . the dramatis personae change until they get to their honest fight'. (Houston) This is only done after the counsellor has helped clients understand that they are not considered 'dangerous animals who have to be ignored or punished because they grip their hands or pull their hair'. Working with the conflicts comes only after they have learned to stay aware of what they are doing at any one moment.

Finally, the Radical counsellor, highly aware of the social origins and implications of this conflict, when appropriate, confronts with ideas and, by pointing up the manifestations of conflict in daily living, validates attempts at alternative solutions.

So in terms of power, in the 'cooperative' models, the counsellor uses her power to draw out and to *build on any perceptible movement towards desired change*. 'People will move towards effective living if they are given enough support to hear inside themselves ... even though that message may be very faint and distorted'. (Inskipp) Power, too, is used to support people while they learn to find their own way forward, and to raise their self-esteem so that they have heart to do so.

In the confronting models, power is used *to make it difficult for people to avoid facing the choices* which are available to them. Co-counselling 'counsellors' use their power to discourage defensive patterns and encourage clients to discharge distress. The Psychoanalytic counsellor leaves the client confronted with his choice. The Gestalt and T.A. models, at least in the case of their representatives here, use their power to encourage clients to make a satisfying choice in either direction – that is either to stay with their present behaviour and value it for its 'payoffs', or to move towards trying new behaviour. The Radical counsellor uses his power to point up the social implications of choice. 'We all depend on the world around us and are part of it. You have to understand in what ways the world around you, and the way you are part of it prevents you. .... At some point that structural effect may be so crippling that it has to be changed ... or has to change. Your world becomes *the* world'. (Osborn)

However, even those counsellors who use a 'confronting' model do not confront arbitrarily. Again in T.A. terms, the powerful Critical Parent is often the postman who delivers messages which start from the counsellor's Adult, especially at times when the client is likely to be suffering from low self-esteem. 'I seem to like that part of you more than you do' (Noonan) or 'Are you always that hen-pecked?' (Wilmot) is not fierce or aggressive confronting. And Tom Osborn says that until real toleration has been established in a group, or safety in a relationship, he supports virtually anything a client wants to do. Only later he may confront with his own reality 'I don't want to be your parent at this moment.' Counsellors are powerful affectors of self-esteem.

This *sense of low self-esteem, or powerlessness*, which is the likely concomitant of seeking help in our culture, is another factor with which counsellors have to contend, if they are to help a person to help himself. 'The more inadequate and unworthy people are made to feel by the social system they are in, the more restricted they become, ... and less able to cope in a changing environment ... and with themselves changing.' (Inskipp) It is for this reason that Dave Wilmot automatically works on raising self-esteem for each individual with whom he works. In order to do this, he does *not* play down his own relative powerfulness, but models taking outright pleasure in his own skill and ability to take care of himself. In Roger's terms (provided, of course, he *is* feeling high in self-esteem at the time he expresses it) this is 'congruence', and is more facilitating for the client than attempts to play down or deny 'phenomenological realities' – in this case the satisfactions of 'coping', *and* the inhibiting effect that that can have on someone who is 'not coping'. Returning, in summary, to the T.A. model, which by its nature is particularly well suited to looking at the power aspects of the counselling interaction, the counsellor need not do the 'switch' on the clients 'I'm not ok, You're ok', by pretending 'No, I'm not ok, you're ok, you've suffered, you're working class etc.', but can most usefully respond with a message which comes across as 'I'm ok and You're ok. You do not have to change, but if you want to, I can help'.

The other resource which a counsellor has which her client cannot have, at the outset, is clear 'attention' which is not shattered by the distress or anxiety of the client. John Heron talks about a client needing to have a certain amount of attention outside the distress on which she is working so that her system is free to discharge the distress. By giving 'free attention' the counsellor 'locks' and reinforces that bit of the client. Ellen Noonan points out that a client usually comes in a state of anxiety or excitement, and by sitting back, not responding to that panic, – containing it – she sees herself helping her client to become reflective about it. The image I have is of the counsellor's strength 'taking the strain' and freeing the client to do what he needs to do.

If these power elements are dealt with cleanly, and the client is increasingly encouraged to share in the task by mobilizing his own resources, then the counsellor correspondingly becomes a person who has the same sort of professional power as any consultant; she gives 'free attention' at a time when the client needs some time and space; developed skills and understanding; and some useful information, which may or may not be used by the client. It is this consultancy role which the action based therapies seem to have so clear.

Feeling, Thinking and Doing

'You can saddle a horse from two sides, either from understanding, and then doing differently, or from doing differently, and then understanding afterwards. Feeling differently afterwards. I don't care which side they get on, so long as they get on the horse'. (Reddy)

Feeling, thinking and doing form the bridge by which a person interacts with his environment. *Feeling*, mediated through sensation, is the *immediate preconscious response* of the body to incoming or internal signals. In response to feeling, the person is 'moved' in some direction. *Thinking* is the system through which such signals and moves are *programmed and adjusted*, according to the way the person perceives his situation at a cognitive level. *Doing* is the *actualising* of the decisions made at precognitive and cognitive levels. All the counselling approaches focus on one or more of these processes (although it is obvious that to give the impression that these processes are 'things' in their own right is to grossly distort the 'wholes' of which they are parts). All contributors claim that, wherever they focus their client's energy and attention, any success in getting one process operating more effectively generalizes to the others. Anyone who learns to reward himself through doing more what he wants to do experiences more feelings of satisfaction and thinks more efficiently. Anyone who learns to listen to, accept and communicate his feelings more accurately will perceive things differently and act more as he wishes to. Anyone who has at his disposal more accurate 'maps' of himself, his environment and his experiencing will feel less confused and act more consistently for himself and others. The question of how and when learning in one area generalises to others is currently the subject of much empirical research.

Several of the approaches in this book suggest focusing in turn on all three processes. The Developmental Counselling mode offers such a framework. First, the focus is on *confusion reduction*, the clarifying of feelings and perceptions; secondly, it is on *choices*, that is helping the client notice and decide about where he is 'moving' himself; and thirdly, it is on *changes*, carrying out those decisions in the world, through action. Social Functioning and Co-counselling also involve focussing on all three processes in sequence. Gestalt, concentrating as it does on awareness, allows for focusing on what is the figure, and what the ground, of the client's 'gestalt' at any one moment. In addition to these 'integrated' models, I think it is useful to take each process separately and look at the way the different models relate to it.

Feeling. Breuer, and later, Freud discovered the dramatic therapeutic effects of catharsis – the release of long held feelings. The energy generated by some feelings has neither been used up in 'moving' the experiencer to action, or, by default, been discharged through the mechanisms which the body provides for disposing of 'waste' energy, (Harvey Jackin's formulation). When Freud helped his patients recollect old traumatic incidents and experiences, he found that they were able to 'let go' of the painful memory, and the defensive structures which had held them from relating to those memories, when they had discharged the emotions associated with it.

This therapeutic re-experiencing of recent or longer term traumatic events is acknowledged by all the counselling models. In the case of Behavioural Counselling, the experience is called 'flooding'. In that model, the accompanying memory or phantasy is not the object of focus, but only the *stimulus* that currently provokes phobic behavior. The client is confronted with this stimulus (e.g., with his consent held with his therapist in a stuck lift) until his anxiety floods and passes, leaving the client unbelievably, to him, intact.

The Co-counselling model has a more comprehensive and large scale 'map' of the process of emotional discharge. It offers a great deal of information on the particular ways that the body discharges minor and major fears, pains, griefs, embarrassments etc. It has also developed a wide variety of self-help techniques for learning to discharge fresh or longstanding distress, against the run of previous conditioning.

Co-counselling differs from Gestalt or Rogerian practice to the extent that defensive patterns are over-ridden, rather than identified with or accepted, as a working part of a person's coping mechanisms. In Gestalt, for example, Gaie Houston says 'I don't condition people . . . to feel they ought to transcend barriers . . . or implode, or explode . . . but . . . condition them to set their own limits'. In this, Co-counselling is closer to the Psycho-analytic model, but where it differs sharply from that model is that it is always the client's choice to work towards 'discharge'. It is also assumed that people can be trusted to handle their own quite strong and long-standing emotional discharge, as and when they learn the skills. However, John Heron does not suggest that everyone is able to do this from the outset, although the majority of people can, with training and support. He believes that those who strongly and consistently 'invalidate' themselves and others are not motivated to use the co-counselling relationship in an effective way. Co-counsellors assert that any work done in counselling without first 'dis-stressing' will be basically stereo-typed and designed, unawarely, to seal in distress, and reinforce rigid holding patterns. In this, the formulations of Harvey Jackins, the founder of Co-counselling, meet up with the work of Wilhelm Reich, whose concept of 'body armouring' suggests that accumulated distress actually shapes and holds the physical body. It also connects with Janov who, in *The Primal Scream* suggests that *only* those who have re-experienced their birth and early traumas can live freely.

This emphasis on the primacy of feeling, often underlined by the whole of the Growth Movement, has already set up its own reaction. Dave Wilmot in his interview talks of the beauty, but impractibility, and even falseness, of 'feeling free to feel'. He sees it as important to help people work on distinguishing thinking from feeling and on communicating feelings clearly, but he distrusts any greater emphasis being put on feeling, than on thinking or action. Michael Reddy in his account of T.A. cari-catures people who may have been to humanistic psychology groups, and come away with the idea that the big thing is to tell people what they feel. 'So they . . . say "I'm really furious with you" – message ... "its now up to you to do something ... I'm crying." As though a baby would have a tantrum and then sit back and say well, that was a great experience'. Their feelings have not 'moved' them in the direction they want to go, by communicating what they want to others.

The Rogerian and Co-counselling models are extremely aware that our culture conditions people not to sense and not to feel, and that it offers inadequate 'labels' for people to use when attempting to communicate their feelings accurately. Transactional Analysis sharpens this insight by pointing out that only certain emotions are 'allowed' by families in certain situations. If for example anger, or tears, or confusion are sanctioned, they become racket feelings. That is, they are both safe to express, and they act as disguises for primary emotions, and even decoys, to lead their experiencer away from those danger areas. These safety manoevres take energy, but secondary rewards or 'payoffs' render the patterns satisfactory enough to their creator to make the choice of encountering say, raw fear or grief, seem risky by contrast. For it is feelings such as these that the 'little person' chose to avoid after particularly painful encounters.

So merely displaying emotion (or 'acting out' in psychoanalytic terms) neither discharges distress, nor does it harness energy for 'moving' in chosen directions. It seems important that clients as well as counsellors become clear about this distinction, so that they can learn, as in Gestalt, to become aware of their own processes, and feel what is helpful in 'moving' them and what is not. To understand, and really 'feel' the distinction needs 'insight', a function of the thinking and perceiving faculties.

The Rogerian, Gestalt, Developmental, Social Functioning, Co-counselling, and Radical models are not *insight* models, but *awareness* models. Clearly, these two are not distinct. But where they do differ, insight is the *recognition* of how one feels by introspection – looking in on oneself from outside – whereas awareness is the *experiencing* of how one feels, and comprehending it. With reference to past events, it is the difference between knowing 'about' how one felt, and re-experiencing, in the present, the power of those feelings. 'Unless you experience the original situation ... feel the terror in your stomach ... no change will take place' says Eugene Heimler, from his personal experience of the aftermath of concentration camp existence. All the humanistic models, with the exception of Rogerian counselling, draw on the *psychodramatic techniques* devised by Moreno to facilitate this encounter with feelings. As we have seen, Gestalt uses 'two chair work' to enable a person to contact the conflicting feelings he is usually unaware of. Co-counselling and Social Functioning and T.A. use similar methods for replaying, and 'finishing' situations in the past which have remained unresolved. The underlying rationale of these methods is, that suspending some or all of the 'givens' in a situation – I am not I, here is not here, now is not now – allows the expression of feeling and perception, and the use of behaviours, that are usually inhibited by the customary structures of a situation, and the responses which they habitually elicit. (In a longer term way, it is exactly the same mechanism that Tom Osborn advocates for people who wish to discover what alternative ways of structuring society there could be. By suspending some of the boundaries of power and ownership, the alternative culture allows fresh patterns to emerge.)

The psychodramatic technique of role-play is also used by all the models which have, or include, an 'action' focus. In these cases, it is used to facilitate rehearsal of *future* events which might trigger feeling responses. Thus, 'bad' learning experiences and traumatic incidents are precluded, as far as possible, by learning to anticipate and develop appropriate behaviour.

Rogerian counselling, relies on what Pat Milner calls '*the holy trinity*' of unconditional regard, warmth, empathy and congruence as offering 'sufficient' conditions for the full experiencing of feelings. This climate, together with the counsellor's basic skill of accurate reflection, enables a person to encounter as he needs, his own hitherto disowned feelings.

So feelings remain as a very important focus in all counselling models. The objective may be to encounter and accept them, to discharge the distress associated with them, to learn to 'handle' them more usefully, to distinguish the feeling process more clearly from the thinking process, to understand and make sense of them, to learn to communicate them more accurately and appropriately, to predict and be fore-armed against them, or to learn to distinguish which are 'originals' and which are 'conversion jobs'.

Dougal Mackay says 'I think profound changes can take place at all levels through behavioural intervention ... (it is) not true to think Behaviourists ignore thoughts and feelings (or phantasies) ... in many cases they are the most important areas to concen-

trate on . . . but (it is) still possible to use a behavioural model'.
Thinking. I use the word 'thinking' here to include all the
cognitive functions – perceiving, imagining, remembering,
judging, reasoning etc. They are all *transitional processes* between
the inner, private, subjective experiencing of the individual and
his public, outer, objective behaviour (to paraphrase Winnicot's
description of 'transitional objects'). As such, they are crucial
to the success with which an individual can become satisfyingly
a social being. It is for this reason that the 'private' end of these
processes – phantasy and perception – are the focus of much
post-Freudian Psychoanalytic attention. The 'public' end –
planning, making choices, exploring consequences, rehearsing
symbolically, devising systems – are the focus of any counselling
models which look, in whole or in part, to the future. Any of
the models may engage imagination, the busy shuttle which
weaves to and fro between the private world where all is possible,
and the public world with all its circumscriptions.

In the previous sections, we have seen that every counselling
approach seeks to *engage the client's imagination and understanding*
at the outset of counselling, in order to help him think about
what he wants, and decide whether the counsellor's way of
working makes sense for him. In addition, every model envisages
the client developing more accurate *cognitive maps* of his own
inner and outer worlds. The phenomenological approaches
encourages him to make his own maps, using his own
imagery and topography. The Psychoanalytically based models
offer ready made maps for use where they seem appropriate and
useful. The Behavioural and Social Functioning models encourage him to map his outer world.

The Psychoanalytic approach is sometimes known as '*insight
therapy*'. Assuming, as it does, that people's irrational behaviour
is caused by unconscious conflicts, it posits that if people understand 'why' they act as they do, they will at least be able to begin
to work more usefully towards greater rationality. 'In . . .
counselling, where there is less time, . . . it . . . is very much at a
thinking, intellectual level. The client's gain understanding rather
than emotional experience of working through . . . (it is) not
very useful, unless it is also emotionally linked'. (Noonan) In
the same way, Michael Reddy, while explaining that T.A. is
'analytical' and highly cognitive in nature, was at pains to say
that it was not 'just' an insight therapy – 'the Child has to be

engaged'. In effect, the head can 'figure out' what seems sensible, and permissible, and unless it is allowed to do so it will be confused. But by itself, it is rather like a computer without enough power. As Gaie Houston points out, intelligence means 'tying together'. It is the necessary process for linking the instinctual responsive energy of the Child (to return to T.A.) usefully, creatively and adaptively with his world.

Any counselling which is entirely symbolic in focus can take flight and lose touch unless it is linked to some sort of 'contacting'. Contact can be achieved by focusing on sensation, the 'real' concommitant of emotion or on 'real' contact with the world through action. Hence the Gestalt dictum 'I don't let them interpret themselves. I think it limits meaning more than it enhances it. I encourage them to be so aware of the moment that they dare to flow or fight into the next moment of the unknown'. (Houston)

It is the usefulness of *insight*, *gained through interpretation*, as a means towards changing behaviour, which is questioned by both humanistic and behavioural practitioners. They do not necessarily question that the content of many Psychoanalytic interpretations are interesting, and even accurate. What they do suggest is that interpreting is not a useful way to facilitate change. Francesca Inskipp says that she finds it frequently creates, rather than lowers, defensiveness. Pat Milner suggests that it actually confuses and sidetracks a person's concentration on making his own sense of his world. Gaie Houston sees it as limiting potential meanings, John Heron sees it as intrusive and presumptuous, and Eugene Heimler as disrespectful. Dave Wilmott considers it takes him past his client's skin, where he has no right or responsibility to go. Francesca Inskipp also shares that very popular criticism of Psychoanalysis, that 'knowing why' so far from helping a person change, often gives them a good excuse for not doing so. It is largely as a reaction to Psychoanalytic over-emphasis on insight that the 'new' therapies have tended to go so far in their emphasis on feeling.

There is no doubt in my mind that both processes need to be engaged in counselling. In writing this book, I went to great lengths to engage readers' thoughts and imagination, in order to open their minds to new ideas. I do not doubt that many people just by reading these interviews will begin to practice differently without even noticing. Others will need to read more, in order to 'get permission' to try out new ways of working. But they still will find themselves able to do that, in some instances, without actual practical instruction and supervision. In other words, mere words and ideas – symbols – can affect people at both feeling and action levels. (Personally, such writers as Freud, Jung, Rogers, Perls, Laing have had this affect on me, as well as writers of fiction and poetry who more actively engage imagination, and suspend traditional constructs.) There must be many people who we can, and have, helped just by offering some new way of looking at their situation.

Returning to the interviews, Francesca Inskipp suggests that the time to offer fresh frameworks for looking at the world is after people have had a chance to make better sense of their own situation in their own terms. In other words, it occurs after the stage of confusion reduction, and during the stage of making choices. In a similar way, the action therapists start to devise alternative 'outer maps' after their clients have decided what they want, or how they want to change. And Eugene Heimler only offers his clients his 'Scale of Social Functioning', as a means for mapping their world, after they have begun to become self-directed.

A client-centred counsellor never intervenes with her maps, but concentrates on helping the client make his own maps.

The Radical therapist also, at that stage of counselling, is going to 'confront with ideas' if that seems appropriate for her client. For it is the radical insight that distress can be occasioned by a cultivated misperception of outer experience, as well as a cultivated misperception of inner experience. In both cases, the counsellor must first of all offer her selected interpretation, for her clients consideration, acceptance or rejection. In both cases, if the interpretation is accepted, the client is then able to begin to work on the distress which such 'cognitive dissonance' (or continuing to *feel* things differently from the way they are now *perceived*) gives rise to. And that means, in psychoanalytic language, 'working it through'. 'Until they find a new resolution which is not self-defeating qualitatively'. (Noonan.)

In the future-oriented approaches – Behavioural, Reality Therapy, Developmental Counselling, Co-counselling, Social Functioning – the clients' cognitive processes are actively engaged in devising ways of fulfilling his objectives. In planning, choosing, forecasting, scheming, mentally rehearsing, imagination is actively engaged. Such exercises allow people to play with the impossible, the improbable and the unlikely but possible. They can 'trick' themselves out of stereotyped behaviour, and forecast the results of risking acting that way in 'real' life. Since imagination, like sensation and feeling, has often been so consistently 'negatively conditioned' as to have been virtually extinguished as a behaviour in many people, the practice of it, in itself, must increase people's ability to relate more inventively to their environment. Imagination is the basis for the skill of lateral thinking, which Dave Wilmot stresses as such essential equipment for counsellors, as well as for human beings in general.

Doing. 'There are hooks out there on which he can hook this internal energy, so the internal becomes externalised. If this flow of energy is not possible, his energy works against the individual rather than for him'. (Heimler.)

This conception, of energy needing to 'make a circuit' between the individual and his environment, underlies all the 'integrated' models. It is not one with which behaviourists would necessarily disagree. The difference is one of focus – where is it most practicable and effective to break in and improve that circuit?

For Dougal Mackay the answer lies mainly in items of behaviour. For Eugene Heimler, the answer lies both at the individual's end, and at the point where action realises itself through role. For Tom Osborn these two would also be main points of focus. For Dave Wilmot the focus is on action as it realises itself through systems for doing things. For Francesca Inskipp, the focus would be first with the individual's experience of himself and would later move through to focussing on any behaviour or action which might respond to desired change.

In every case, the methods employed rely heavily on the behavioural approach. Very briefly, they entail the clear formulating of objectives, the cutting down of these to 'bite-sized chunks', systematic control of anxiety, tangible and clear rewards, practical contracts, under rather than over-aiming, conscious 'modelling', 'shaping' of behaviour through overt, and sometimes covert, conditioning. The method is always directive, but not, as Dougal Mackay is at pains to point out, authoritarian. Direction is (at any rate said to be) always towards the clients' objectives. They rely heavily, at the outset, on the creativity of the counsellor, but aim to engage the clients' inventiveness on his own behalf.

Children, by nature, are more at home in the 'real world' of action, rather than in the world of words and ideas. For this reason, Pat Milner and Francesca Inskipp always have 'things' for them to play with available, and work (like any mother might expect) on finding things that they can usefully 'do' to help themselves. Unless people are socialized and educated to the verbal, symbolic mode of relating to the world, verbal counselling sessions may, in themselves, be experiences for which they have no adequate 'behavioural repertoire'. It is not surprising that Dave Wilmot's 'multi problem families' can more easily relate to an action model of counselling.

In conclusion, I think it is interesting to think about 'roles' and 'systems'. Both these are 'structures' which are intangible and symbolic – perpetuated by the ideas and expectations of people relating to them. But, they have the power of determining behaviour, until awareness intervenes and allows choice. 'Little boys don't do that'. 'All counsellors are accepting of their clients'. 'Counselling lasts an hour, is in a room, the participants sit opposite each other, and they never touch'. Tom Osborn, John Heron and Gaie Houston all talk about the limiting effect of accustomed role behaviour, and also the way acting can change, when roles are differently perceived. Either way, if change is to take place, it has to affect both the behaviour and the conception of the role or system. It is another instance of the horse being able to be mounted from either side. 'I do not think any form of human liberation from internal problems can come about until changes have taken place in the external world.' (Heimler.)

Monitoring

I have one major dissatisfaction with my original questionnaire. When I composed it, I did not ask my contributors how they knew whether their client's, and their own, objectives in counselling had been met. Nor did I ask them how they monitored their long term skill and personal satisfaction as a counsellor. Tied in with those questions, too, is when and how do they terminate a counselling contact.

Dougal Mackay and Dave Wilmot point out in their interviews that making a contract about objectives has the inbuilt advantage of knowing when and if objectives have been met. That also takes care of the question of termination. Heimler has the 'Scale of Social Functioning' as a monitoring device, and speaks of long term follow-up of clients. In Co-counselling, where the responsibility is on the client to meet her own objectives, the client gives feed-back on how well her partner 'gave attention' and facilitated her in meeting her objectives. My other contributors do, I know, have their own methods of evaluating their short and long term effectiveness – client questionnaires and feed-back sheets, review sessions, and records, as short term self-evaluators; and supervisors, peer support systems, refresher courses etc. as long term monitoring devices.

If I work in the Gestalt mode, I always look for what is *not* there, and it often tells the client a great deal more than what is there. My omission of these questions reminds me that I found the issue of evaluation and monitoring difficult at the time I devised the questionnaire. As a Psychoanalytically trained worker, I had been taught to keep records – *my* assessment of the client's strengths and weaknesses, *my* treatment plan for the client, three monthly progress summaries, and session by session reports. I never succeeded in keeping them regularly, even though I appreciated their purpose. Working in a client-centred way, I have enjoyed the freedom from setting goals for someone else, and evaluating them by my standards. I enjoy, when it seems appropriate, setting up Behavioural contracts with clients, and I value that clarity. I do not see that as always the most effective way of working – I am not yet at ease or experienced enough in that style not to get pushed into a 'Critical Parent' role, when the person I am working with fails in his objectives. In addition, although those objectives do measure what was done, they do not indicate what might have been done better, or what temporary or permanent blindspots I may have.

Underneath that there is a more fundamental question. It is really very difficult to measure, to report, to notice what is going on in the counselling interaction. Gestalt awareness exercises remind us of the infinitude of movement and change that goes on within each of us, all the time and every second. Tom Osborn talks about this in his interview. Michael Reddy remarks how, as a teacher, it was sometimes the boy in the class who had not been in his awareness at all who later told how much he had learned from him, while the boy for whom he had a clear therapeutic intent apparently learned little. How often have we all heard a client tell us of *the* significant moment of breakthrough, which turns out not to be that marvellous insight we had and shared, but something we said when we were tired and bored or absent minded, and that we have difficulty in recalling when it is repeated. Or equally, moments when we were unaware until much later how much we had hurt him or deterred an initiative.

Related to that is the therapeutic value of the immediacy of personal contact – how the client and the counsellor feel about each other. Ellen Noonan quotes Winnicot as saying much the same thing in relation to a mother with her child. Counselling often does provide, for the first time in someone's life, a warm and nourishing relationship. Often this need only be experienced for a very few sessions for the results to be dramatic, and there does not need to be a long drawn out dependency. It is difficult to be sure what are the effective ingredients in that, though the Rogerians have done a good job of clarifying and measuring various of them.

Also, how do I measure if I work more effectively when, for example, my energy is high, rather than when I am low? Listening to my contributors, I get a very clear feel of counsellors being human. Sometimes they are content with their way of working, sometimes they are beginning to feel restless and look about for more effective ways of working, sometimes they are at a point of minor or major transition, relinquishing old certainties and not yet centred in new ones. Yet other times they are both relaxed and invigorated, having made a transition, and assimilated 'good new food'. Counselling students, for instance, often undergo drastic and unsettling transitions. In our culture, it often needs something like a training course to give people 'permission' to make overdue changes in the way they are and the way they see the world. Often, at the same time other factors are changing too – jobs, friends, being away from home. Does that make for good counselling work? Better than at other times? Are there times for all of us that we do not have enough 'free attention' to work? How do we judge, and what do we do about it if we are employed, for instance?

Also, how much is, and should the way I work be, the result of the kind of person I am? Reality therapy meets Dave Wilmot's needs, as he says unabashedly. It uses his talents to the full and no doubt helps him avoid areas and relationships that frustrate and worry him. That makes him an excellent therapist, but it does not necessarily mean that Reality Therapy is the best way of helping all families. Nor does it mean that in other hands it would be equally effective. I think it not a coincidence that all the *solely* action based models in this book are represented by men, and that three of the partially action-based ones are too. (Heimler, Heron and Osborn.) Only Francesca Inskipp is not, and her model very clearly starts with a process orientation. All the process-based models are represented by women. I think few would disagree that in our culture it is still probably easier for men to use and be accepted in an active role, and women to take and be accepted in a receptive role and mode. I do not think this should be so, but I do believe most women have to work harder to work directively, and sensitively, and most men have to practice hard to be receptive and remain sinewy. So the choice arises, for everyone who counsels, whether it is more sensible to use time and energy in the mode that they know and like, or, in the interests of being more flexible and varied in what they can offer, they should develop other ways of working. If they do, will they ever work as well in the new ways as in the ways in which they may have great experience? Ellen Noonan raises this issue when she talks of her dilemmas in counselling. It is the recurrent choice between specialisation and generalisation, each with its own advantages and limitations.

As an illustration of these issues, I would like to ask the readers to use their imagination for a minute. If each of the contributors to this book and I were to establish a peer counselling group, can you imagine what the resulting 'pairs' would look and sound like at work? Each of us would bring our own agenda as a client and would more or less know what our different partners would have 'on offer'. I am sure that when those links were made, they would result in a series of totally different experiences. I dare say that almost all of them would be highly effective working sessions for the client. It would not be hard to decide if we were effective for each other. It would be hard to know what was 'most effective' since we would almost certainly have selected awarely, or unawarely, what to work on, with whom. In that situation, it would be possible to devise some way of checking. In most day-to-day situations such comparisons are just not possible.

In raising these issues, I do not want to despair of the possibility, nor reject the desirability, of evaluation and monitoring. I just want to remind myself and others that in going for the appearance of 'scientific monitoring' we must be careful not to

do so at the expense of actual monitoring, however untidy it
might seem.

Basic Skills

Self-evaluating and monitoring, with the help of peers, mentors
and clients starts in training (if the counsellor has any.) There
seems a high degree of consent among my contributors about
what a student should develop in training. Among the most
important are the following:
- *An ability to listen*
- *An ability to discriminate in what she is hearing, according to
  some theoretical framework*
- *An ability to communicate effectively and creatively what has
  been heard*
- *An ability to share with the client what she sees herself offering,
  and anything else that needs saying or sharing*
- *A particular set of skills which will vary according to the
  training model.*
- *Appropriate tools, if these are necessary within the training
  model, and judgement in using them properly.*
- *Clarity about what she is trying to do and how she does it*
- *Some knowledge of 'alternative maps', information and resources
  which may help her make sense of her own and her clients
  experience*
- *Overall, an openness to herself and others which allows her to
  appreciate her own strengths and limitations.*

These are all things which can be monitored on initial courses,
refresher courses, with peer groups or with a supervisor, as well,
of course, as with clients. Video and tape recorders make for
the possibility of a regular check on these abilities being a
genuinely self-monitoring exercise.

Development

Beyond that level of maintenance of basic skills, lies the level of
development. Could I be more effective? Could I be working
in different ways? Am I getting locked into unhelpful patterns?
Am I steady enough/too dull? Am I responsive to the needs of
my clients or rather to my preferred way of working?
These interviews have clarified for me the kind of questions that

I want to ask myself at some stage or stages of each counselling contract.

- *What is my client wanting?*
- *What am I trying to do?*
- *What does the climate feel like?*
- *Where is the focus?*
  - *Time (past, present, future)*
  - *Place (feelings, thoughts, actions, awareness)*
- *What skills do I seem to be using?*
  - *Are there others I could usefully try?*
- *What ego states (Parent, Adult and Child) do I and my client move in and out of?*
  - *When? does it feel right? are there other states that would feel more comfortable for him/me? more useful?*
- *How long does my client expect to work for?*
  - *How long do I envisage?*
  - *How will this client and I know when to stop?*
- *Are we both working well and having fun?*
  - *If not, could we usefully unbore ourselves?*
  - *Am I taking care of myself? would I feel safer, more effective using more structure, less structure, outside support etc.*
- *How do I know what is happening for my client?*
  - *How will I know, when he is finished, how this experience was for him?*
  - *How will I know how it was for me?*
- *What are the particular things I have learned about my working/myself since I last checked?*
  - *Is there any learning objective I want to set myself as a result?*

These questions would increase my awareness without 'judging' my performance. They would provide information which I could appropriately share with my client. To answer them fully would entail helping my client devise his own simple monitoring devices, and devising some scale by which I can monitor myself over time. If enough readers of this book devised their own check-list and worked imaginatively enough meanwhile, I think it would soon be possible to get some very clear indications about what methods work for what clients and when.

Counselling and Psychotherapy

Finally, no book about counselling can avoid looking at definitions. Reading through these interviews, I suggest that it is possible to arrive at shared ground about the *objectives* of counselling. Very broadly, all the contributors see it as in some way offering individuals greater freedom of their personal and social life. There is further agreement that how this freedom is defined *is in terms of the particular objectives of the individual* seeking counselling. There are some *distinctions* between the counselling role and other roles about which there is considerable agreement. It would be difficult at this stage to arrive at a shared definition of *how* those objectives are met through counselling. I can see a possible eventual definition being in terms of 'the provision of experiential learning structures', but such a hypothesis would need to be explored much more fully than is possible here. There is no possibility of agreement about the *limits* of counselling and psychotherapy. The fairly clear distinction between the two which some practitioners recognize is not useful or relevant to the formulations made by practitioners with different assumptions or focus of practice.

Looking at the answers to the question 'So what do you see as the objectives of the counselling task?', the following replies emerge: to offer a man freedom to be his own guide; to free him to be that self he truly is; to increase his behavioural repertoire; to enable the individual to understand the patterns of his life so that this insight leads to some sort of mastery or control; to train a person to take charge of his feelings and to provide him with skills for discharging anger, fear, grief, etc. so that he is not driven by compulsive, disoriented behaviour; to help him live more effectively for himself and for others since he is a social being and his well-being depends on the co-operation of others; to help him to freedom, through awareness – not the freedom of irresponsibility, but of super-responsibility; to help him feel he is allowed to want things and to help him discover how to go about getting them; to build on strengths and skills so he can take the actions he wants to take; to free him from the internal prison he is in, and offer him a chance to remake early decisions which are now not useful to him.

Together, these objectives seem to add up to offering people opportunities to feel happier and freer with themselves, and more competent to be the way they want to be in their personal and social life.

The theoretical approaches discussed here are the basis for

other fields of practice than counselling. Such an aim might be shared by many whose work is in the area of social and personal facilitation. Teachers, social workers, those with pastoral care responsibilities, even managers, might see such a broad objective as being at least part of their general objectives, even when the task they are undertaking is not one that they, or contributors to this book, might call counselling. What does seem to distinguish counselling is the understanding that the client himself asks for help, and that he then decides what, within the general objective of greater personal freedom, are his particular aims.

Although in theory there is agreement about this, in practice it presents difficulties. Firstly, the process-based approaches suggest that a client has to learn to discover, in Gestalt terms, 'his own right-mindedness, below the level of conditioning'. This is particularly difficult with children in school, where the development of self-esteem may depend on helping them alter their behaviour in more socially acceptable ways. But it is also possible with adults, to pursue objectives which are determined by 'oughts' rather than 'wants', like Michael Reddy's lady who thought she wanted to be pregnant and Dougal Mackay's client who thought he wanted to alter his sexual orientation. Dave Wilmot, too, points out that self-esteem for most people is built on satisfactory contacts with other people within roles and systems.

There seem to be three ways of dealing with this dilemma. One is to allow a kind of 'introductory offer' of exploration while the client begins to get clearer what his objectives might be. (Milner, Heimler, Inskipp, Osborn.) The second way is to be happily prepared to buy into 'ought' contracts, which can be altered later on, when they show for what they are. This reinforces the message that, in *this* interaction, it really *is* what the client says that matters. It will not be converted into the counsellor's currency. This would also accord with the humanist and existential belief that what people need to learn about is their own *processes*, however maladaptive, so that they can be forewarned and take more direct paths to their objectives in future. The third way is to be a known specialist, so that people know something about the aims and methods of the particular approach before using it. They are then able to formulate suitable objectives, in terms of that method. While there are only 'counsellors', and the public is relatively uninformed about the aims and methods available, and while many counsellors only offer one way of working, there is little choice for the client. Either they have what they bring 'made over' into behavioural or process objectives, or they continue to suffer. 'They didn't really want to change' used to be the way of dealing with 'non-returners' when I was training. That might be true, but it could be that the way offered felt alien, or insufficiently safe for that person at that time.

Theoretically then, the objective of counselling is to help a client towards greater personal freedom, through working with him to relieve dissatisfactions, frustrations or distresses or to realise objectives, which he himself has specified. This begins to point up the distinction between counselling and other roles and tasks with which various contributors compared it. Friendship, for instance, was not seen as task centred, or as focused in the objectives of one participant rather than the other. In Michael Reddy's words, 'a friend can give you a powerful bit of loving, or a powerful therapeutic kick in the pants'. But friendships are seen as both more appropriately collusive than counselling, and also relationships of full mutual sharing. Tom Osborn and Francesca Inskipp both suggest that friends, or colleagues, can enter into peer counselling relationships, usefully and appropriately, but that for that purpose the contract is overtly a counselling one, specifying time and objectives, and boundaries. The Co-counselling training includes teaching on the differences between Co-counselling and friendship. Francesca Inskipp points out that the friendly climate which most approaches cultivate can actually make the distinction one that is hard for clients and counsellors to appreciate, especially in unstructured counselling situations. It is noticeable in the interviews that there are almost no 'rules' set up, offering prescriptions to counsellors. Rather, there is clear delineation of *task* – the time is the client's time, he can expect full attention, etc – and of responsibility of a counsellor to herself – to take care of herself, to have good relationships outside work, to know her own boundaries.

The *social work task* is one that must have a large overlap with counselling, using the same skills and insights in many instances. Like the counsellor in a school, a social worker may sometimes suffer confusion as to whether her task is one of care or of control. Dave Wilmot suggests that this is a confusion which permeates all our 'helping' systems. It seems likely that both social workers and counsellors in institutions may have certain tasks which are about delivering the demands, as well as the resources, of the system to the individual. These tasks, should, in my opinion, be seen as *pastoral care* tasks. Pastoral care has the implications of trying to mutually adjust the objectives of the individual and of the system, so that both can find ways of meeting each others legitimate, developing needs, in maximally satisfying ways.

Enlightened *management*, too, can employ skills and insights very similar to those developed by counsellors. Tom Osborn points out that, in organizations, the objectives of the individual are only paramount when they do not conflict with the objectives of the organization. 'Counselling' is a task which increasingly appears in job descriptions without being defined. In my experience, it is almost always taken to mean 'talking with an employee in a sympathetic and sensitive way, so that he can be helped to do better the job which he has to do'. This seems to be quite distinct from 'counselling' as used by my contributors.

No one mentioned the use of the word 'counselling' by organizations with specifically defined moral values in certain areas e.g., abortion, homosexuality etc. I suggest that when such organizations cater to 'their own' – that is, those who share their moral convictions – such 'counselling' is what I would call pastoral care, – that is a genuine concern for a 'person-within-a-specific-system'. Where such counselling is for the general public, it is a more or less overt attempt to influence choices. As such, it is not counselling within the terms defined here. But in saying that, I am acutely aware that I have spelled out how all the counselling approaches offer clients norms which conflict with the covert norms of our society. To the extent that any of those alternate norms are 'pushed' rather than overtly offered, – with real, rather than apparent, choice to refuse them, – any of the approaches in this book are equally able to be used to persuade rather than 'counsel'.

Another related task is that of *psychological testing*. Dougal Mackay sees such a task as being about clarifying choices for clients, by means of various tests. But he also recognizes that testing can be used for giving information to 'experts' in order to 'diagnose' – that is as an adjunct to the medical model of treatment of psychiatric disorders. Heimler, too, refers to such testing as being intrinsically different from his Scale of Social

Functioning. Thus some testing is an adjunct to the counselling task, and other testing is quite different in its objectives.

The other task that counselling is most frequently compared with is that of *teaching*. Several contributors make a clear definition between *teaching as the imparting of information* and counselling, which although it may entail some of that, is not primarily information giving. However, Gaie Houston, Tom Osborn, John Heron, Eugene Heimler and Francesca Inskipp, all suggest that counselling is about offering carefully structured learning situations. In each case the learning is 'experiential learning'. That is, it offers people an opportunity either to explore and make choices about alternative solutions to problematic or frustrating situations, or to make sense of certain experiences by devising their own theories, with or without the aid of previously formulated theory. I want to return to this idea later, and test whether it has validity for other approaches too. It is significant that these four all see clear continuity between their counselling, and their *training* roles.

The remaining role which was explored and contrasted with counselling was *the psychotherapeutic role*. About this distinction, there can be no agreement at the present time. The usual distinction is the one based on 'depth of intervention', which arises out of Psychoanalytical assumptions. Carl Rogers does not recognize a distinction, and nor do the majority of humanistic and existential approaches. Some practitioners consider that there are some people with 'chronic patterns' of destruction or invalidation who require 'therapy' as opposed to counselling. Behavioural and Reality Therapists use the word 'therapy' while working entirely in a way that 'responsibility stops at the client's skin'. (Wilmot)

Ellen Noonan offers her version of the Psychoanalytic distinction between counselling and therapy. She sees them both calling on much the same resources. However, since, in this framework, the client requires the help of a skilled worker to gain access to his own unconscious, and recognize his defensive mechanisms, the more work is directed at the unconscious, the more unequal the relationship becomes. The more limited goals of counselling can be reached by mobilizing the 'ego resources' of the client, but for large scale modification of personality, the 'alliance is about trusting me at the more primitive level'. The language she goes on to use is very similar to that a T.A. therapist might use, and she and Michael Reddy are in agreement with each other. Both see the Adult part of the client sharing, and in Michael Reddy's case, directing the counselling process, while in therapy, at times the Child is worked with directly, with all the implications of working with an actual child. I think there is a distinction in that, in T.A., agreement to work in that way is always by overt contract – the client's Adult has arranged with the therapist to temporarily relinquish hold to the therapist. Presumably, this arrangement is also entered into in Psychoanalytic counselling, but since there is less concentrated 'teaching of the language' in the first place, it may not be an arrangement which is so fully understood by the client. It is in this 'therapeutic contract' that the transference of early feelings into the relationship with the therapist becomes the focus of attention. Again, in T.A., the theory of 'script' and the expectation that this may show in the way the client relates with the analyst has been fully explored with the client, who has 'discovered' his own script, by script analysis. He is not therefore dependent in the same way on the counsellors 'interpretation'.

A further difference between these two approaches is that T.A. provides for 'reparenting' contracts, which Michael Reddy sees as at the extreme 'therapeutic' end of the spectrum. In these the client empowers the therapist to give him the 'permissions' which were withheld in the first instance, so that the client can feel safe to do the growing he needs to do. This sounds very similar to, though more structured than, the way that Ellen Noonan works with very 'disturbed patients', which she describes as 'a relationship protecting the client from impingements, so that he can have a sense that he exists and continues to exist'. This, in its turn, sounds remarkably similar to the intent of Rogerian work, whether it is termed 'counselling' or 'psychotherapy'.

Two other contributors, Francesca Inskipp and Tom Osborn, define 'therapy' as taking place when the 'therapist' is using skills and insights which are not available in 'everyday' life. For both of them this means specialised knowledge of the way energy is distributed and held in the body, and the skills which contribute to freeing that energy, through body work. Tom Osborn points out that in body work it is possible to work 'deep' without working with transference.

The non-analytic approaches do not consider that it is necessary for the counsellor to have specialised therapeutic skill and knowledge which enables her to introduce a client to his own unconscious. They all consider that people do have the knowledge and ability to handle and make use of their own sensations, feelings, phantasies, belief systems and actions if they are given the safety and information to allow them to do so. For all except Co-counselling, this safety, as we have seen, lies in the client not being encouraged to override defensive, or safety, mechanisms, but to encounter acknowledge and make overt choices about them. 'They may be gaining something all the time by this way of doing it and . . . decide . . . "the costs are too great to change" – I try to make the issues as explicit as possible'. (Inskipp) The safety in Co-counselling is in the client's responsibility for focus and 'depth' of work.

This is the qualitative difference between the analytic and phenomenological approaches, at least in their 'pure' forms. The phenomenologists go on to point out that by considering that any 'expert' has the key to another person's psyche, the Psychoanalytic school has mystified and de-powered 'ordinary' people in their search for their own meanings. To offer clients alternative ways of viewing their experience is considered useful by all but Rogerian and Gestalt therapists and Co-counsellors, but to interpret disagreement with that interpretation as 'resistance to change' and to see the relationship between two people as having more to do with one person's past than with their mutual present, is not considered useful. It is seen as perpetuating the distinction between 'helper' and 'helped', and reinforcing dependent ways of relating by sealing them in societal role structures.

Almost all contributors agree that people do recreate old relationships in counselling as elsewhere, but only the analytic approach actively encourages that tendency, for learning purposes. Pat Milner says 'I do not encourage it by being enigmatic, withdrawing myself as a person from what is going on. I would help people be aware of them, like other feelings which arise . . . gradually leading on to explore other attitudes involved . . .' and Francesca Inskipp relates to 'what's happening now between myself and the client as something that is actually happening, not interpeting it as something from the past'. Tom Osborn says that anyone who works non-directively is bound to become involved in transference, since people seek approval, love and support in all kinds of accustomed ways. He tries not to reinforce that dependent way of relating by focussing on it, but rather sidesteps it and helps people to interdependent ways of relating. Eugene Heimler 'bounces it back' to the significant person in the client's outside life, from whom he could realistically ask for those things. Dougal Mackay focuses on the task, rather than on the relationship, by using alternative therapists, and Dave Wilmot just does not bring transference into focus. It seems to me that by these determinedly 'Adult' ways of relating to dependency – accepting and exploring it, making contracts about it, recognizing its here-and-now reality base, discouraging it, teaching new ways of relating – non-analytic counsellors avoid a relationship which allows of a qualitative distinction between counselling and therapy.

Nevertheless, Francesca Inskipp and John Heron acknowledge that there are 'chronic patterns' of invalidation and destructiveness of self and others which need 'expert' help before positive energy can be reached and worked with. They imply that particularly safe, long term climates need to be provided for people who use these patterns – perhaps in the same kind of ways that Michael Reddy talks about in re-parenting, or Tom Osborn when he talks about the methods of R. D. Laing. As in analytic psychotherapy, the two conditions – confrontation with new permissions, or interpretations, in extreme safety – seem to be the requisite conditions of change.

For the most part, the qualitative difference is that the psychoanalytic approach focuses on 'what has gone wrong' even when in the counselling, as opposed to therapeutic, encounter it seeks 'to mobilise ego resources'. (Noonan) The humanist and existential, as well as the behavioural, approaches, posit '. . . the healthy parts may be very faint and very distorted because of things which have happened in the past . . . but (there is) this belief that there are enough internal resources'. (Inskipp) Reality Therapy 'builds on healthy seeking towards self-esteem, and 'proper wanting things for himself'. Since both Behaviourists and Reality Therapists call their work therapy, the Psychoanalytic definition of therapy cannot be used universally. For, although both Behavioural and Reality Therapists own special skills, they believe them to be ones that can quite easily be shared with clients.

At this stage, I would like to return to the idea that both counselling and what, for those who acknowledge a difference, is considered therapy are ways of offering to the individual client carefully tailored 'structures for learning'. Each of the approaches in this book has devised particular structures for 'pointing up' certain areas of a client's total experience. It is this 'structuring' which is 'artificial' – literally a devised artifact. What happens within that structure is 'real' – an arranged opportunity for an encounter of one person with another, with himself, with parts of himself, or with other people. Within that structure, the individual may be encouraged to 'make sense' of what he experiences, either in his own terms (Rogers, Gestalt, Developmental and Social Functioning), or in terms of other frames of reference (T.A., Psychoanalytic, Radical Therapy). Or he may be encouraged to try out new behaviour, and to explore and experiment with new solutions (Behavioural, Reality Therapy, Social Functioning, Developmental Counselling, Gestalt, Radical Therapy, Co-counselling).

All of these frameworks are of much wider application than counselling or psychotherapy. Most of them lend themselves to 'package deals' which are, or could be, useful for anyone who is interested in living more freely or enjoyably. The particular difference between such 'human relations and skills training' and counselling and psychotherapy is the degree of frustration and distress which clients are likely to be undergoing when they seek help. The particular skills and capacities of counsellors and psychotherapists, in that case, are those of special sensitivity to vulnerability, and to patterns by which people prevent themselves from using learning situations well. 'She needs to develop very aware skills of human judgement, rather than to develop professional expertise' in the words of John Heron – to treat clients with respect and to remain open and genuine herself.

This judgement needs to be increasingly well-developed if counsellors choose to make decisions whether to focus on (1) the here and now, using such 'mini learning structures' as reflection or clarification; (2) the future, by offering such mini structures as contracts and role-play, or other structures for experimenting with new solutions; or (3) on stuck patterns their clients have developed, which prevent them relating usefully to the offered learning structure, using the mini structures of confrontation and interpretation. This experiential learning framework seems to me to be one that ties in the different counselling and therapy approaches usefully with each other, and also serves to demystify counselling and psychotherapy in relation to such tasks as teaching, training and managing.

It does not, of course, devalue the skill and sensitivity required by all counsellors. For instance, to pick up Pat Milner's remark, 'Rogerian counselling is 'one of the easiest approaches to learn, but the hardest to be'. Through client–centred methods, students can quite quickly become skilled in helping a client encounter and handle those strong emotions which the Psychoanalytic school would call 'unconscious.' In terms of humanistic and existential psychology, these are feelings and sensations that he may have chosen not to encounter previously because of the pain and fear with which they are associated. It may be very hard, however, for an inexperienced counsellor to trust in practice, as she does in theory, that her client can support such strong feelings, given sufficient safety. It is at just this point that she is likely to fear and distrust her own responses – fear, perhaps, or anxiety, repulsion, distress, or love – or to be unable to find appropriate ways of allowing for them within the relationship. Ellen Noonan points out that the respect and humility of new counsellors often helps them to be particularly safe and receptive at this point. Tom Osborn points out that when a client's experience seems un-understandable it is particularly necessary to be accepting. It is also at this stage that an inexperienced counsellor may, in T.A. terms, find that her own 'script' may become confusingly enmeshed with the client's 'script' – or in psychoanalytic terms, she may lose touch with what is her own 'material' and what the client's. In Rogerian terms, it is sufficient at this stage for the counsellor to remain 'congruent'. If she does so, Rogers suggests that the client will find his own way to handle his experience, no matter how damaged he may be.

Perhaps, therefore, a phenomenological definition of 'therapy' as opposed to counselling might be '*therapy* is entered into at whatever point in a counselling relationship that a particular *counsellor* needs to seek support and help in order to take care of herself and continue or begin to offer her client sufficient safe acceptance and warmth.' This is a mischievous definition, at one level. At another, it is a serious attempt to recognize that the current definitions of counselling and therapy are only useful or applicable to practitioners working within a Psychoanalytical framework. Yet a counsellor working in a humanist or existential framework experiences times when she seems 'at sea' rather than on land. Those experiences are often interpreted in terms of the client 'needing therapy'. However, they clearly depend at least as much on the counsellor's congruence, experience and clear-sightedness as they do on the client's 'pathology'. If it should prove that a climate of safety and respect for the client is 'sufficient' for healing and development to take place within the client, then a counsellor's respect for her own ability to offer, or fail to offer, such a climate would be more relevant to the process than an attempt to make demarcation lines between counselling and psychotherapy based on the 'origins' of the client's 'material'.

In concluding this section, it may be appropriate to look at the kind of support a counsellor may seek under such circumstances. Clearly, she can refer the client to someone, or some place, where the necessary safety is available. She can ask the help of a supervisor, or of her peers who, in Michael Reddy's words, can be trusted not to tell her she is necessarily doing fine. The trouble is, that where 'prescriptions' have been instilled in training – 'you ought not to get over-involved' for instance – it is at the point of most anxiety that counsellors may feel reluctant to seek help. Counsellors may need their own safe places of support and freedom from external evaluation in order to dare to look at their experience with their clients.

Finally, Psychoanalytic counsellors and therapists have always looked to undergoing psychoanalysis as the most useful long term resource for their practice. Through analysis, they are confronted with their own defence mechanisms, and work through the conflicts underlying them. The phenomenological counsellors and therapists in these interviews may look to regular peer counselling or Co-counselling, in which they have consistent opportunities to discharge the distress which may accumulate in their work, and re-evaluate their practice and living. They may find ways of 'ordering' their energy in accordance with wider systems of universal energy, through oriental arts, through meditation, or through themselves working in any of the approaches talked about here, in the client role. They may look to ways of working through the 'body armouring' that holds their energy in non-productive ways. They may explore for themselves, in women's groups, or gay groups, or hopefully, men's groups, those structures within society that hold energy in dysfunctional ways, and explore less alienating ways of living.

In conclusion, I want to reiterate that this attempt, to open up the different approaches to each other through the exploration of themes, is not intended to be a more authoritative look at counselling. It is as subjective and partial as are any of the contributors' interviews. I intend it as a model of how to go about using the differing approaches (or, if you prefer, how not to). It has been a useful exploration for me, and I hope it may suggest some fruitful connections to others.

3   Conclusion and Acknowledgements

A BOOK has to have a navel – a belly button which marks where it passed from being a private, inner, subjective experience to becoming a public, shared, objective experience. In most books it is the Preface, but for me, it needs to come at the end, because that is the place of passing. The process, for me, has been very like the counselling experience. Limitless possibilities become transformed into limited realities. The structure has both allowed certain things to happen, and prevented other things from happening. That happened when I devised the questionnaire – my concepts and language allowed and inhibited the contact I could make with my contributors. It has happened as those spoken ideas have been transformed into paper, and print, with a price. Together, we had forged a common language and set of norms, but at some stage this had to meet the accepted language and norms and boundaries of the outside world. In the real power struggle that went on at that point – nothing nasty, just minor victories, relinquishments and compromises – what was really important enough to author, contributors or publisher made it into print. What we lacked the courage or certainty to fight for found the waste-paper basket.

So the conflict model of human interacting has made a lot of sense to me, but so has the cooperative model. Once satisfactory structures had been devised, and norms established, what could happen in those spaces was very satisfying. Fighting the right fights, as Perls suggests, allows the underlying (or overarching) integrations to emerge.

I think this is the place to put in those acknowledgements which I have always thought so boring, but which I now understand the necessity for. Because 'books' – those things which seem such solid, respectable, reliable 'things' – are in fact newly-set processes. Don't let them fool you – they are as important or as superfluous as your own thoughts, and in order for them to have structure, a good deal of energy which is not the author's has to be expended. So firstly, I want to thank the contributors. Thank you, Ellen, Pat, Dougal, Francesca, Gaie, Dave,

Eugene, John and Tom. This is your book as much as mine
You gave time, thought and energy to the interviews, editing,
and 'business' and your thoughts and ideas have enriched my
thinking, working and living.

Then, the family. You have said that this will be the only book
where the author *doesn't* say how much the family has helped,
and sometimes I thought it would be. But when I really needed
it, you rallied round and could not have been more patient and
accepting. Thank you, you are all lovely. And Brian, thank you
for being the only one who could help when I was really in
trouble, despite the fact that you would have preferred to have an
argument about the contents. The really painful conflicts we have
had about the style and contents, have forged it into something
more real than image. To colleagues and students and clients, who
have always let me try out ideas which sometimes seemed to
loose touch with 'real life', and whose experience vastly supple-
ments my own, thank you. Finally, to Farrell Burnett who had
to wet nurse me a lot more than must ordinarily be the case, and
whose intervention prevented the book probably being still born,
thank you.

I have put the acknowledgements in the middle of a general
piece to readers in order to make the point that learning is never
divorced from life. It is out of the stuff of an individual's choices
and changes, achievements and disappointments that history
is forged. This book has allowed me to immerse myself in my
own inner dialogues. I hope, and think, that that does not make
it any less a useful vehicle for furthering the dialogues going on in
the wider system of the counselling world. Perhaps it might even
add some small power to the wider dialogue about the ways that
it is most useful and satisfying to interact in Western democracies
in 1978.

I emerge more certain that the 'right' place to put my energy
is into devising simple maps and simple structures which can be
used in schools, colleges, workplaces, and especially in professional training – structures that allow people to become
aware of some of the choices and possibilities which these interviews open up, so that they can make good choices for themselves.
It seems very stupid that often only those who are almost too
frightened or damaged to dare to learn are those to whom that
learning is available. Specific counselling skills are needed in
this more general education. There are not many people who

have not been conditioned to distrust psychology and suspect those who practice it in any form. In my experience it is necessary to understand, before offering maps and structures, what it is those particular people want and need in their situation. It is also essential to trust them to make their own choices. And it is useful to help them recognise that they will learn more if they have some ideas, at the outset, about what they would like to learn; and if they enjoy themselves doing it. These are all simple and important messages which the contributors to this book have helped me understand.

Appendix

Questionnaire

Section I	The Game Strategy of the Counselling Task

QUESTIONS	ISSUES EXPLORED IN THIS SECTION
1. Looking through the particular pair of conceptual spectacles, you are adopting for the purpose of this interview, what come into relief as the nature of human beings, and the relationship between individuals and the groups, social systems and ecological systems of which they are a part.	The 'models' of the human species which counsellors have in their minds, which determine the assumptions 1. on which they are aware of acting and 2. which they make about others actions.
2. What do you see as the purpose of human energy?	The social climate and personal situations out of which these particular set of perceptions were developed. What errors or omissions in the current models did they remedy or fill?
3. Can you tell me briefly how, where and when your approach to counselling originated?	
4. What processes or structures within British society today stand out as being helpful to the realisation of your 'proper' purposes of humanity?	The light these insights cast on our existing social systems and on an individuals experience of them.
5. What processes or structures appear to impede their realisation?	
6. So what do you see as the objective of the counselling task?	Overall counselling objectives.

CONCERNS AND ASSUMPTIONS
BEHIND THE RAISING OF THESE
ISSUES

DIFFICULTIES IN FRAMING
QUESTIONS AROUND THESE ISSUES

To explore and clarify the extent to which counselling is viewed as remedial as opposed to developmental. To look at the other side of the coin – is our social system 'sick' or 'healthy' in meeting the needs of the species?

To demonstrate at the outset that all actions are based on assumptions. To the extent that I am unaware of the assumptions on which I act, I am confusing to myself and other people. To open the issue that even the simplest counselling is inherently political – that is, that by acting publicly on the assumptions I do, I am adding some power to whatever social energy supports or opposes my assumptions.

To give contributors and readers an opportunity to explore how far their actual counselling practice is informed by their public assumptions. To demonstrate how partially, and culturally conditioned, any one person or group of people are obliged to view fundamental questions.
To suggest that most powerful insights are at one level universally significant, at another level locally significant, and yet another level, personal to their originator.

I am conscious that the idea of 'conceptual spectacles' is not familiar to many people. We are mostly taught that this or that 'is' the way things 'are'.

To ask for a thumbnail philosophy of human nature and counselling is to invite caricature. However, good caricature is useful if the main signals are transmitted forcefully and fairly without doing violence to the subject.

Language is the chief problem. It is packed with so many assumptions and associations. (By using the word 'I'. I assume a separate entity which some cultures do not acknowledge by a word). The language I use is bound to incorporate assumptions of which I am unaware and associations personal to you. When I am aware of this happening, I try to reduce the word to lower common denominator for clarity. For instance I have not used the word 'values'. Sometimes I have used 'jargon' words, e.g. social systems, when I feel they have been coined to embody fresh assumptions which I share. Since I cannot write totally freshly, I fear that when my language is an 'in-group' signal – for instance I use unaware rather than unconscious – I will switch off (another group signal) readers I would like to keep tuned in.

Section   The Game Rules
II   of the Counselling Task

QUESTIONS	ISSUES EXPLORED IN THIS SECTION
7. What resources do you see yourself bringing to the counselling task?	The counselling interaction
	Its similarities to and differences from other personal encounters.
8. What do you see as being the responsibilities of the client and the counsellor in the counselling interaction?	
9. Is the counselling encounter different from encounters you have in other roles?	Where authority and responsibility are perceived as belonging in that interaction. What the explicit or implicit contract is between the participants.
10. Do you have ways of trying to ensure that your client and you have similar assumptions and objectives about the nature of the task and the interaction?	

CONCERNS AND ASSUMPTIONS
BEHIND THE RAISING OF THESE
ISSUES

DIFFICULTIES IN FRAMING
QUESTIONS AROUND THESE ISSUES

I am fascinated by the way in which a counselling interaction seems to be felt as both extremely familiar to people and very strange to them. I hope these questions will allow contributors space to explore what lies behind that ambivalence.

There is ambivalence too, among counsellors and public, towards what counsellors have to offer. I am interested to discover where contributors believe their skill and authority to counsel derive from.

I am concerned to discover how much contributors consider their own sort of insights about the human species are potentially available to all, or are likely to, or should, remain the province of particular people. I have not used the words 'professional' or 'ethics', but there is high concern for 'the protection of the public' and also high concern to educate children and others, in human relations. I hope these questions will allow contributors to explore the hopes and fears that lie behind the sometimes conflicting pressures towards professionalism and dissemination.

Relationship is one of the words I decided to avoid, as concealing rather than revealing. Encounter and transaction both of which feel appropriate to me carry in-group signals with which I do not fully identify. I settled for 'interaction', which seems to make very few assumptions, but for me, personally, feels a bit too clinical.

I am aware that most of the contributors are counselling, or training others to counsel, for the greater part of their working life. However, the book is offered as being useful to those who carry counselling responsibilities as only part of their professional duties, or who are voluntary counsellors. In this and other sections, I am conscious of exploring questions in a depth which may seem irrelevant to them. On the other hand, when people do wear 'two hats' it is my experience that confusion about the 'rules' of the different games can be exhausting to them and confusing to their colleagues and those with whom they counsel. Clarity is important and I think that means exploring fully the issues involved.

Section III   The Game Tactics of the Counselling Task

QUESTIONS

ISSUES EXPLORED IN THIS SECTION

11. Counsellors tend to focus on certain aspects of the clients total interaction with the environment. Do you focus on any particular processes or engage some faculties more than others?

12. What kind of climate do you seek to develop and how do you see it being important for your joint task?

13. Does the idea that people tend to re-create old patterns of relating in a counselling relationship, i.e. transference, have much significance for you? If so, what do you do about it?

14. Do you regard yourself as a model for the 'client'? If so, what do you model?

15. What kind of behaviour do you expect, sanction, encourage in the client, and are you aware of positively conditioning certain communications and negatively conditioning others?

16. Are there any other patterns of interaction, which you would identify as a process, which you habitually recognise and or make use of?

17. Given that there are a fairly limited number of ways that we can respond to a request for personal help, or seek to intervene in another's personal exploration, are there any responses that you have worked on being able to use effectively?

18. Any that you have deliberately soft-pedalled?

The extent to which the counselling task is focused and the way that focus is determined.

The processes which are recognised as taking place between people in interaction and the extent to which these are recognised, acknowledged or used in the counselling task.

The 'techniques' or counselling styles which can be employed.

CONCERNS AND ASSUMPTIONS
BEHIND THE RAISING OF THESE
ISSUES

DIFFICULTIES IN FRAMING
QUESTIONS AROUND THESE ISSUES

I assume that it is impossible to reapond to another human being other than selectively. To the extent that I believe I am being non selective I will be being unawarely selective in my focus. I am concerned to give contributors space to make explicit the areas in which their training and assumptions lead them to focus.

It interests me to know if there are processes of human development and interaction which are acknowledged and used by counsellors with different 'models'.

I have not used the terms 'directive' or 'non-directive' because they can refer either to the question explored in the last section, or to counselling style and the same person need not be 'directive' or 'non-directive' in both areas. Of the styles of reaponse, I can identify four broad categories which I might call prescriptive, exploratory, supportive, confronting. I am interested to discover if these or other responses, are recognizably associated with different models of counselling.

Overall, I hope that the answers to these questions will clarify to what extent the rules and 'tactics' used by the different contributors are inevitable because they flow out of their 'model', or how much they are 'traditional' and therefore negotiable.

Terms that I have in mind to describe what I mean by 'area of focus' worry me with their vagueness. On the other hand, to be more exact (but still very vague) is to risk categorizing in a way that invites very splintered and segmented descriptions of what is possibly in experience a smooth flowing interaction. These decisions must be for the contributor to make but the section points up the difficulty of understanding a moving, developing film by looking at selected stills.

The 'areas of focus' I do have in mind are for instance, feeling and emotion, fantasy and imagination, behaviour, awareness – of sensation and environment – communication skills, goal setting, decision making, social and personal perceptions, concepts and assumptions, role performance, social interactions. I am sure there are other areas of focus, too, and that these areas would not be considered as discrete entities by all contributors. The section also seems to highlight another set of conflicting attitudes as I try to formulate it. There is an assumption that there is a quality of authenticity which is an essential ingredient of 'helping encounters', which may be damaged by developing self-consciousness and by 'learning' techniques.

Section IV   Limits of the Counselling Task

QUESTIONS	ISSUES EXPLORED IN THIS SECTION
19. Do you see any demarcation between counselling and therapy within your framework?	Whether there are definable differences between counselling and therapy.
20. If so, what are the dangers of the unitiated going beyond it?	The anxieties that underly the heat generated by this topic.

CONCERNS AND ASSUMPTIONS
BEHIND THE RAISING OF THESE
ISSUES

DIFFICULTIES IN FRAMING
QUESTIONS AROUND THESE ISSUES

I hope that the discussion will help
to de-mystify an issue around
which the sometimes magical
hopes and fears in relation to
counselling interactions tend to
focus.

Section V   Personal Considerations

QUESTIONS	ISSUES EXPLORED IN THIS SECTION
21. Does the client group with which your work (or have largely worked) influence the way you view counselling?	The interaction between the person who carries a model and the work experience.
22. Have you any personal dilemmas in your counselling work?	
23. Do you feel that the framework offered by these questions has slanted the presentation of your practice and experience? If so, anything to add in correction?	

CONCERNS AND ASSUMPTIONS
BEHIND THE RAISING OF THESE
ISSUES

DIFFICULTIES IN FRAMING
QUESTIONS AROUND THESE ISSUES

I assume that the model a person
carries at the start of their
counselling work will be variably
useful in the situation she finds
herself working and I want to
check how contributors find this
interaction.

I hope that with prior warning of
the questions and this opportunity
to share any feeling of having been
'rail roaded', the answer to the
questions will be a fair
representation of the contributors
thinking and experience.

This sections highlights the
difficulty and frustration of asking
a person to wear a 'model hat' and
expecting fresh and authentic
replies. It may be that the
answers to this section will show
that the whole exercise has been
unduly restrictive and is not
useful for gaining access to people's
personal counselling experience.